Reflective Interviewing

Reflective Interviewing

A Guide to Theory and Practice

Kathryn Roulston

SAGE

Los Angeles | London | New Delhi
Singapore | Washington DC

First published 2010

Reprinted 2012, 2013

SAGE Publications Ltd
1 Oliver's Yard
55 City Road
London EC1Y 1SP

SAGE Publications Inc.
2455 Teller Road
Thousand Oaks, California 91320

SAGE Publications India Pvt Ltd
B 1/I 1 Mohan Cooperative Industrial Area
Mathura Road
New Delhi 110 044

SAGE Publications Asia-Pacific Pte Ltd
3 Church Street
#10-04 Samsung Hub
Singapore 049483

Library of Congress Control Number: 2009930844

British Library Cataloguing in Publication data

A catalogue record for this book is available from
the British Library

ISBN 978-1-4129-4856-2
ISBN 978-1-4129-4857-9 (pbk)

Typeset by C&M Digitals (P) Ltd, Chennai, India
Printed in Great Britain by CPI Group (UK) Ltd, Croydon, CR0 4YY
Printed on paper from sustainable resources

Contents

Acknowledgements

Numerous people have assisted in the formulation of the ideas presented in this book. I would like to extend heartfelt thanks to the following people.

Colleagues and friends have been generous in discussing their use of research interviews and how we might go about working with students: Derrick Alridge, Kathleen deMarrais, Melissa Freeman, Linda Harklau, Thomas Hébert, Juanita Johnson-Bailey, Sharan Merriam, and Judith Preissle. Deep gratitude to colleagues and friends with whom I have spent time examining transcriptions of interviews and focus groups: the late Carolyn Baker, Anna Liljestrom, Kathleen deMarrais, and Jamie B. Lewis. I would also like to thank colleagues and friends who have provided insightful comments on earlier drafts of various sections of this book: especially Bob Fecho, Jodi Kaufmann and Janice Fournillier. I would like to extend special thanks to Melissa Freeman who was generous in providing feedback throughout the development of the manuscript, and Kathleen deMarrais and Judith Preissle for helping me learn how to interview, and learn how to teach interviewing. Former students too numerous to mention who have used interviews in their research, collaborated on projects with me, talked and written about their interviews and asked questions have helped me think about issues discussed in this book. Thanks to graduate researchers whose assistance in locating relevant literature was invaluable: Myungweon Choi and Mitsunori Misawa. Special thanks to Myungweon Choi for assisting me in thinking about how qualitative researchers account for their interview practice and for her systematic and thorough reading of earlier versions of this manuscript.

I also wish to express thanks to my family for providing encouragement and support to complete this project: my parents Pat and Reg who kept asking me when the manuscript would be finished; Suzanne Mulliss for assistance with indexing; and my husband Mike Healy for his encouragement and continuing support throughout this project.

Also thanks to Patrick Brindle, Anna Coatman and Ian Antcliff of SAGE Publications for their timely advice and guidance; and Jeremy Toynbee for assistance with copy-editing.

I would like to thank the following for their permission to reproduce material in this book: Cengage Learning Inc., Elsevier, Jonathan Lynn and Anthony Jay, Random House Group Ltd, Taylor & Francis Informa UK Ltd and Taylor & Francis Group LLC.

Introduction

The purpose of this book is to assist newcomers to qualitative research methods to think about the variety of ways that qualitative interviews have been used by researchers working from different theoretical approaches, and how these might be applied in their own research studies. Interviews are a format to which we are so accustomed in contemporary society that it is difficult to imagine a world without them. Excerpts from interviews published in newspapers and magazines provide evidence for claims about what happens in our world. At work we interview others in order to gain information about their professional capabilities. Children conduct interviews in order to find information to present in school projects; journalists interview politicians; nightly news anchors interview journalists; parents interview teachers; and physicians interview their patients. We participate as witnesses to others' interviews, as well as take part in interviews as interviewers and interviewees. There are few places, it seems, where we are immune from the questions and answers that characterize the interview as a particular kind of social interaction. By making visible the assumptions underlying the different ways in which qualitative interviews have been theorized in social research, in this book I aim to assist researchers using interviews for the first time to consider the connections between theory and practice and to examine critically the use of interview data for research purposes.

The approach that I outline in this book entails the researcher's consideration of three interrelated issues:

> the researcher's theoretical conception of the research interview;
> the researcher's subject positions in relation to the project and participants; and
> methodological examinations of interview interaction to inform research design.

I argue that reflection on each of these issues will contribute to advancing the practice of both qualitative interviewing and qualitative inquiry. Through developing sophisticated understandings of qualitative interview practice, qualitative researchers are better positioned to design and conduct quality research projects that provide researchers and communities with significant findings concerning social problems.

Background

In academic work, the interview has been used extensively by social researchers as a method for generating data concerning research problems (for a selective history of the interview see Platt [2002]). For social researchers, there is a wide range of methodological literature that provides guidance on how to design and conduct all kinds of interviews – from standardized structured protocols conducted by telephone, to open-ended conversations. Yet, our everyday exposure to the 'Interview Society' in which the interview is central to the construction of the modern individual obscures the complexity of conducting interviews for research purposes (Atkinson and Silverman, 1997; Gubrium and Holstein, 2002). It is easy to see the research interview as simply a series of questions followed by responses – all we need to do as researchers is to ask the right questions of willing interviewees and we will extract the information we need to answer our research questions. This perspective of interviewing has been seriously questioned in the methodological literature and there are longstanding critiques of social researchers' use of the interview method.

Critics of qualitative interviews maintain that research interviewers who contribute their personal perspectives in interview interaction *bias* data and produce studies that lack *validity*. Some researchers argue that human subjects cannot be relied upon to provide *accurate* or *truthful* accounts. This view is supported by studies that have found mismatches between what people say in interviews and what they do in everyday life. Methodologists have also critiqued the quality of research in which interview data has been insufficiently analyzed and under-theorized (see for example, Atkinson and Coffey, 2002). Radical critiques of interviewing (see Potter and Hepburn, 2005, for an example, and Hammersley, 2003 for a review) criticize reports from qualitative interview studies on epistemological and methodological grounds. These critiques of interviewing reject the notion that peoples' talk accurately represents what they are thinking (that is, thoughts, beliefs, attitudes, and opinions), are skeptical that interview accounts can actually reflect either what is *inside* people's heads, or what actually happens out there in a *real* world, and posit that interviews are not satisfactory substitutes for direct observation and are heavily context-dependent, making them unreliable sources of evidence (Hammersley and Gomm, 2008). Finally, postmodern critiques of qualitative interview studies and methodological writing question the modernist assumptions of the human subject embedded in theorizations of interviewing, and analyses and interpretations of interview data (Scheurich, 1995).

Should researchers give up on the qualitative interview? David Silverman (2005: 238–40, 2007), for example, calls on qualitative researchers to take care to justify their use of interviews as the preferred method for gaining access to people's experiences and, like Jonathan Potter and Alexa Hepburn (2005), makes the case for the use of naturally occurring data (Silverman, 2005: 119–21). Martyn Hammersley (2003: 124) suggests that it would be ill advised to either uncritically adopt radical critiques of interviewing, or to ignore the problematic methodological issues inherent in the use of qualitative interviews. Yet, given the proliferation of methodological advice concerning qualitative interviews, how might beginning researchers proceed? This book provides novices to qualitative research methods with some starting points by offering a theoretically informed guide to interview practice that will assist researchers to develop as reflective interviewers, and showing how the design of research projects might be approached to ensure quality work.

A Proposal for Advancing the Practice of Qualitative Interviewing

The theoretical assumptions of the researcher – whether explicit or not – inform the design of interview studies and interview questions, as well as the analysis and representation of data. Researchers need to consider various theorizations of the interview as they design their studies in order to grasp the implications of their theoretical assumptions for the generation, interpretation, and representation of data. Thinking about these issues during data analysis may be too late. The danger of overlooking the important links between theory and practice in the planning and conduct of interviews is that resulting research reports can be – as critics have pointed out – under-theorized and of poor quality. It is crucial for qualitative researchers to have an understanding of and an ability to theorize the application of qualitative interviews to investigate research problems in social science research, and the researcher-relationships inherent in each research study. But what does it mean to 'theorize,' and how might a researcher go about doing that? Figure I.1 illustrates one model of the necessary components for researchers to accomplish this task.

Theories are simply statements that explain connections between concepts, and tell us something about the way things work and how things happen (LeCompte and Preissle, 1993: 118). Theorizing, then, is the process by which we go about constructing these statements in relation to what is already known about an issue. In relation to the issues concerning interviewing listed above, to 'theorize' means to consider relevant issues and implications for research design related to what interview data can tell us about a specific topic; how interview data are generated; who the interviewer is in relation to the research topic and the study's participants; how the theoretical assumptions underlying the research design relate to data analysis, interpretation, and representation; and finally, how the quality of the final report will be judged within a particular field of inquiry.

Theory and Interviewing

There is no shortage of literature discussing the theory and methods of qualitative research. Novice researchers, however, may have difficulty in synthesizing and applying what may be learned from the rapidly growing literature on theory and methods to their interview practice. Too much emphasis on theory may

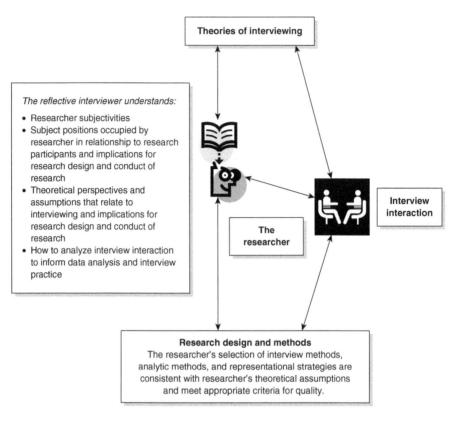

Figure I.1   The reflective researcher

result in beginning researchers experiencing paralysis in the creative process, through striving to first know everything of relevance concerning theory in relation to their prospective studies. The problem here is one of difficulties in getting to the practicalities of doing research. For students with little interest in engaging in academic discourses on theory, too little theory may result in simplistic interview studies in which an unreflective researcher produces naïve analyses of data. Seeing interviews as merely a sequence of questions followed by answers – a transparent stimulus–response medium for gathering facts, opinions, and beliefs – and failing to understand the complex nature of interview interaction between interviewers and interviewees, the researcher who does not consider theory may generate data that does not inform his or her research questions. Yet, other beginning researchers, in attempting to follow innumerable prescriptions concerning what to do in order to generate rich descriptions, become entangled in agonized reflective dialogues about what happened in their interviews, their relationships with their participants, and the ethical issues of doing qualitative research with human subjects. Thinking about the possible theorizations of qualitative interviewing will assist beginning researchers to contextualize their use of interviews within the broader array of social theory that qualitative researchers use to inform research design. Another key step is to consider the place of the researcher in relation to the research project.

Theorizing the Researcher

Researchers bring different conversational styles to their research interviews with unique individual participants on diverse topics, and researchers approach their work from a variety of theoretical perspectives. Any guidelines for 'good' interview practice, therefore, must be taken up with respect to each researcher's particular context and his or her subject positions (that is, race, class, gender, culture, language, status in relation to each interviewee; and prior experiences and relationships with the participant among other social locations). This is not news – indeed Lewis Dexter wrote many years ago that 'What may be suicidal or impractical for one interviewer or in one situation may be feasible or even the best way to proceed for another interviewer or in another situation' (1970: 24). In this book, I offer suggestions for how researchers can become more mindful of what they bring to their research project, and how that intersects with particular participants in the process of conducting interview research.

Examining Interview Interaction Methodologically

A next step in learning about interviewing is for researchers to reflect critically on their interaction with others within the research setting through close examination of their interview transcripts. Qualitative methodologists have frequently used models and transcripts of both exemplary and problematic interviews in teaching beginning researchers the skills of interviewing. In this book I argue not only for the continued usefulness of data sets that exemplify common problems faced by novice interviewers, but that researchers themselves be encouraged to look at problematic moments in their own interviews to unpack them. Rather than discarding this kind of data as worthless, in this book I outline an approach to developing an interview practice that researchers might use to think about research interviews methodologically and theoretically. Problematic interactions and difficult data provide rich materials for examination and further development of one's own interview practice through asking questions concerning *how* data are collaboratively generated by speakers. Researchers can reflect on the answers to these questions and inform decision-making concerning research design and methods, the formulation of interview questions, and appropriate ways to analyze and represent interview data.

Learning about Qualitative Interviewing

A common approach to introducing qualitative interviewing to novice researchers is that of providing advice based on the researcher's personal experience as an interviewer. This is so whether the researcher is based in anthropology (McCracken, 1988), education (Seidman, 2006), educational anthropology (Wolcott, 1995), psychology (Kvale, 1996; Kvale and Brinkmann, 2009; Moustakas, 1994), social psychology (Mishler, 1986), sociolinguistics (Briggs, 1986), or sociology (Douglas, 1985; Weiss, 1994; Wengraf, 2001). It is clear from these accounts that qualitative interviewers and social researchers learn by doing, and reflection on doing. Newcomers to research are no different to their more experienced qualitative colleagues. Thus any program for developing research skills must involve novice researchers in conducting authentic interviews, and reflecting on those experiences. To assist with this task, throughout the book I include suggested practical activities that can be used in coursework, or, alternatively, by individual researchers. In short, this book recommends that researchers ask questions – of their theoretical assumptions about interviews, of themselves, and of what happens in their interview interaction with others.

Outline of the Book

Chapter 1 reviews the question–answer sequence as the basic unit of interviews, as well as different approaches to thinking about individual interviews. This includes the 'structure' of the interview, as well as the approaches to asking questions that have developed in ethnographic, phenomenological, feminist, oral and life history, and dialogic traditions.

Chapter 2 provides a series of considerations for researchers who would like to use group interviews or focus groups in their studies. The chapter draws distinctions between group interviews and focus groups and reviews focus groups in more detail. Excerpts of talk from focus groups to illustrate various issues that arise in the facilitation of group interaction are included.

Chapter 3 discusses various theoretical assumptions that underlie different conceptions of interviewing. I include examples of research demonstrating six conceptions of the research interview: neo-positivist; romantic; constructionist; postmodern; transformative; and decolonizing. I discuss how each conception of the research interview relates to different theoretical assumptions about human subjects and interview data, the implications for data analysis and representation of findings, and provide examples of research exemplifying different approaches.

Chapter 4 reviews steps entailed in the research design process, including identifying research topics, formulating research questions, and selecting and sampling populations. Given that researchers must consider how judgments concerning the value, or quality of research are made, this issue is discussed in relation to the conceptions of interviews outlined in Chapter 3.

Chapter 5 discusses some of the procedural issues to do with conducting interview research. Before interviewing, researchers must gain consent for the study, and follow appropriate procedures for conducting ethical research. Recruitment of participants, preparation for interviews, and issues arising in conducting interviews are discussed. Recording options, transcription practice, and considerations concerning the use of translated data are reviewed. Suggestions for further reading concerning interviewing specific populations are included.

In Chapter 6, I explore methods that individual researchers might use to examine themselves as researchers. Here I consider reflection as an integral feature of well-designed research, and provide a number of different strategies that researchers can use to develop a reflexive research practice. These include examining subject positions as researchers through writing subjectivity statements, keeping researcher journals, being interviewed as a researcher, and analyzing the interviewer's 'work' in interviews. The chapter provides further reading concerning reflexive practices in social science research.

Chapter 7 outlines an approach that interviewers can use to develop an increased awareness of what they do and say in interaction through inspecting both problematic and effective moments in interview transcripts. A series of interview excerpts are used to show how interviewers can use methods drawn from conversation analysis to examine their interview practice. I argue that this approach assists interviewers to see possibilities for how they formulate and ask questions in future research interviews, as well as to think about research design and the use of interview data.

Chapter 8 provides an overview of different approaches to the analysis of interview data. I provide brief reviews of a selection of approaches to the analysis, interpretation, and representation of interview data. These include thematic analysis, grounded theory analysis, ethnographic analysis, phenomenological analysis, narrative analysis, and ethnomethodological and conversation analysis. I conclude the chapter by reviewing resources one might turn to in order to learn more about poststructural and postmodern approaches to the analysis of data, as well as the use of arts-based approaches to representation.

Chapter 9 concludes the book with accounts of interviewing practice from experienced researchers, as well as advice for beginning interviewers.

The aim of this book is to provide guidance to researchers about how they might develop interview skills in keeping with their theoretical assumptions. Throughout the book, readers will find multiple data excerpts that illustrate the different kinds of events that occur in research interviews, reflections on interviewing from qualitative researchers who use interviews, and suggestions for further reading.

I have employed two approaches to transcribing interview excerpts. When the focal point of attention is *how* the talk-in-interaction was generated, paralinguistic features of talk such as pauses, hesitations, and slips are notated using transcription conventions developed by Gail Jefferson (Psathas and Anderson, 1990; see Appendix 1). Where these features of talk are not relevant to the discussion, they are not included. Activities that might be either incorporated into course work on qualitative research methodology or used by individual researchers are included at the conclusion of each chapter to assist readers with developing their interview practice.

ONE

Asking Questions and Individual Interviews

This chapter introduces:

- Question and answer sequences: *closed* and *open* questions and follow-up questions or *probes*.
- *Structure* in interviews.
- Forms of interviewing, including *phenomenological, ethnographic, feminist, oral* and *life history*, and *dialogic* interviewing.

In the film *Surname Viet, Given Name Nam*, Trinh T. Minh-ha (1989) purposefully upsets our assumptions about interviewing by juxtaposing English-language interviews of Vietnamese women that at first *look* to be real, against interviews conducted in Vietnamese with English subtitles of – we find out as the film unfolds – authentic interviews of people who have acted the parts of the interviews we have seen earlier in the film. In a further twist, we find out that Trinh has translated transcriptions of interviews from a Vietnamese book to form the basis of the scripts for interviews of the Vietnamese women who introduce the film with their touching, evocative, and sometimes heart-rending narratives. In but one of the themes explored in this film, Trinh cleverly asks questions of both the interview as method, and how researchers translate the voices of others into visual, oral, and written texts.

In this chapter, I begin my exploration of the interview as a research method by first examining 'questions' and 'answers' as a basic conversational sequence. Second, I discuss different structures for interviewing, including structured, semi-structured, and unstructured interviews. Third, I review a variety of approaches to individual interviewing practice used by qualitative researchers. In contemporary qualitative research practice, there are numerous forms for conducting individual interviews as well as labels to characterize them. These include semi-structured, unstructured, and structured interviews; formal and informal interviews; long, creative, open-ended, depth, and in-depth interviews; life history, oral history, and biographic interviews; feminist interviews; ethnographic interviews; phenomenological interviews; and dialogical, conversational, and epistemic interviews. And this is by no means an exhaustive list! The purpose of reviewing a variety of approaches to interviewing is to assist researchers to make sense of the labels used in the methodological literature. Researchers may then select the kind of interview structure and form that is both consistent with their theoretical assumptions, and appropriate to generate data to answer research questions.

An Introduction to Qualitative Interviews

Qualitative interviews may be conducted individually or in groups; face-to-face, via telephone, or online via synchronous or asynchronous computer mediated interaction. In this book, I focus on qualitative interviews in which an interviewer generates talk with an interviewee or interviewees for the purposes of eliciting spoken, rather than written data to examine research problems (for those interested in learning about synchronous and asynchronous online interviews, see Beck, 2005; Davis et al., 2004; Egan et al., 2006; Hamilton and Bowers, 2006; James, 2007; James and Busher, 2006).

Information concerning the design and conduct of structured interviews or standardized surveys is not the focus of this book, since the purpose of these interviews – often administered via telephone – is to generate responses that may be coded to a fixed set of categories, and analyzed quantitatively. Much research has investigated the standardized survey methodologically (Houtkoop-Steenstra, 2000; Maynard et al., 2002; Schaeffer and Maynard, 2002; Suchman and Jordan, 1990); and advice is also plentiful with respect to construction and administering of surveys and questionnaires (see for example, Brenner, 1985; Foddy, 1993; Genovese, 2004). Interestingly, many suggestions for conducting an effective survey interview are reiterated in recommendations for conducting 'good' qualitative interviews.

The term *interviews* is used to encompass many forms of talk – including professional interviews such as counseling and therapeutic interviews, job interviews, journalistic interviews, and so forth. What all of these forms of talk have in common is that parties are engaged in asking and answering questions. Whatever the structure or format of an interview, or medium used for an interview (such as telephone, face-to-face, or computer-mediated), the basic unit of interaction is the question–answer sequence. Given that researchers pose questions to participants with the aim of eliciting answers, it is useful to examine in more detail how 'closed' and 'open' questions work, and how they can generate different kinds of responses.

Questions and Answers

Questions are particular kinds of statements that request a reply – although posing a question does not necessarily mean an answer will be forthcoming, or that the answer will relate to the particular question posed. In his analysis of conversation, sociologist Harvey Sacks (1992) located a class of utterances that he labeled 'adjacency pairs' (see Appendix 2 for a glossary of terms used in conversation analysis). In an adjacency pair, when a first-pair part (in this case, question) has been uttered, it sets up the expectancy that a second-pair part (an answer) will be forthcoming.

Interviews are built on the assumption that questions asked by the interviewer will be followed by answers provided by the interviewee. Two kinds of questions that are routinely used in interviews are closed and open questions.

Closed Questions

Understanding questions is simple – isn't it? Maybe not. Although we immediately recognize or understand when a question has been posed in interaction, how to ask interview questions that are comprehended by others and answered in ways that generate relevant data is more complex than initially apparent. Some question structures have been found to have a certain kind of *preference* for the response. That is, response types might be marked or unmarked for certain kinds of adjacency pairs. For example, invitations *prefer* acceptances, and declinations are typically followed by accounts, or are 'marked.' Self-deprecations *prefer* disagreements, whereas agreements present an interactional difficulty to be negotiated by speakers. The question beginning this section is posed as an assertion with a tag, 'isn't it?' This question formulation implies a particular kind of response, which, in this case is confirmation ('yes'). The response that follows the statement above is the 'dispreferred' response, or disagreement. Researchers have found that dispreferred responses (such as when an invitation is declined) are usually followed by accounts, or explanations (as demonstrated in this paragraph). Although this closed question is formulated as an assertion that implies confirmation, the response generated is neither yes nor no! Thus, we can express something about the format of this particular question–answer sequence as shown in Figure 1.1 below. Note that that dotted arrow from the dispreferred response to the account or explanation indicates that a speaker *may* provide an explanation, although this does not always occur.

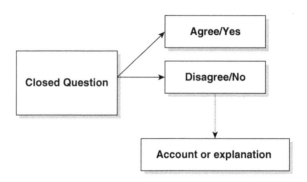

Figure 1.1   A closed question and possible ways of responding

Many methodological texts advise qualitative interviewers to ask *open*, rather than *closed* questions because closed questions have the possibility of generating short one-word answers corresponding with yes/no or factual information implied by the question (for example, What time is it? One fifteen). Thus, closed questions are those in which the implied response is restricted in some way. For example, the closed question I posed below is answered by a single-word affirmation from the participant:

Excerpt 1.1[1]

Interviewer (IR) And, do you have choruses at school yourself?
Interviewee (IE) Uh-huh.

Interviewees may respond to closed questions as if they were open by providing further description. For example, in response to the following probe that I posed as a closed question, the interviewee in Excerpt 1.2 provided further explanation, rather than supplying a one-word affirmation such as 'yes.'

Excerpt 1.2

IR   Now you mentioned that you started taking private lessons yourself. Had you had formal music training prior to that?
IE   At a very early age, my father had enrolled me in a piano class. And I begged him to let me drop out. And he said, 'Well the only way I'll let you drop out is if you play a sport.' So I started playing soccer, so that I would not have to play the piano.
IR: Huh.
IE: That was probably the dumbest decision that either one of us ever made.

In Excerpt 1.2, we see that even closed questions can generate significant explanation, rather than simple yes/no responses. Thus, while closed questions may imply yes/no responses – they are not always taken up in that way. Yet, it is a wise move for novice interviewers seeking to generate in-depth descriptions of people's perceptions and experiences to learn how to pose open, rather than closed questions. This should not be taken to mean that there is no place for closed questions in a qualitative interview. In Excerpt 1.2, a closed question is used as a follow up question to clarify an aspect of a preceding narrative that was not central to the research topic. Therefore, closed questions can also be used judiciously by qualitative interviewers to clarify their understanding of details provided by interviewees.

Open Questions

Open questions are those that provide broad parameters within which interviewees can formulate answers in their own words concerning topics specified by the interviewer. Questions beginning 'Tell me about …' invite interviewees to tell a story, and can generate detailed descriptions about topics of interest to the interviewer. These descriptions can be further explored when the interviewer follows up on what has already been said by asking further open-ended follow up questions, or 'probes' that incorporate the interviewee's words. For example, I have used the following kinds of questions in interviewing to clarify topics, and elicit further description:

> You mentioned that you had _____; could you tell me more about that.
> You mentioned when you were doing ____, ____ happened. Could you give me a specific example of that?

---

[1]Unless otherwise noted, all interview extracts included in the text are drawn from studies in which the author was principal investigator, and for which informed consent from interviewees was obtained.

Thinking back to that time, what was that like for you?
You mentioned earlier that you _____. Could you describe in detail what happened?

Probes frequently *use the participant's own words* to generate questions that elicit further description. This is an important point, because in everyday conversation, we regularly use 'formulations' of what others have said to us to clarify our understanding of prior interactions. There is a distinct difference between using formulations to sum up our understanding of others' talk and using the participants' words to generate questions. In the former, interviewers use their own terms to sum up what they have heard (through a process of preserving, deleting, and transforming aspects of what has already been said, see Heritage and Watson [1979] and Appendix 2 for further information). By formulating talk, interviewers are likely to introduce words into the conversation that the participants themselves may not use. Just as in everyday conversation, interviewees may take up the researcher's terms at a later point in the talk – in effect recycling what the interviewer has said rather than selecting their own words. This is avoided when interviewers use the participants' words to generate probes. In Excerpt 1.3, we see in an interview that I conducted how I formulated talk in a way that my research participant commented on.

Excerpt 1.3

IR   Yeah, so the, like the identification of the vocal timbre.
IE   Right.
IR   Gets identified with sexual orientation.
IE   Exactly.
IR   Yeah.
IE   Look at you. Putting that into big words, you know.

In this example, I formulated the interviewee's previous talk concerning how she had overheard comments from fifth-grade boys that boys who sang sounded gay as 'the identification of the vocal timbre gets identified with sexual orientation.' In this instance, the interviewee commented on how this formulation had transformed her comments into 'big words.' Here I elicited agreement to my formulation from the interviewee; however, another way of approaching this talk could have been to generate more detail concerning the interviewee's response. There are many probes using the participant's words that could have been used, however, perhaps the simplest probe is: tell me more about that.

When asking open ended questions, interviewers need to be sure that the topic is sufficiently specific so that the interviewee will be able to respond. If topics have not been explained, or are unclear to interviewees, they may have difficulty in answering broad open-ended questions. When interviewees and interviewers both feel comfortable talking to one another, it can take as few as four or five key interview questions with appropriate probes to generate talk of an hour or more. A possible sequence of open questions can be illustrated diagrammatically (see Figure 1.2).

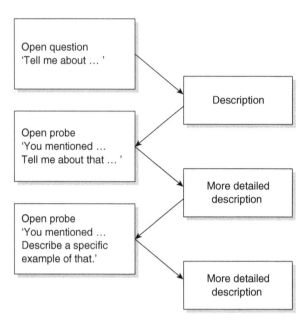

Figure 1.2   An open question and possible ways of responding

'Structure' and Interview Talk

Broadly speaking, research interviews for the purposes of social research range across a spectrum from structured, tightly scripted interviews in which interviewers pose closed questions worded in particular ways in specific sequences, to open-ended, loosely guided interviews that have little or no pre-planned structure in terms of what questions and topics are discussed (see Table 1.1).

Table 1.1   Range of interviews

Structured interviews ↔	Semi-structured interviews ↔	Unstructured interviews
The interviewer follows scripted questions in a particular sequence	Interview protocol is used as a 'guide' and questions may not always be asked in the same order; the interviewer initiates questions and poses follow up 'probes' in response to the interviewee's descriptions and accounts	Both interviewer and interviewee initiate questions and discuss topics
The interviewee chooses responses from a range of fixed options that are coded quantitatively; responses are provided by interviewer	The interviewee selects own terms to formulate answers to questions; responses are guided by the interviewer's questions	The interviewee selects own terms to participate in free-flowing conversation
Asymmetrical structure	Asymmetrical structure	Possibly less asymmetrical structure

Table 1.1   (Continued)

Structured interviews ↔	Semi-structured interviews ↔	Unstructured interviews
Data analyzed via deductive analysis for hypothesis testing in multivariate studies[a]	Data analyzed via inductive analytic methods for descriptions and interpretations in interpretive studies	

Note: [a]Alford (1998: 38) explains that multivariate arguments attempt to measure factors that explain a 'particular social phenomenon', while 'interpretive' arguments are those that 'combine an empirical focus on the language and gestures of human interactions with a theoretical concern with their symbolic meanings and how the ongoing social order is negotiated and maintained' (1998: 42). Interpretive arguments may also 'focus on ideologies, discourses, cultural frameworks' (1998: 42).

Respondents of *structured interviews* are called upon to select their answer from those listed by the interviewer (see Foddy [1993] and Fontana and Prokos [2007] for more detail on structured interviews). Interview researchers using a standardized format of interview are advised not to deviate from the script, although conversation analytic studies of talk generated in standardized survey interviews suggest that this is technically very difficult to do, given that interviewees may not understand questions, and speakers may demonstrate a variety of other interactional difficulties in the administration of survey instruments (see, for example, Houtkoop-Steenstra, 2000; Houtkoop-Steenstra and Antaki, 1997; Suchman and Jordan, 1990).

Another point on the spectrum of structured to unstructured interviews is that of *semi-structured interviews*. In these kinds of interviews, interviewers refer to a prepared interview guide that includes a number of questions. These questions are usually open-ended, and after posing each question to the research participant, the interviewer follows up with probes seeking further detail and description about what has been said. Although the interview guide provides the same starting point for each semi-structured interview given that it assumes a common set of discussable topics – each interview will vary according to what was said by individual interviewees, and how each interviewer used follow up questions to elicit further description. Similarly to other interview structures, interviewers using semi-structured interviews must have highly developed listening skills to be able to both ascertain whether the research topics have been addressed by the interviewee, and when and how it is appropriate to follow up on the accounts given.

Unstructured interviews, in contrast, are those in which interviewers proceed with no formal interview guides. Questions are posed in relation to both ongoing ethnographic field work (i.e. participant observation) as well as the talk that takes place in spontaneous conversations, rather than from pre-specified topics outlined in an interview guide. Nevertheless, interviewers using unstructured interviews have research topics in mind, and are likely to steer conversations towards topics of interest to them. The talk generated from unstructured interviews resembles conversation, and the interviewees are freer to ask questions of the interviewers, who may divulge personal details and opinions of their own. Like conversation, unstructured interview talk may appear to be less asymmetrical than structured and semi-structured forms of talk in which the interviewer has greater rights to ask pre-designated questions. In that conversations can sometimes turn into arguments or interrogations, it is impossible to predict whether unstructured interviews – nor for that matter, any interview format – will go smoothly, or resemble free-flowing conversation. A drawback of using an unstructured format for interviewing is that the talk may not generate useful data, given that any and every topic can be introduced at any point by either of the speakers, and topics may not be relevant to the researcher's interests. For researchers to generate usable data to examine research questions using unstructured interviews, they are likely to carry these out on repeated occasions during an extended period of fieldwork in which they have focused on specific topics and aspects of analysis (see Lofland et al., 2006).

Interviews Used in Qualitative Research

While some social science researchers characterize their use of qualitative interviews in terms of 'structure' – that is, they use structured, semi-structured, or unstructured interviews – researchers often specify the form further in accordance with the kind of content they seek to elicit. In the next section I review a number of forms for qualitative interviewing used in social science research. Each is used for different purposes, corresponds with different theoretical assumptions about how we might learn about the social world, and may entail particular approaches to data analysis and representation. In this chapter, suggestions for each interview form are not intended to be taken up as prescriptions for interview practice. In each individual interview setting, the interviewer must exercise wisdom in judging when it is necessary to talk about his or her own experiences in order to develop rapport. This differs on each and every interview occasion. Below I discuss the phenomenological interview, the ethnographic interview, feminist interviews, oral and life history interviews, and the dialogic or confrontational interview. Although these interviews share some common characteristics, they also have some distinctive features in relation to the kinds of content sought by researchers.

Phenomenological Interviewing

Social science researchers who focus on generating data to examine participants' lived experiences have made frequent use of phenomenological interviews. The purpose of this kind of interview is to generate detailed and in-depth descriptions of human experiences. Thus, questions that generate detailed information concerning these experiences as well as the participant's responses to the phenomenon of investigation are crucial. Since researchers want to understand the participants' feelings, perceptions and understandings, open questions are particularly useful in providing a format for interviewees to answer in their own words. To begin the interview, an open question could be posed as follows:

Think of a time when you experienced _____ and describe that in as much detail as possible.

Possible follow up questions include:

You mentioned _____ tell me what that was like for you.
You mentioned _____ describe that in more detail for me.

To use phenomenological interviews effectively, it is essential that the interviewer has identified participants who have both experienced, and are able to talk about the particular lived experience under examination.

Some researchers using phenomenological interviews are informed philosophically by phenomenological theory. According to Catherine Adams and Max van Manen, the focus of phenomenological interviews is to elicit the 'direct description of a particular situation or event as it is lived through without offering causal explanations or interpretive generalizations' (2008: 618). Adams and van Manen distinguish between two inter-related forms of interview – the 'phenomenological interview' that explores and gathers descriptions of lived experience, and the 'hermeneutic interview' that seeks to examine the 'interpretive meaning aspects of lived experience material' (2008: 618). Researchers informed by phenomenological theory may use phenomenological reduction to analyze and represent the findings in the form of descriptions of the structures of meaning relevant to a lived experience (for an example, see Fischer and Wertz's [1980/2002] description of being criminally victimized). Yet, some researchers draw on the form of phenomenological interviews in order to gain detailed descriptions that may be subject to other forms of analysis – such as narrative analysis and constant comparative analysis, and may not be conducting research informed by various strands of phenomenological theory. Thus, in some work the term 'phenomenological' is used as a synonym for 'qualitative,' rather than to refer to the kind of work described by Adams and van Manen, and other researchers who conduct phenomenological inquiries.

In terms of 'structure,' the phenomenological interview is relatively unstructured and open-ended, and may be guided by only one or two interview questions. For example, Fischer and Wertz state that the questions used in their study of the experience of being criminally victimized were 'what was going on prior to the crime, what it was like to be victimized, and what happened then. Questions were restricted to requests for clarification or elaboration of what the victim had already said' (1980/2002: 279).

Interviewers may also conduct multiple interviews with each participant. For example, Seidman (2006) describes a phenomenologically informed interview sequence in which the interviewer conducts three separate 90-minute interviews over a two- to three-week period. In phenomenological interviews, the interviewer takes a neutral but interested stance, and the relationship between interviewer and interviewee is sometimes described as pedagogical, in that the interviewer's role is to be a student of the interviewee, learning as much about the topic of inquiry as possible through sensitive questioning (see, for example, Van Manen, 1990). In this kind of interview, the interviewer must listen carefully, follow up on participant's responses without interrupting the story flow to gain specific details of the participant's experience, and generally exercise reservation in contributing to the talk. This would usually mean refraining from evaluating or challenging the participant's responses. In sum, in phenomenological interviews as traditionally discussed and understood, the interviewer's responsibility is to provide a supportive, non-therapeutic environment in which the participant feels comfortable to provide in-depth descriptions of the life experiences of interest to the researcher.

Christine Sorrell Dinkins (2005) has provided an alternative form for phenomenological interviewing that she calls the 'Socratic-Hermeneutic Inter-view.' In this form of interview, the interviewer and interviewee (referred to as 'co-inquirer') 'engage in a dialogue through questions and responses that encourage the researcher and co-inquirer to reflect together on the concepts that are emerging and taking shape within the interview itself' (2005: 112–13). In this description, Dinkins refers to a central focus of hermeneutic study, that of examining the process of understanding and interpretation. Drawing on the hermeneutic phenomenology of Hans-Georg Gadamer and Martin Heidegger, Dinkins rejects the neutral stance taken by phenomenological researchers seeking detailed stories about specific experiences. Instead, Dinkins makes use of a Socratic method of inquiry in which speakers question one another in order to clarify understandings, and search for and develop insight concerning research topics. In this kind of dialogue,

> Socrates puts himself very much into the inquiry. He expresses surprise when an interlocutor says something he didn't expect, he challenges beliefs that seem to conflict, and he acknowledges his own assumptions and allows them to affect the dialogue. He is never passive, and he never simply asks a question and lets the answer lie. (Dinkins, 2005: 116)

Although the kinds of research questions posed may be similar to those of other phenomenological studies, the way in which the kind of interview proposed by Dinkins will unfold is radically different to the phenomenological interview described in numerous methodological texts. It is worth exploring further some of the concrete suggestions that Dinkins draws from Socratic dialogues that might be used to generate data for phenomenological and hermeneutic inquiries.

Similarly to Socratic dialogues, the Socratic-Hermeneutic Inter-view begins with definitions. That is, the interviewer first asks the research participant to provide a definition for the phenomenon that is the focus of the investigation. Like Socrates in his dialogues, interviewers will make use of analogies to help interviewees think about difficult questions and clarify what they believe and mean by terms used in descriptions; use examples to explore the co-inquirer's descriptions; point out conflicting statements in an effort to have participants explore what that means; re-word co-inquirers' statements in the researcher's words in order to identify potential misunderstandings on the part of the researcher; and ask participants for their ideas about 'ideal' experiences in addition to those that are 'actual.' Dinkins proposes that the structure of this kind of interview is a back and forth process of 'continual reexamination' that resembles Heidegger's hermeneutic circle (2005: 137–40). Finally, in this kind of interview, interpretation is seen to be part of the interview process itself, rather than a separate phase that takes place after the interview when the researcher analyzes data and writes the report from her study. Dinkins suggests that the interpretations from this kind of interview are likely to be incomplete or lacking in resolution, with interviewees having gained insights about their experiences that they reflect on further, and researchers left with more questions to ask (2005: 142–3).

As we can see here, traditional models of interviewing are being continuously revisited, and researchers are suggesting alternatives and innovations – some of which draw on ancient understandings and practice. It is useful, then, to think of the various forms of interviews described in this chapter not as fixed practices, but flexible forms that researchers take up, alter, and reformulate to align with the theoretical presuppositions upon which they base their work.

Ethnographic Interviewing

The purpose of ethnographic interviewing is to explore the meanings that people ascribe to actions and events in their cultural worlds, expressed in their own language. Whereas the focus of phenomenological interviews is to gain descriptions of particular lived experiences, the focus of ethnographic interviews is on generating participants' descriptions of key aspects related to the cultural world of which he or she is a part – that is space, time, events, people, activities, and objects (Spradley, 1979). Thus, researchers must generate data that not only includes participants' 'folk' terms and language to describe that culture, but explanations and definitions of those terms and how they are routinely used by members of the culture studied. Drawing on two ethnographies in which he was involved (Spradley, 1970; Spradley and Mann, 1975), James Spradley describes how to develop and conduct ethnographic interviews for the purpose of writing ethnography (Spradley, 1979). Embedded in extended field work involving participant observation (Spradley, 1980), Spradley comments that ethnographic interviews share similarities with friendly conversations; the key difference being that the researcher introduces 'ethnographic elements' to 'assist informants to respond as informants' (1979: 58–68). Because of the conversational style, ethnographic interviewing appears to be highly unstructured, yet this kind of interviewing relies on the researcher's ongoing analyses of data generated via field notes of observations, participation in the research settings, development of rapport with informants, and multiple interviews over extended periods of time.

Although ethnographic interviews may resemble everyday conversations, the researcher is focused on findings answers to very specific questions. Spradley (1979) divides questions that can be asked in ethnographic interviews into (1) descriptive (2) structural, and (3) contrast questions. In the early stages of ethnographic fieldwork, the researcher focuses on asking open-ended questions aimed at gaining participants' descriptions of space, time, events, people, activities, and objects (Spradley, 1979). Spradley describes five different kinds of descriptive questions that can be asked of participants to get at the details of participants' cultural worlds. The exemplar questions provided in Box 1.1 are drawn from Spradley's study of men who had been arrested for public drunkenness (1970), and James Spradley and Brenda Mann's study of the world of a cocktail waitress (1975).

Box 1.1   Types of descriptive questions

(1) Grand tour questions
     Could you describe the inside of the jail for me?
(2) Mini-tour questions
     Could you describe what you do when you take a break at Brady's Bar?
(3) Example questions
     'I was arrested while pooling': Q: 'Can you give me an example of pooling?
(4) Experience questions
     You've probably had some interesting experiences in jail, can you recall any of them?
     Native-language questions
(5) How would you refer to the jail? (Spradley, 1979: 78–91)[2]

After analysis of data generated from early interviews, Spradley provides examples of structural and contrast interview questions that can be generated from information already gleaned. The researcher uses these kinds of questions to verify or disconfirm hypotheses generated from data analysis. In this way, the researcher seeks to generate data in succeeding interviews to systematically check his or her understandings of what participants have already said, and refine ongoing analyses and interpretations of data.

There is some debate as to what counts as ethnographic interviewing. For example, some researchers who claim to have used ethnographic interviews do not engage in extensive fieldwork, nor do they engage in analyses with the purpose of gaining an understanding of how people use language and make meaning of events and objects in specific cultural settings. Rather than use the term ethnographic interviews as a loose synonym for qualitative interviews in research studies that do not exemplify the kinds of ethnographic fieldwork commonly practiced by anthropologists and sociologists (see, for example, DeWalt and DeWalt, 2002; Emerson et al., 1995; Lofland et al., 2006), novice researchers might consider how their use of ethnographic interviews aligns with or challenges the ethnographic traditions that have been developed in the fields of cultural anthropology and qualitative sociology.

Data generated from ethnographic interviews may be analyzed in a number of ways, including ethnographic analytic methods such as domain analysis, taxonomic analysis, componential analysis (Spradley, 1979, 1980), grounded theory

---

[2]I have included only one example of each of the five kinds of description questions here. Spradley provides many sub-categories for each of these that are worth reviewing by those seeking to do ethnography.

methods (Glaser and Strauss, 1967), or a more open process described by Harry Wolcott as 'transforming qualitative data' (1994). Given the emphasis on culture and symbolic meaning, many studies also make use of symbolic interactionist theory as an interpretive lens (for a review of symbolic interactionist studies that have used a variety of interview methods including structured, semi-structured, and unstructured interviews as well as focus groups, see Herman-Kinney and Verschaeve, 2003).

Researchers using ethnographic interviews frequently become participants in the settings that they are studying. For example, Mitch Duneier's (2000) study of street vendors in Greenwich Village in New York City combined participation observation and ethnographic interviews. His questions developed from what he observed and experienced during his fieldwork, and were frequently undertaken during the course of everyday business; for example, one chapter deals with the reasons why some street vendors chose to sleep on the sidewalk.

Feminist Interviewing

Feminist interviewing as a specific label developed in the 1970s and 1980s when feminist researchers began to use open-ended, intensive, and unstructured interviews as an alternative to the social scientific standardized survey (see DeVault and Gross, 2007 for examples). Ann Oakley's (1981) influential article 'Interviewing women: A contradiction in terms' was one of a number of critiques arguing that research methodologies and the tools of social scientific inquiry alienated and objectified women, and contributed to the development of knowledge that reinforced patriarchy (see also Finch, 1984). In the 1970s and 1980s, feminist researchers were promoting the development of a sociology for women, and feminist standpoint theory emerged (Harding, 2007; Reinharz, 1992; Smith, 1987). For some feminist researchers, this has meant exclusive use of qualitative research methods, such as ethnography and unstructured interviews, while others have argued that this has ultimately hindered feminist causes (see, for example, Oakley, 1998, 2000). In her much-cited 1981 article, Oakley provided specific recommendations for how feminist interviewing might be undertaken, including establishment of intimacy and openness through self-disclosure on the part of the researcher, and a willingness to engage in continuing relationships with research participants beyond the conclusion of the study. Much attention has been paid to this kind of advice by feminist researchers conducting qualitative interviews.

In the writing of the 1980s and early 1990s, open-ended interviews were thought to provide a context that promoted an egalitarian relationship among women researchers and women participants with the aim of producing knowledge about previously unknown and unstudied facets of women's lives. Instead of asymmetrical relationships in which the researcher reserved the right of topic selection, and posed the kinds of questions of relevance to researchers, feminists argued for a qualitative or feminist interview that promoted equitable relationships between researchers and participants, in which the conversation was guided by the interviewee, rather than interviewer. Furthermore, some argued that for some topics, only women interviewers could interview women (Reinharz, 1992: 23–6; although see Harding, 1987).

In recent decades, feminist qualitative researchers have embraced the use of semi-structured interviews, as well as unstructured, in-depth, and open-ended interviews (Reinharz, 1992), life history interviews (see, for example, Behar, 1993), and focus groups (Wilkinson, 1999), and many prefer to use the label 'feminist interviews' to describe their methods. Interview research framed as feminist has made frequent use of open-ended questions, and multiple, rather than one-off interviews.

Readers may be asking the question: Given that feminist interviewers use semi-structured and unstructured interviews, what distinguishes the feminist interview from other kinds of qualitative interviews? As in every other area of scholarly research, there is considerable debate about this question (see, for example, DeVault and Gross, 2007; Harding, 1987). A number of issues have been highlighted with respect to what feminist interviews involve (Reinharz, 1992; Reinharz and Chase, 2002). Feminist interviewers:

- Maintain that ethical issues are heightened in doing social science research.
- Argue that participants should be believed (Reinharz, 1992: 27–30).
- Work to ensure that they are trusted by research participants (Reinharz, 1992: 29–30).

Others have argued that these are problematic positions, and that the shared category of woman does not necessarily mean that researchers can generate meaningful data from women who ascribe importance to other category positions (for example, race, class, status, or sexual orientation among others), or that interactions in interview contexts will always go smoothly (see, for example, Best, 2003; Johnson-Bailey, 1999; Kezar, 2003; Naples, 1996; Riessman, 1987; Tang, 2002). Sandra Harding (2007) has also outlined a number of 'futile strategies' used by feminist researchers that she argues do not serve the purposes of feminist work well. These include use of 'empathy, careful listening, or "going native,"' in an attempt to erase the power differentials inherent in the researcher–researched relationship (Harding, 2007: 53); use of confessional subjectivity statements to locate the position of the researcher in relation to the topic and research participants; and finally, attempts to omit 'theoretical or conceptual input into the research process itself' by simply recording women's voices (2007: 54). Although these strategies relate to research more generally, they may be noted frequently in feminist interview research. Harding's critiques, therefore, are useful to consider for researchers taking a feminist approach to interview research. Yet, the critiques of feminist practice outlined above provide productive avenues for development of feminist methods.

For example, Marjorie DeVault (1990) has argued that in order to engage in respectful and ethical ways with others in feminist research, there are a number of concrete strategies that researchers might follow. DeVault's recommendations for engaging in feminist interview research focus on language-use, both within the interview setting, and beyond, as the researcher represents others in research reports. These include:

- Using the terms and categories used by women in their daily lives, rather than the research 'topics established by the discipline' (DeVault, 1990: 101). Here, researchers work to 'interview in ways that allow the exploration of incompletely articulated aspects of women's experiences' (DeVault, 1990: 100).

- Listening carefully to how women construct their accounts in order to examine 'not-quite-articulated experience' (DeVault, 1990: 103). This involves researchers in noticing 'ambiguity and problems of expression' within the interview interaction, and then drawing on their experience within the research context to fill in 'what has been incompletely said' (DeVault, 1990: 104).
- Considering carefully how women's speech is represented in order to portray participants respectfully (DeVault, 1990: 109).
- Representing research in a way that can be understood by new audiences to feminist work. DeVault asserts that '[p]art of the task of feminist writing, then, should be to instruct a newly forming audience about how to read and hear our words' (1990: 112).

Harding's (2007: 54) advice to feminist researchers to guard against the colonizing effects of social science research at each stage of the research process through the use of feminist standpoint theory is useful in thinking about how feminist researchers can use interviews in ways that align with feminist assumptions. The four stages reviewed by Harding are the selection of the research problem and design of the study; the conduct of the research; interpretation and representation of findings; and dissemination of the research. The strategies outlined by DeVault show possible ways that researchers can address the issues that Harding outlines within the research process.

In summary, unlike phenomenological and ethnographic interviews, feminist interviews do not identify with particular ways of asking questions, or structuring interviews, although oral history, life history, and semi- and unstructured interviews have been frequently used. The distinguishing feature of feminist interviews is that they are used for the purpose of doing feminist work, and contributing to the advancement of women's causes in a patriarchal, capitalist society. Rather than re-produce the exploitive relationships of traditional forms of social scientific research, feminists aim to work with participants in respectful and ethical ways that allow women's voices to be heard.

Ongoing scholarship in this area shows that the self-reflexive critique with which feminist work has long been identified has produced insightful findings about how interview interaction is accomplished, and how we might use interviews for feminist purposes (see, for example, DeVault and Gross, 2007; Hesse-Biber and Leavy, 2007; Moss, 2007). Above all, in writing on feminist interviewing, we see a focus on particular kinds of relationships that researchers strive to develop with interviewees – those that are ethical, non-exploitive, sincere, and genuinely interested in free and open dialogue with women participants.

Oral History Interviewing

Oral history involves the collection of oral narratives from ordinary people in order to chronicle peoples' lives and past events. There has been a proliferation of terms often used synonymously: life story, biography, personal narrative, and memoir (Yow, 2005: 3–4). Whereas the audio- and video-recordings of qualitative research interviews are frequently erased (this is frequently required by Institutional Review

Boards in the US), in oral history, interviews are often transcribed in addition to being indexed and deposited in archival collections in libraries and museums for public access (see Ritchie [2003] for further information on archiving oral history interviews). With the proliferation of information in the digital age, oral history work is frequently accomplished by members of community groups with the purpose of recording local history (see, for example, one archive at http://www.centerforthequilt.org/qsos/qsos.html in which members of quilting guilds are encouraged to collect oral histories of local quilt makers).

One historian, William Moss, argues for the need for using other forms of evidence in conjunction with oral histories in order to construct 'good history' (1977/1996: 113). What Moss is referring to here is the need for verification of the information provided by interviewees in oral history in order to construct realist accounts. This is accomplished through checking and comparing information from interviews with other kinds of historical evidence, including *transaction records* such as laws, contracts, deeds, wills, treaties, diplomas, certificates, licenses, patents, proclamations, orders, instructions, advertisements, and so forth (1977/1996: 109); *contemporary descriptions*, including audio and video recordings of events, still photographs, or running descriptions (e.g. from broadcasts) (1977/1996: 109); *recollections* in the form of diaries, stories told by grandparents to children, information gained from eyewitnesses by investigators, and information from other oral history narrators (1977/1996: 110–11); *reflections* in which narrators simultaneously recollect events and actions from the past, and make these relevant to the present; and *accounts* by historians, journalists, writers of government reports, and others that have involved careful and critical examination and comparison of records (1977/1996: 113).

Two common features appear in the literature on oral history, these are that oral history narratives and personal commentaries form collective memories that contribute to documentation of 'public history' (Ritchie, 2003), and that these are recorded and made available for posterity. While historians such as Moss argue that an integral feature of doing oral history interviews is to verify the information provided by interviewees, others disagree. Dunaway, for example, stresses the interdisciplinary nature of oral history, and comments that the fourth generation of oral historians draws on postmodern and critical theories, and makes use of modern technologies (1996: 7).

Shifts in theoretical perspectives used by historians has meant a move from 'presenting facts as received wisdom to presenting theoretical analyses as specific to a given time and place and society' (Dunaway, 1996: 9). Thus, not all researchers using oral history interviewing aim to construct realist accounts. For example, feminist researcher Delores Delgado Bernal (1998) used oral history interviews to generate stories and memories of women's experiences of the East Los Angeles Blowouts, which occurred in 1968 when thousands of students walked out of schools to protest inferior educational opportunities. Delgado Bernal states that 'I was used to my grandmothers' storytelling in which absolute "Truth" was less important to me than hearing and recording their life experiences' (1998: 571). Here, Delgado Bernal's espoused theory as a Chicana feminist informs her use of oral history interviews, rather than using various forms of interview and documentary data as a means to construct an accurate and truthful historical account of what may have actually happened.

Life History Interviewing

Although oral history and life history interviews are similar in some respects, they are not necessarily the same. While life history interviews may contribute to the production of oral history, life history interviews are used in many disciplines other than history, and for purposes other than contributing to oral history. Ardra Cole and Gary Knowles define life history inquiry broadly, commenting that this kind of research aims to understand the:

> human condition by coming to know and understand the experiences of other humans. It is about understanding a situation, profession, condition, or institution through coming to know how individuals walk, talk, live, and work within a particular context. (2001: 11)

The 'life narrative or life story' is a 'written or oral account of a life or segment of a life as told by an individual' (Cole and Knowles, 2001: 18). Donald Ritchie defines a life history interview as one in which interviewees 'relate their entire life, from childhood to the present' (2003: 40). Robert Miller (2000: 19) teases out some of the transitions in terminology that have transpired in the later decades of the 20th century. He comments that *life story* originally referred to 'the account given by an individual about his or her life' (2000: 19). When validated by external sources, the story was called a *life history*. With the influence of narrative work, Miller argues that 'life history' is now used to refer to 'a series of substantive events arranged in chronological order. Confirmation or validation by external sources is no longer a necessary requirement for a life history' (2000: 19).

Life history research typically involves small numbers of participants over a lengthy period of time. Oral history, in contrast, may not necessarily be restricted to small numbers of participants, particularly when the purpose is to archive recollections of specific events, periods of time, or groups of people. For example, in the US, the Federal Writers' Project undertook oral history interviews across 17 states during the 1930s with 2000 former slaves about their experiences of slavery (Waters, 2000).

Given that biographical research is often conducted with older people, interviewers are likely to schedule multiple meetings to allow participants time to reflect, and recount their stories, and interviews are likely to take many hours to complete. Similarly to oral history research, multiple forms of data are used – including interviews, field notes of observations, and documents and artifacts (Cole and Knowles, 2001: 13), although the focus of the use of other data may not be on verification of evidence as described by oral historians. Cole and Knowles comment that:

> These data are then thematically interpreted and considered in relation to relevant discipline-based theories and represented in the form of detailed and rich life history accounts. These accounts represent both the researcher's interpretation of the research participants' lives, and the researcher's theorizing about those lives in relation to broader contextual situations and issues. (2001: 13)

Using Miller's typology of approaches to biographical and family history research – 'realist,' 'neo-positivist,' and 'narrative' – Cole and Knowles are situated in a 'narrative' approach to life history, in which data are jointly constructed by interviewer and interviewee, and 'questions of fact take second place to understanding the individual's unique and changing perception' (Miller, 2000: 13). This is a decidedly different perspective on research than that taken by a realist oral historian, who seeks to construct participants' accounts based on factual empirical material, or the neo-positivist researcher seeking to test theories using factual data (Miller, 2000: 13).

Dialogic and Confrontational Interviewing

In the approaches to interviews outlined above, with the exception of oral history interviews in which the interviewer is advised to ask challenging questions of interviewees in order to pursue topics when necessary (Ritchie, 2003) and the Socratic-Hermeneutic Inter-view proposed by Dinkins (2005), interviewers are usually described as taking non-adversarial roles in relation to interviewees. We are familiar from watching journalists' encounters with politicians, however, with interviewers who take confrontational and combative roles. There are few descriptions available in the social science literature of research interviewers who purposefully take on an oppositional role with interviewees. Given that researchers rely on the good will of people to engage in social science research, and there are limited direct benefits of participating in inquiries, this is hardly surprising. Yet some researchers have discussed how participants resist the interviewer's role by 'fighting back' and disagreeing with assumptions embedded in interview questions. In addition, researchers have begun to think about how they might instigate dialogue, and perhaps even arguments in their conversations with research participants.

Svend Brinkmann and Steinar Kvale have outlined a contrasting perspective to 'warm, empathic, and caring interviews,' that, they argue, 'neglect real power relations' (2005: 170). Alternatives to these kinds of interviews include the psychoanalytic interview in which the therapist intervenes on behalf of the client by actively creating conflict, the Platonic dialogue in which speakers provide 'reciprocal critique of what the other says', agonistic interviews in which the interviewer 'deliberately provokes conflicts and divergences of interests', dissensus research, which exposes the arguments of opposing sides, and advocacy research, in which representatives of different positions in a social setting (e.g. managers and workers, teachers and students) 'critically interpret the texts, and potentially, as in court, cross-examine the witnesses' (Brinkmann and Kvale, 2005: 171, 172, see also Kvale, 2006). These models of interaction are very different to the kinds of research interview outlined earlier in this chapter. While some of these kinds of talk are clearly not research interviews (e.g., Platonic dialogues, or therapeutic psychoanalytic interviews), these researchers seek to purposefully introduce 'challenge' in interviewer–interviewee interaction for the purpose of social research. Below, I examine these proposals in further detail.

Writing from the field of psychology, and similarly to Dinkins (2005), Brinkmann (2007) has forwarded the idea of 'epistemic interviews' inspired by Socratic dialogues as an alternative to those interviews informed by a therapeutic Rogerian model. The purpose of Socratic dialogues was to move conversationalists 'from a state of being simply *opinionated* to being capable of *questioning* and *justifying* what they believe is the case' (Brinkmann, 2007: 2, emphasis in original). Here, Brinkmann (2007: 4) has extended Holstein and Gubrium's (1995, 2004) notion of the active interview – in which interviews are viewed as interactional and interpretive – to focus on an interview practice that *develops knowledge* rather than simply *conveying experience*. An example of this kind of interviewing that is used by Brinkmann (2007: 16) is the well known study *Habits of the Heart* (Bellah et al., 1985), in which the researchers aimed to investigate public and private life in the US with a view to examining the 'relationship between character and society' (1985: vii). Bellah et al. argue for 'social science as public philosophy,' and state that they used an 'active, Socratic' approach to interviewing in which, while seeking not to impose their views on their participants, they 'did attempt to uncover assumptions, to make explicit what the person [they] were talking to might rather have left implicit' (1985: 304).

Another example used by Brinkmann in his argument for epistemic interviews is that of Pierre Bourdieu et al.'s (1999) *The Weight of the World: Social Suffering in Contemporary Society*. In one of the cases presented, Bourdieu actively interviews two young men from the north of France, openly challenging them to justify their accounts (Bourdieu et al., 1999: 64–76). Bourdieu also draws on a Socratic notion of dialogue in his discussion of interview methods, stating that it is the interviewer's responsibility to offer:

> the respondent an absolutely exceptional situation for communication, freed from the usual constraints (particularly of time) that weigh on most everyday interchanges, and opening up alternatives which prompt or authorize the articulation of worries, needs or wishes discovered through this very articulation, the researcher helps create the conditions for an extraordinary discourse, which might never have been spoken, but which was already there, merely awaiting the conditions of its actualization. (Bourdieu et al., 1999: 614)

Brinkmann cautions that this kind of interviewing is neither suitable for all research purposes, nor certain kinds of interviewees. The use of epistemic interviews, then, rests on the researcher's interest in promoting interaction between interviewers and interviewees that seeks to foster public dialogue on topics of concern. In this kind of dialogue, interested citizens – including the interviewer – must be willing to justify, argue, defend, and perhaps even change, their accounts.

Similarly, Lene Tanggaard (2007, 2008) has outlined adversarial roles for interviewers and their participants, also building on Holstein and Gubrium's (1995) notion of the active interview. Tanggaard (2007) uses the metaphor of 'discourses crossing swords' in a 'battlefield' to envision the 'antagonistic character of conversations' and encounters that take place in qualitative interviews. Here, rather than a site of consonance and agreement between interviewer and interviewee, interaction is analyzable as a site of dissonance in which 'discourses cross each other' (Tanggaard, 2008: 18). Both Tanggaard (2007, 2008) and Brinkmann (2007) point to the possibilities of producing more objective understandings of data when the dialogues produced and interpreted show how both interviewers and interviewees challenge one another, and interpret topics within the interview interaction itself, rather than leaving interpretation as a sole feat performed by the researcher after the interview has been completed. Here, Tanggaard and Brinkmann are using Latour's (2000) notion of 'objectivity' in which the subject of research is able to 'object' to the researcher, just as objects of study in the natural sciences object to scientists' claims by 'behaving in the most undisciplined ways, blocking the experiments, disappearing from view, dying, refusing to replicate, or exploding the laboratory to pieces' (Latour, 2000: 116).

In the examples of interview interaction given by Tanggaard (2007, 2008), she shows confrontational dialogue between interviewers and interviewees in which the interviewer asks leading questions, and the interviewee disagrees and disputes the researcher's interpretations. Tanggaard (2008) asserts that through confrontational interactions such as these, in which the interviewer and interviewee challenge each others' assumptions and inquire into one another's viewpoints, that knowledge is produced. Brinkmann (2007) cautions that ethical practice requires that participants to these kinds of interviews must know what it is that they are participating in, and argues that researchers can proceed ethically with epistemic interviews, given that they too take risks by participating fully in the dialogues.

Through the use of dialogic and confrontational interviews, these researchers are seeking to generate data in which people's reasoning practices and justifications are made explicit in the ongoing dialogue. At this point in time, there are few examples of qualitative interviewers who have discussed this kind of approach in their practice – although Dinkins' (2005) adaptation of the Socratic dialogue for use in phenomenological interviews is one resource. Key questions, among others, concerning this kind of interview relate to how researchers might use this approach in an ethical manner in which participants are fully informed, what kinds of topics are best suited to this approach, and what analytic methods best represent the talk generated.

Conclusion

In this chapter, I have outlined a number of different interview forms used by qualitative researchers. Beginning with an examination of question–answer sequences, I showed how research interviews are built on sequences of open and closed questions, usually arranged in semi-structured or unstructured ways. I then reviewed different kinds of interview formats, including the phenomenological, ethnographic, feminist, oral history and life history, and dialogic or confrontational interview. While each of these forms uses questions and answers, the research purposes differ. Phenomenological interviews are commonly used to elicit detail concerning descriptions of concrete lived experiences. Ethnographic interviews are frequently used by ethnographers studying questions to do with culture. A multitude of interview formats, including life history, semi- and unstructured, ethnographic, and phenomenological interviews have been used by feminist researchers as a way to contribute to work that benefits women. One way to think about the feminist interview is that it is conducted in a way that is consonant with the theoretical assumptions associated with the strand of feminist theory underpinning a researcher's work. Oral history interviews have been used by historians to construct historical accounts, and contribute to public knowledge concerning events and people's lives. Life history interviews are used by researchers from a wide range of disciplines to capture the range of people's experiences in the examination of a multitude of topics. Finally, dialogical or confrontational interviews have been proposed by researchers as an alternative to 'neutral' interviews that aim to elicit descriptions of individuals' psychological and interior states. In contrast, these researchers want to investigate participants' justification and reasoning practices, show how interviewers themselves are implicated in the production of research accounts, and both instigate and examine public discourse and dialogue about research topics.

The forms of interviewing that I have discussed in this chapter might also employ stimulus texts and photographs to elicit data. That is, the researcher either brings texts or images to an interview setting, or participants generate images such as drawings, time lines, or photographs according to guidelines provided by the researcher. In both cases, the images and texts become topics of talk for the interview. These methods have been used effectively to work with children, battered women, and people with illnesses, although these methods are by no means restricted to these kinds of populations (Clark-Ibáñez, 2004; Frith and Harcourt, 2007; Frohmann, 2005).

In the next chapter, with my co-author, Anna Liljestrom, I discuss group interview formats, and what researchers have learned about designing and conducting interview studies with multiple participants. I specifically discuss focus groups as one particular form of group format.

Further Reading

Phenomenological Interviewing

deMarrais, K. (2007) 'Qualitative interview studies: Learning through experience', in K. deMarrais and S.P. Lapan (eds), *Foundations for Research. Methods of Inquiry in Education and the Social Sciences*. Mahwah, NJ: Lawrence Erlbaum Associates. pp. 51–68.

Kvale, S. (1996) *Interviews: An Introduction to Qualitative Research Interviewing.* Thousand Oaks, CA: Sage.

Seidman, I. (2006) *Interviewing as Qualitative Research: A Guide for Researchers in Education and the Social Sciences*, 3rd edn. New York: Teachers College.

Ethnographic Interviewing

De Leon, J.P. and Cohen, J.H. (2005) 'Object and walking probes in ethnographic interviewing', *Field Methods*, 17 (2): 200–4.

Heyl, B.S. (2001) 'Ethnographic interviewing', in P. Atkinson, A. Coffey, S. Delamont, J. Lofland and L. Lofland (eds), *Handbook of Ethnography*. Thousand Oaks, CA: Sage. pp. 369–83.

Feminist Interviewing

DeVault, M.L. and Gross, G. (2007) 'Feminist interviewing: Experience, talk, and knowledge', in S.N. Hesse-Biber (ed.), *Handbook of Feminist Research: Theory and Praxis*. Thousand Oaks, CA: Sage. pp. 143–54.

Reinharz, S. and Chase, S.E. (2002) 'Interviewing women', in J. Gubrium and J.A. Holstein (eds), *Handbook of Interviewing: Context and Method*. Thousand Oaks, CA: Sage. pp. 221–38.

Oral History and Life History

Frisch, M. (2008) 'Three dimensions and more: Oral history beyond the paradoxes of method', in S.N. Hesse-Biber and P. Leavy (eds), *Handbook of Emergent Methods*. New York & London: The Guilford Press. pp. 221–38.

Starr, L. (1977/1996) 'Oral history', in D.K. Dunaway and W.K. Baum (eds), *Oral History: An Interdisciplinary Anthology*. Walnut Creek, London & New Delhi: Altamira Press. pp. 39–61. Reprinted from the *Encylopedia of Library and Information Sciences*, 20: 440–63.

Digital Archives

University of Southern California, Shoah Foundation Institute
http://college.usc.edu/vhi/

This website contains videos of oral history interviews conducted with Holocaust survivors. Numerous oral history projects are located at national archives, and audiofiles and transcriptions of interviews are accessible via the Internet, for example:

The Smithsonian Institution – http://www.si.edu/
The British Library – http://www.bl.uk/
National Library of Australia – http://www.nla.gov.au/digicoll/audio.html
Library and Archives Canada – http://www.collectionscanada.gc.ca/

Photo Elicitation and Use of Stimulus Texts

Cappello, M. (2005) 'Photo interviews: Eliciting data through conversations with children', *Field Methods*, 17 (2): 170–82.

Clark-Ibáñez, M. (2004) 'Framing the social world with photo-elicitation interviews', *American Behavioral Scientist*, 47 (12): 1507–27.

Crilly, N., Blackwell, A.F. and Clarkson, P.J. (2006) 'Graphic elicitation: Using research diagrams as interview stimuli', *Qualitative Research*, 6 (3), 341–66.

Frith, H. and Harcourt, D. (2007) 'Using photographs to capture women's experiences of chemotherapy: Reflecting on the method', *Qualitative Health Research*, 17 (10): 1340–50.

Frohmann, L. (2005) 'The Framing Safety project: Photographs and narratives by battered women', *Violence Against Women*, 11 (11): 1396–419.

Radley, A. and Taylor, D. (2003) 'Remembering one's stay in hospital: A study in photography, recovery and forgetting', *Health: An Interdisciplinary Journal for the Social Study of Health, Illness and Medicine*, 7 (2): 129–59.

Torronen, J. (2002) 'Semiotic theory on qualitative interviewing using stimulus texts', *Qualitative Research*, 2 (3): 343–62.

Interview Practice

Select one or more of the following types of interviews, and practice interviewing another person. Audio-record the meeting, aiming for a 45–60 minute interview.

Activity 1.1   Exploring phenomenological interviews

Arrange to interview a friend or relative about one of the topics listed.

- *The experience of transformation*
- *The experience of joy*
- *The experience of frustration*
- *The experience of learning*

You will need to check if your interviewee has had the kind of experience that you have selected before you start. If not, select another topic. One way to start the interview is to elicit a story using the following question:

Think of a time when you had a _____ experience. I would like you to tell me about that in as much detail as possible.

Possible probes that you can use to follow up on your interviewee's description are:

- *You mentioned _____ tell me more about that.*
- *You mentioned _____ what was that like for you?*
- *You mentioned that you _____ walk me through what that was like for you.*

Activity 1.2   Exploring ethnographic interviews

Consider a 'cultural' group with which you are familiar. This might be a group that you belong to or a community in which you live. Using the exemplars of 'descriptive' questions included in the section on ethnographic interviews in this chapter, formulate some questions that might be asked about group members' use of space and time, or events common to the group, as well as people, activities and objects.

Conduct a conversational ethnographic interview in which you pose questions to a member of the group in order to elicit descriptions of cultural knowledge. The ethnographic interview could entail observational activities, and demonstrations of routine activities. For example, a member of a potters' group might demonstrate how clay is routinely prepared for a project in addition to describing the process orally. A resident of a retirement home might take you on a tour of the building while describing a 'typical' daily routine.

Activity 1.3   Exploring feminist interviews

Using an unstructured format, interview a woman in order to elicit descriptions of her daily life. Consider how you might incorporate spaces for your interviewee to ask questions of you, as well as providing opportunities for her to steer the conversation towards topics of interest to her.

Activity 1.4   Exploring oral history or life history interviews

Interview a person you know in order to gain descriptions of a significant event that has taken place in the community in which you live. If possible, search for other kinds of data that might be used to complement the interviewee's narrative, including photographs, newspaper accounts, and historical records. Try to elicit data that answers questions concerning who, what, where, when, how, and possibly why. Possible topics might relate to the weather (e.g., floods, droughts or storms), or community events (e.g., workers' strikes, building projects, celebrations).

Activity 1.5   Exploring dialogic interviews

Select a topic that is currently of public interest. Make a note of the issues related to the topic that you might discuss with another person. Explain your interest in facilitating a 'dialogue' concerning this topic with a participant. In your dialogue, ask questions that call upon your participant to justify their opinions and clarify their understandings. Make sure to let your participant know that they can question you and call on you to explain your viewpoints and defend your statements.

Activity 1.6   Debriefing questions

- Which interview format felt most comfortable to you as an interviewer? Why?
- Which interview format felt most uncomfortable to you as an interviewer? Why?
- What did you notice about interviewees' responses to your questions?
- What did you notice about your responses to interviewees?
- Is there anything you would change about the way you conducted your interview? If so, what? Why?

TWO

Interviews with Groups

with Anna Liljestrom

This chapter introduces:

- Group formats for interviews: *brainstorming, nominal group technique, Delphi* groups, *informal* and *formal* groups, *focus groups.*
- Considerations in using focus groups: working with groups, discussing sensitive issues in groups, formulating questions and encouraging participation.

This chapter reviews the considerations qualitative researchers need to take into account when generating data with groups of people. We begin by briefly discussing several approaches to group interviews before examining one form, the focus group, in more detail. We then outline issues to consider in using focus groups for the purposes of social research, ideas for planning question guides, and suggestions for how group members' participation might be encouraged by focus group moderators.

While it could be assumed that skills used in asking questions in face-to-face individual interviews apply equally to interviews with groups of people, when researchers interview more than one person at a time, unless they are using a specific group technique designed to minimize or eliminate group interaction, they will likely call on additional, if not different, skills to effectively manage talk. Group interaction complicates turn-taking, since speakers are likely to take different roles within the group, and participants will orient to what others have said. Even though multi-party talk is complex, interviewers are unlikely to notice how turns in conversation are accomplished unless some kind of problem in interaction arises – for example, if one speaker monopolizes the conversation, if speakers talk at the same time, if someone constantly interrupts others, if side conversations emerge, or if certain participants remain silent. Of course, these kinds of actions are not confined to group interviews – some can also occur in individual interviews involving two speakers. How interviewers work out what to do next when faced with problems in interaction among multiple speakers is a task that may be complicated by group members' responses.

Formats for Working with Groups

There are a number of formats that may be used to elicit information from multiple participants. These include brain-storming, the nominal group technique, the Delphi technique, informal, and formal group interviews (Frey and Fontana, 1993), and focus groups. James Frey and Andrea Fontana (1993: 30) suggest that group interviews may be compared on four dimensions: (1) interviewer role (directive–non-directive); (2) question format (structure–unstructured); (3) purpose (exploratory, pretest–phenomenological); and (4) setting (formal–natural). Each of the techniques we review below differs according to each of these dimensions in the ways in which data are generated.

Researchers use group formats to gain information for a variety of reasons. These include an interest in learning about group dynamics and the ways in which particular groups talk about topics among themselves (Stewart et al., 2007); or the belief that group talk and the presence of others will provide the kind of environment in which people are willing to self-disclose (Krueger and Casey, 2000; MacPhail, 2001). Some techniques are organized to eliminate the impact of group participation on the data generated, while for others, group interaction is a key feature. Thus, when considering the use of group interview techniques, researchers must first clarify the purpose of the project, consider if group interaction is desirable, and what it will contribute to examination of the research questions, and structure group interaction in a way that will effectively fulfill the requirements of the project.

Brain-storming sessions are groups facilitated for the purpose of generating and exploring new ideas in an unstructured format. Here, the group interaction assists in the generation of a large number of ideas – the more the better – as people respond to one another's contributions (MacPhail, 2001). While brain-storming sessions are dissimilar in many ways to interviews, they may provide an option for researchers who want to glean a large number of ideas in a short time period about topics from particular groups that they would like to work with in future. This kind of group interaction could be effectively used in the early phase of a study to explore ideas among groups in informal settings. The interviewer would likely take a less directive role in the generation of data, and use unstructured questions to gain a wide variety of views (Frey and Fontana, 1993: 30).

Nominal groups are those in which the researcher minimizes interaction among group members, or eliminates it altogether. This technique avoids the problem posed by group members who dominate interaction when talking with others, and provides researchers with a method of obtaining information in a way that is not influenced by what others say. Ann MacPhail (2001) describes her use of the nominal group technique (NGT) to elicit young peoples' views about physical education. Students completed individual written responses to a series of statements, which were then collated and presented back to students, who then selected and ranked statements in a format specified by the researcher in a second round of data generation. The researcher takes a directive role in this technique, asking questions of participants in a structured format.

Delphi groups are those in which a panel of experts is convened to respond to the researcher's questions via successive rounds of structured questionnaires. The participants – who are unlikely to meet face-to-face – receive the results from each round of data generation, and the aim of the researcher is to come to consensus concerning the topic discussed (see Hasson et al. [2000] for an account of this approach). Like the NGT, the Delphi technique is highly structured, with the researcher taking a directive role, and asking structured questions to elicit specific information about the topic concerned.

Frey and Fontana (1993) also list natural and formal field interviews as another group interview technique. Here, researchers conduct spontaneous and unstructured interviews with naturally occurring groups – as opposed to researcher-selected groups – in ongoing fieldwork. They might also arrange to meet with these groups on planned occasions to conduct more formal interviews (Frey and Fontana, 1993: 30–1). While natural interviews are likely to be unstructured, and conducted at an early phase in the study for exploratory purposes, formal field interviews are more likely to take place at a later stage in a study, with the interviewer taking a more directive role in search of specific information.

In focus groups, a group of people are brought together by an interviewer, or 'moderator,' to discuss their views and opinions about a selected topic with one another. In that group interaction is deliberately fostered by the moderator, focus groups differ from the formats described above. Below, we discuss this format in more detail and review its origin, before outlining steps that social science researchers might consider in designing studies that use focus groups for research purposes.

Focus Groups

In response to the growing popularity of focus groups in the social sciences, health professions, and marketing and consumer research, there has been a proliferation of publications that provides a range of theoretical perspectives on methodological issues involved in the use of focus groups, as well as the practicalities of designing and conducting studies using this method (see, for example, Barbour, 2007; Barbour and Kitzinger, 1999; Kamberelis and Dimitriadis, 2005; Litoselliti, 2003; Morgan, 1993, 1997, 2002; Morgan and Krueger, 1998; Puchta and Potter, 2004; Smithson, 2000; Stewart et al., 2007; Wilkinson, 1998, 2004). We begin with a definition of terms.

As noted above, focus groups bring a group of people together to discuss a set of topics introduced by the moderator. Jenny Kitzinger and Rosaline Barbour note that participants are 'focused' on a particular activity, and make 'explicit use of group interaction to generate data' (1999: 4). They continue:

> Instead of asking questions of each person in turn, focus group researchers encourage participants to talk to one another; asking questions, exchanging anecdotes, and commenting on each others' experiences and points of view. (1999: 4)

The development of focus groups is frequently traced to the work of Robert K. Merton et al. (1956/1990), described in the text, *The Focused Interview: A Manual of Problems and Procedures*. Merton himself did not distinguish between the use of focused interviews with groups or individuals, and preferred the term 'focussed interviews'. As described by Merton, the focused interview was originally used to generate information concerning participants' responses to particular experiences and situations (such as watching a film, or listening to a radio program) (Merton, 1990: xxi), and the criteria for measuring quality related to whether descriptions provided by participants were sufficiently detailed with respect to the dimensions of range, specificity, depth, and personal context. Thus, the manual provides sequences of interaction drawn from focused interviews to show how effective interviewers generated data according to these criteria; typical problems and situations that interviewers encountered; and guidelines for interviewers for how to generate data more effectively.

Much of the current writing on focus groups takes a stance similar to that articulated by Kitzinger and Barbour (1999) and cited earlier; meanwhile overlooking the 'discontinuity between the focussed interview and its modified version in the form of focus groups' (Merton, 1990: xxix–xxx). One of the challenges in learning how to use focus groups for the purposes of social research is that of discerning what advice is methodologically appropriate for a particular study. This is because there is a great diversity in the purposes for which focus groups are used.

Variations in the Use of Focus Groups

The use of focus groups in a variety of fields has led to a multitude of procedural advice relevant to differing theoretical and practical issues of concern. Focus groups have been used for the purposes of informing military intelligence, marketing and consumer research, academic work, evaluation studies, public/non-profit work, participatory agendas, and emancipatory and feminist pedagogy (Kamberelis and Dimitriadis, 2005; Krueger and Casey, 2000). These applications of focus groups will entail quite different work on the part of the facilitator or moderator.

For example, in marketing, moderators frequently conduct focus groups with product samples, or artifacts (such as images for advertising campaigns), asking participants to respond to these objects in the moment. Thus, the topics of talk – that is, peoples' views and opinions – frequently orient to external objects (e.g., mock-ups of a website, product samples, advertising slogans, etc.). Participants are paid for their participation at the conclusion of the focus group. In this context, focus groups are usually conducted with people who are unknown to one another – and participants are likely to have less concern for how others view what they have said. The talk is usually videotaped and undertaken in a setting in which the client group (i.e., representatives of the company seeking information) may view the interactions from a viewing booth. Moderators may not necessarily transcribe the interaction, rather presenting client groups with videos of interaction, and a written report of impressions developed concerning participants' responses. The appeal of focus groups for market researchers lies in the potential of group interaction to provide researchers with data that demonstrates participants' responses and opinions about products, services, or other phenomena of interest (see Stewart et al., 2007).

Televised focus groups in political campaigns provide another example of the ways in which focus groups might be conducted. Here, journalists and opinion pollsters are seen to access participants' opinions and attitudes as they respond to the moderator's questions. Given that sometimes these groups are very large, the talk generated in these kinds of groups is often highly structured, with the moderator calling upon particular people to respond, and sometimes seeking responses from participants in pre-specified orders. In instances where the focus group simulates a fire-side chat with a moderator, the editing of talk for the public venue of television is hidden from viewers. How talk is generated in these instances differs in important ways to how social science researchers commonly moderate focus groups.

Groups have long been used by social activists for pedagogical and political purposes. George Kamberelis and Greg Dimitriadis (2005) include Paulo Freire's 'study circles' and feminist 'consciousness-raising groups' as examples of focus groups used for these sorts of purposes. This use of group talk might not necessarily contribute to research, however, given that the primary focus is the instigation of critical dialogue and helping people to imagine – and ultimately, live in – the world differently. Yet social science researchers pursuing emancipatory agendas have drawn on these kinds of applications of group interaction to inform their research practices.

In the examples described above, group interaction has been used to examine consumers' responses for the purpose of marketing products and audiences' perceptions of political campaigns to inform opinion polls. Freire used group interaction in study circles to facilitate critical dialogue among Brazilian workers. Similarly, feminist activists have facilitated consciousness-raising among groups of women for political purposes. Clearly, these are distinctly different applications of group interaction that entail thoughtful reflection on how groups might be facilitated.

Although many of the steps to design a study using individual interviews apply equally to the use of focus groups, working with groups entails several issues not relevant to individual interviewing. In the next section, we discuss issues involved in using focus groups for the purposes of social science research, including designing the study, scheduling interviews, and organizing groups.

Designing a Study Using Focus Groups

Prior to beginning a study, consideration should be given to the following questions:

- Will focus group data be sufficient to adequately address the research questions?
- If not, what other methods of data generation in addition to focus groups might be employed? (For example, individual interviews, naturally-occurring interaction, documents and texts, field notes of observations.)

Focus groups are particularly useful for researchers who want to examine the possible ways that people talk about and make sense of topics, and the kinds of issues that they see as relevant. There are a variety of ways in which they may be incorporated by researchers. These include as an adjunct to other methods; as a single source of data; and as a way of facilitating dialogic interaction. Below we discuss these in more detail.

Focus Groups Used to Generate Data in Conjunction with Other Methods

Because focus groups are useful for generating a range of opinions and ideas in a short period of time, they are frequently used in mixed-methods research, especially when researchers want to generate ideas in order to develop interventions or large-scale surveys and test instruments, or ascertain what topics are relevant to people with whom they are working (Brody et al., 2003). When used to generate ideas, focus groups are used in the preliminary phase of a study's design. The data are used to inform the design of instruments to be used in a larger study; or inform program design and implementation. Focus groups may also be used in the latter phases of a study to explore a study's findings. Researchers can convene focus groups to examine findings that emerged from analysis of other data sets – whether qualitative interviews, or surveys that have been analyzed quantitatively.

Focus Groups as Single Source of Data

In some studies, focus groups are used as a single source of data to examine specific topics (for examples see Morgan, 1997: 18–21). Methodologists provide different views on whether or not focus groups should be used as the single source of data for a project. Whether one does this will depend on one's theoretical assumptions about how knowledge is produced. Some research has demonstrated that people may provide different kinds of information in focus groups than if individually interviewed (Agar and McDonald, 1995; Maynard-Tucker, 2000). This does not mean that individuals are necessarily providing untruthful information. Rather, this may be seen as a product of group interaction – in which people provide comments that orient to what others have said, as well as tailor their accounts in particular ways to other group members as over-hearing audiences. In a group, people provide particular self-representations which may differ from those provided in a one-on-one setting. If researchers take a neo-positivist perspective towards interviews, then it is unlikely that focus groups – particularly if they are one-off interviews – will provide sufficient information to generate valid and reliable data.

Focus Groups as Dialogic Interaction

For researchers working from participatory, critical, and feminist perspectives, the venue provided by focus groups presents opportunities for dialogue, consciousness-raising, and deliberate discussion of topics brought forth by both participants and researchers. A key assumption of this kind of work is that the very nature of focus groups – with participants out-numbering the moderator – provides opportunities to deliberately upset the asymmetrical relationships usually assumed by researchers with participants of studies. Group interviews are seen to accomplish this through providing opportunities for participants, rather than the moderator, to set the agenda and pose questions, and to respond to one another's utterances in free-ranging ways. Another assumption of this perspective of focus groups is that all participants, including moderators, can transform their understandings of topics by engaging in dialogue with others.

Recruiting Participants and Organizing Groups

Participants are recruited for focus groups using similar methods as for individual interviews. Strategies include sending invitations to selected populations, advertising for participants, or using established networks or groups as a basis for group participation (see Farquhar and Das, 1999; Krueger and Casey, 2000: 167, for examples). In cases in which participants are recruited from a single setting, participants may already be known to one another. Participants who already know one another bring pre-established relationships to the interaction, and also take away impressions of and information concerning others that have been generated within the group. This poses a number of issues for researchers.

First, participants are likely to orient to others within the group according to existing relationships. People who know one another prior to the group will talk in ways that reflect their roles and relationships outside the group – conversation analysts refer to this ubiquitous feature of all talk as *recipient design* (see Appendix 2). This can be both beneficial and detrimental for the generation of data for research purposes. For example, if working with groups who are well-known to one another, the moderator may have little work to do in order to establish a comfortable environment in which group members are willing to freely discuss topics of interest. Yet, it is also possible that in such groups, group members will enact particular identities occupied outside the group and position their perspectives in particular ways for other members of the group. For researchers taking a constructionist approach to interview interaction, this is all data, and can be a topic of analysis. If researchers are aiming to elicit individuals' opinions and views about particular topics, this is likely to be problematic, and focus groups may not generate useful data. Take for example, the following excerpt from a focus group conducted for a study in which all participants were known to one another and work together.

Excerpt 2.1 (October 2007)

P: Participant
M: Moderator

1.   P   I'm just saying from what ev- from we've all said from [those
2.   M   [uh huh

3. P   who have spoken I would say that we've all said you know [we were
4. M   [I see
5. P   positive and I think that's how we feel so I can't speak for the ones who
6.   haven't spoken=
7. M   =sure

In this interaction we see a focus group participant providing a positive evaluation concerning the topic discussed. In her formulation of this view, there is explicit recognition in lines 3 and 5 that not all members of the group had provided views on the topic. In this particular focus group, analysis of the group's interaction indicated that several members of the group were comfortable in expressing their views, while other members were not – contributing little to the interaction. If the purpose of the study is to elicit responses from all members of a particular group in which there are divergent views, it is possible that some people may be uncomfortable in presenting their views publicly. The problem posed for group members in presenting divergent or unpopular views within the format of the group is heightened further when the topics discussed are sensitive, or when group members have strongly held views concerning controversial topics. Thus, in the evaluation study from which Excerpt 2.1 was taken, given that there were several instances in which the transcription of the focus group showed that some members dominated the talk, while certain participants were reticent to discuss their views, the research design was revised to include individual interviews in additional rounds of data collection. By using individual interviews to explore the topic further, the researcher was able to gain more information concerning how the views and opinions of participants involved in this group diverged.

A second issue relevant for focus groups, particularly those in which members are already known to one another, is that of confidentiality. Although researchers assure participants of research studies that they will treat the data generated in focus groups confidentially and may request that participants keep information shared within the focus group private, researchers cannot ensure that this will occur. Therefore, for topics that seek to elicit personal experiences concerning sensitive topics, researchers might consider using individual, rather than focus groups.

Another related issue to consider when organizing focus groups is that of the heterogeneity or homogeneity of group members. What constitutes 'homogeneity' or 'heterogeneity' in a group may be difficult to gauge prior to generating and analyzing interaction. While researchers frequently make use of established sociological categories (such as gender, age, socio-economic status, or race and ethnicity) in order to group people, participants themselves may not view themselves in the way that researchers do. To provide a simple example, the group 'international students in a US setting' might be comprised of students from many countries, yet also include people from Western as well as non-Western countries, whose native language may or may not be English. Thus, to organize a group on the basis of one category (e.g., that of occupying an identity as an 'international student'), may overlook other relevant social locations (e.g., native language or country of origin) that may be of relevance to both participants and the topic studied. This issue highlights one of the key differences in how Robert Merton has described the use of focused interviews in examinations of peoples' responses to media messages in the 1940s to how focus groups are frequently used in research in the social sciences today.

Whereas Merton and his colleagues asked questions that focused on an *experience* that participants all shared (e.g., listening to a radio broadcast); in many cases, social science researchers want to learn about the views concerning a phenomenon expressed by members of a particular group who they have identified by a sociological category (e.g., gender, race, ethnicity, age). Although researchers may assume that people who occupy a specific social location share experiences, this may not be so. Thus, organizing groups of people to participate in focus groups involves more than scheduling a time and place. Researchers need to think about the ways participants identify themselves, and from what social category the researcher is seeking individuals to speak.

For moderators who are beginning to work with focus groups, it is useful to consider the following questions in relation to recruitment of participants for focus groups:

- Are group members already known to one another?
- If so, what is known about these peoples' relationships?
- What are the implications of prior relationships for the production of talk?
- What are the implications for group interaction of discussing the topic selected?

In some studies the answers to these questions may not be known prior to conducting a focus group – therefore, it may be wise to either conduct a pilot study to try out the methods used, or, if appropriate to the research question, to use other forms of data collection (such as individual interviews, document review, or participant observations) to complement focus groups. Even then, focus groups may not always generate the kinds of data that are needed to examine research questions. Therefore, by examining data while it is being collected, researchers can make adjustments to the research design that will ensure that data will be purposefully generated.

Scheduling Interviews

There is a range of advice on the appropriate number of participants that should be included in focus groups. A frequent recommendation in the literature is to recruit 8–12 members for groups, with the proviso that smaller groups of 4–6 may work better for some topics (e.g., Krueger and Casey, 2000: 73–4). Given that multiple people are involved in focus groups, scheduling a common time in which they might all meet is a complex task. When scheduling a meeting time for groups that do not meet regularly, it is wise to recruit more members than required in order to ensure that enough people will attend at the scheduled time. Researchers need to be prepared for the eventuality that not all people who agree to participate actually will. For researchers who are working in institutional or workplace settings, scheduling focus groups may be an easier task, given that they may be slotted into the routine schedule (e.g., at a regular meeting). Because of the complexity of arranging meetings with multiple people, often this scheduling may need to be facilitated by a member of the organization in which the study is being conducted. If focus groups are scheduled at meal-times, researchers might consider providing drinks, snacks, or meals for participants. Researchers need to consider relevant circumstances that may mitigate participation – in some cases this might necessitate providing childcare for parents who attend; in others, transportation of participants to and from the venue for the interview may need to be arranged.

Sensitive Topics

Some authors have argued that focus groups may be effectively used to study sensitive topics (e.g., Farquhar and Das, 1999; Hoppe and Wells, 1995; Zeller, 1993). Moderators undertaking such work must be able to effectively facilitate talk in such a way that group members feel comfortable in expressing opinions that diverge from those of others, and facilitate an environment in which participants are comfortable to discuss sensitive topics. Richard Zeller (1993) provides examples of interaction in which the moderator uses the introduction to the focus group to make remarks or narrate stories that represent self-disclosure about sensitive topics – in this case, sexual decision-making – that set the tone for self-disclosure on the part of participants. This technique draws on a feature of ordinary conversation – in that when one person tells a story, frequently a listener will provide a 'second story' (Sacks, 1992), which closely aligns with the first.

Zeller's (1993) three recommendations for eliciting interaction concerning topics that participants may be reluctant to talk about involve (1) the use of a screening questionnaire to stimulate thinking prior to the focus group, (2) self-disclosure by the moderator, and (3) responding to participants' comments in ways that legitimate contributions from all group members. Whether participants self-disclose in response to moderators' acts of self-disclosure is very much dependent on how participants perceive the moderator. Although working mainly with individual interview data, Jackie Abell and her colleagues found that in some instances, interviewers' self-disclosure was perceived as a display of difference by participants, and these researchers propose that the identity of the researcher is as 'much a focus of study as that of the interviewee' (2006: 241). Thus, researchers who want to use focus groups to discuss sensitive topics need to consider the ethical implications involved in having participants share information perceived to be sensitive with others, in addition to how they will moderate the discussion in ways that will facilitate talk.

Developing Questions and Topic Guides

As in individual interviews, there are numerous ways to formulate and ask questions of participants. The following recommendations concerning how to structure topic guides and formulate questions should be viewed as guidelines rather than prescriptions, since the relevance of questions will depend on the topic of study, the theoretical perspectives taken by the researcher, the research questions to be examined, and the purpose of the study. Morgan writes that in an ideal group, 'the moderator would have to ask only the first and last questions' (2002: 148), suggesting that the most effective focus group is one in which talk is unstructured, and participants become so engaged in discussing the topic that they need little assistance from the moderator. While this is a model to work towards, as a starting point, we draw on Krueger and Casey (2000) to suggest four sets of questions that researchers might formulate in order to structure the topic or interview guide.

Opening Groups and Introducing Discussion Topics

Methodologists agree that the opening moments of focus groups are important for setting the agenda for interaction to come. Thus, to ensure participation of all group members, moderators are advised to foster a genial social environment. Suggestions provided by various authors include setting an informal and relaxed tone by providing snacks and drinks for participants, and joke-telling on the part of the moderator. Other authors have emphasized the importance of explaining the ground rules for talk to participants at the outset of the session, as well as the inclusion of introductory activities to orient participants to the group's task.

Openings might begin with participants' self-introductions. This, of course, assumes that participants are unknown to one another – which while a common feature of focus groups in marketing, may not be the case in studies in which researchers make use of pre-existing networks and groups. In cases where group members are already known to one another it makes little sense for them to introduce themselves to one another – in this case, moderators might use name tags to identify different participants; or alternatively, ask participants to introduce something about themselves that is unknown to other participants. Thus, introductions need to be tailored to the composition of specific groups. For example, if there are status differentials among group members who are unknown to one another that would be highlighted through providing personal introductions, researchers might include an orienting activity in which equal participation from all members is required.

Michael Bloor, Jane Frankland, Michelle Thomas and Kate Robson (2001: 45) recommend that initial questions should focus people's attention on the topic of subsequent interaction and suggest orienting activities that entail participants responding to various items provided by the moderator (e.g., a list of items, an opening vignette, a news bulletin exercise, or a set of photographs). Nicola Robinson (1999: 907–8, citing Kitzinger, 1990 and Brook, 1988) recommends three activities for inclusion in focus group research, including the card game (in which group members sort a set of statements provided by the moderator); the news game (in which group members produce a 'news' item in relation to a set of pictures); and the 'advert exercise' (in which group members guess the intent of advertisements produced without slogans). Given the immense possibilities provided by information available on the World Wide Web, researchers have many sources from which to draw if they would like to use visual images, or audio- and/or video-clips to open focus groups and prompt discussion by group members.

After the opening sequence in which participants introduce themselves, or in which the moderator has provided some orienting activity, researchers usually introduce the topic of talk for the focus group by posing a question. Exemplar questions provided by various authors indicate that these are usually open-ended questions that provide a wide range of possibilities for participants to respond. For example, Krueger and Casey suggest the following as a starter for an opening question: 'What is the first thing that comes to mind when you hear ...' (2000: 45). One alternative to answering questions aloud is to have participants write down their responses, and then, after reading these aloud, the moderator can follow up on the kinds of ideas that have been generated among the group. Again, how moderators introduce a topic is significant for how participants will orient to forthcoming questions, and many writers agree that the opening moments of a focus group will impact the kind of data generated and its quality (Krueger, 1998; Krueger and Casey, 2000; Morgan, 1993, 1997).

Focus Questions

Focus questions are those that seek information to inform the primary research questions that the researcher is aiming to study. Krueger and Casey (2000: 45) use the term 'key questions,' and propose that 10–20 minutes be allowed for discussion of each one. These authors suggest that a typical focus group of 60–90 minutes will likely need from two to five questions to discuss the central topics of interest. Many texts on focus groups recommend that interview guides be constructed to lead from general questions to more specific questions. Stewart et al. (2007: 61) also suggest that questions should be ordered by level of importance, that is, more important questions should be included earlier on the topic guide to allow appropriate time for discussion.

Clarification Questions and Transition Statements

Clarification questions include both open and closed questions in which the moderator checks his or her understanding of prior talk, or seeks to elicit further information from participants in order to expand on what has been said. Examples include:

- You've told me that _____. Is that accurate?
- You talked about _____. Does this mean that _____?
- When you say _____, do you mean _____?
- You mentioned _____. Tell me a bit more about what you mean by that term.
- You talked about _____. Does anyone have an example of that?
- Does anyone have any other stories about _____ that you would like to share?

Note that many of these questions use the participants' words in order to clarify the moderator's understanding of what has been said, or to prompt further elaboration.

Transition statements are used to move discussion from one topic to the next. When posed as questions, they provide an opportunity for others to contribute their ideas before moving to the next topic for discussion. For example:

- We've heard _____, what are other views about that?
- Before we move on, would anyone else like to add to what has been said about _____?
- You've told me about _____, now I'd like to learn about your views on _____.

Summarizing Statements and Closing Questions

Summarizing statements signal that the focus group is moving towards closure, and the moderator can provide opportunities for participants to add final comments. For example:

- Now just to sum up what you've said. What I've heard is _____. Is there anything you'd like to add to that?
- Are there any relevant topics that you'd like to discuss that I've missed?
- Are there any questions that I haven't asked that we should have talked about?

The questions that are described in the section above may not work for all applications of focus groups. For example, for researchers aiming to stimulate dialogical interaction among speakers, other methods might be more appropriate (see, for example, Freeman, 2006). For novice researchers who would like to experiment with focus groups, however, this section may be used as a framework to generate initial questions that can be used to facilitate talk among a group of people.

Managing Focus Group Interaction

Puchta and Potter (2004) have used excerpts from focus groups conducted for marketing purposes to investigate how moderators effectively manage group interaction. As a result, they have outlined specific strategies that might be used by moderators to generate group interaction and participation. Although the data they have used to generate these recommendations is drawn from marketing focus groups, it is useful to consider how these ideas might be applied in social sciences research. Puchta and Potter (2004) describe the conversational resources and techniques used by effective moderators to (1) produce informality, (2) produce participation, and (3) produce opinions that are both useful and varied. We examine these suggestions in more detail below, and include excerpts from focus groups conducted by novice moderators in the social sciences to show what these strategies might look like in practice.

Producing Informality

First, Puchta and Potter (2004: 46) suggest that informality is produced through a number of conversational resources, including the use of idiomatic and slang terms, and laughter. They recommend that moderators avoid using scripts in talk, since they contribute to a sense of formality. In contrast, moderators are advised to cultivate spontaneity by referring to notes or a checklist (Puchta and Potter, 2004: 46). Excerpt 2.2 from an interview conducted by a novice moderator concerning teachers' professional development exemplifies how informal talk might be used by a moderator to facilitate interaction and participation of her interviewees.[1] The sequence is taken from the opening section of a focus group in which the moderator had asked her participants to describe their teaching history as an introduction to the topic of talk. As discussed above, the strategy of seeking some introductory comments about one's personal background is one way to introduce a group, and establish a comfortable environment in which to introduce the focus questions.

Excerpt 2.2 [FG9:05/25/01]

P: Participant
M: Moderator

 1. P16   OK (.) I taught high school remedial English and Math for
 2.   two years taught English as a Foreign Language for a year
 3.   in [Eastern Europe] (.) I taught high school LDPD for a year (.) that
 4.   was all I could take (.)=
 5. P8   =heh heh heh heh heh heh heh
 6. P16   hhh. ↑then I taught ↑fifth grade for ↑three years (.) all subjects and
 7.   I've been teaching college education methods courses now (1.0) for
 8.   (1.0)
 9. P16   ↑five years
10.   (2.0)
11. P16   so I've been teaching for 12 years
12.   (1.0)
13. M9   °mm wow° wow
14. ALL   heh heh heh heh
15. M9   and you look so ↑young ((reaches out to touch P16's arm))
16. P16   heh heh heh heh heh I started teaching at eighteen
17. P8   I love it
18. M9   and ↑how about ↓you ((turns to P8 and touches the desk in front))
19. P8   oh Lord have mercy (.) uhm I taught for five years so (.) uhm
20. P16   I feel like a ↑grandma
21. P15   heh heh heh

Throughout this interaction, we see laughter (lines 5, 14, 16, 21) from multiple participants, including the moderator. The moderator shows her appreciation for the contribution of P16 (line 13), and jokes about P16's length of experience (line 15). P16 responds to this by joking about her age (line 16), before the moderator assigns the turn to a new speaker (P8, line 18). The informal and spontaneous nature of this excerpt was characteristic of the interview as a whole. Turns were rarely allocated, but rather were taken by members in no specific order. Participants' accounts were interspersed with comments, assessments, laughter, and appreciation

---

[1]Excerpts 2.2–2.3 are drawn from a study conducted by Kathryn Roulston and Kathleen deMarrais on how researchers learn to interview. See Roulston et al. (2003) for one report. In these excerpts, both moderators and participants gave their consent for publication of data.

tokens from both the moderator and group members (in this excerpt, see lines 5, 13, 14, 16, 17, 21). Throughout the focus group, this moderator, as visible on line 18, focused the topic of talk by allocating turns that oriented participants to their task. In this excerpt we see how a moderator can contribute to the interaction in a spontaneous way that works to produce an informal atmosphere in the opening moments of a focus group, thereby setting a casual tone for members' interaction.

Producing Participation

In contrast to the advice from many other writers to ask short, open questions, Puchta and Potter (2004) suggest that moderators make use of 'elaborate questions.' These authors found by looking at examples of data from actual focus groups that moderators tended to ask complex questions that provided multiple response options, prior to asking simple follow up questions. Puchta and Potter argue that elaborate questions are an effective means of managing interaction in that they 'display informality, guide participants without forcing them, secure participation, and manage asymmetry between moderator and participant' (2004: 52). The examples that these authors provide are all drawn from marketing focus groups, so it is difficult to ascertain whether the same holds true for the use of elaborate questions for the purposes of social research. Given an example discussed in Chapter 7 (see Excerpt 7.3), however, it is quite possible that if used purposefully, elaborate questions could be effectively used in social sciences interviews and focus groups in the way that Puchta and Potter describe. In reference to elaborate questions, Puchta and Potter make the following suggestion to moderators:

> At the start of new topics and themes ask elaborate questions in a way that shows uncertainty both about the answer and the type of answer. Unpack it as it goes along. Include a range of candidate answers. Make the participants experts by focusing on views, opinions or feelings. (2004: 46)

Another suggestion for securing participation is one that is echoed throughout the literature: 'Pay attention to the participants' (Puchta and Potter, 2004: 65). In the excerpt below, we show an example of how a moderator might demonstrate this kind of attention by distributing turns to speakers who have participated minimally.

When speakers in a group have pre-existing relationships and friendships, they may dominate the talk. In Excerpt 2.3 from a focus group moderated by a beginning researcher, two of the participants (P2 and P9) repeatedly took lengthy turns, at times freely conversed with one another, and even posed questions probing for further details of one another's accounts. Another participant in this group of four, P7, took turns less frequently, and on two occasions in this focus group, was nominated by the moderator. Below is an example of how the moderator, by paying attention to the ongoing interaction, nominated P7 for a turn in the context of interaction dominated by other speakers.

Excerpt 2.3 [FG 6:05/25/01]

1. M6 so you mentioned a few things u::m (.) problems with colleagues ↑or
2.   administrators↑(.) and uh (I also noticed) you had a bit of

3.		a problem with a colleague too=
4.	P9	=yeah it was a problem with a colleague and that's what (that's what
5.		happened)
6.	M6	yeah (.) do you have a similar experience Lauren? [with a colleague or an
7.	P7	[with a colleague?
8.	M6	administrator?
9.	P7	yeah with admin- with administrators mostly maybe it's because I'm
10.		coming from a different school background

In lines 9–10, P7 responded to the moderator by taking a turn which oriented to one of the two options provided by the moderator (line 8, 'administrator'). She then proceeded to give an account of her experience (not included here). It is impossible to know whether P7 would have produced this account had she not been nominated for the turn by the moderator. It is safe to assume, however, that in cases where a speaker remains silent in group talk, if moderators do not assign turns in a way that encourages them to participate, they will be unlikely to take the turn themselves. An allocation of turns to reticent speakers is just one way that moderators show that they are attending to participants. Other ways this is achieved include use of continuers such as 'mm hm' and 'uh huh,' and asking follow-up and clarification questions that orient to what speakers have said.

Producing Opinions

The production of 'opinions' is especially pertinent in marketing research, as moderators seek to elicit people's 'perceptions, opinions, beliefs and attitudes' (POBAs) (Henderson, 1991 cited by Puchta and Potter, 2004: 66). Thus, Puchta and Potter advise moderators to:

> Monitor carefully breakdowns where participants start to make knowledge and truth claims, and become concerned with evidence and the moderator's own knowledge. Reiterate the focus on POBAs as needed. (2004: 88)

They recommend asking questions that specifically seek evaluations to prompt interaction, and if talk becomes too 'lively,' 'ask for descriptions' (Puchta and Potter, 2004: 88). Again, these are useful recommendations for generating data for very specific purposes. The generation of POBAs is required if the research purposes are to provide information to client groups about consumers' perspectives of products, services, and programs. For qualitative researchers conducting focus groups for the purposes of evaluation of a program, these kinds of questions are particularly useful. Not all social science research is geared to these kinds of questions, however, so researchers must ask themselves what kinds of data they seek to elicit, how they intend to use it, and formulate questions with that purpose in mind.

Conclusion

In this chapter, we reviewed some formats for working with groups. We briefly reviewed the techniques of brain-storming, nominal groups, Delphi groups, and informal and formal group interviews as ways to elicit data from groups. We then provided further detail concerning issues to consider in the use of focus groups, in addition to some suggestions for how one might secure participation from group members. A well-conducted focus group looks deceptively easy – however, managing talk in a way that will generate data that will serve the researcher's purposes may not always go smoothly. With careful and thoughtful planning for how the group is structured and what kinds of questions will generate the data required to respond to research questions, researchers can use focus groups to generate useful data for analysis. Given the complexity of group interaction, researchers might also consider analyzing the talk for how group members interact with one another – asking questions about the topics that were taken up or ignored by others, and how group members managed disagreements.

In the next chapter, six different conceptions of interviewing are reviewed in relation to the kinds of research questions that might be posed, as well as implications for analytic and representational strategies.

Further Reading

General Introductions to Focus Groups

Barbour, R. (2007) *Doing Focus Groups*. Thousand Oaks, CA: Sage.

Bloor, M., Frankland, J., Thomas, M. and Robson, K. (2001) *Focus Groups in Social Research*. Thousand Oaks, CA: Sage.

Krueger, R.A. and Casey, M.A. (2000) *Focus Groups: A Practical Guide for Applied Research*. Thousand Oaks, CA: Sage.

Litoselliti, L. (2003) *Using Focus Groups in Research*. London: Continuum.

Morgan, D.L. (1997) *Focus Groups as Qualitative Research*, 2nd edn. Newbury Park, CA: Sage.

Morgan, D.L. (2002) 'Focus group interviewing', in J.F. Gubrium and J.A. Holstein (eds), *Handbook of Interview Research: Context and Method*. Thousand Oaks, CA: Sage. pp. 141–60.

Morgan, D.L. and Krueger, R.A. (1998) *The Focus Group Kit*. Thousand Oaks, CA: Sage.

Focus Groups in Marketing and Consumer Research

Puchta, C. and Potter, J. (2004) *Focus Group Practice*. London: Sage.

Stewart, D.W., Shamdasani, P.N. and Rook, D.W. (2007) *Focus Groups: Theory and Practice*, Vol. 20. Thousand Oaks, CA: Sage.

Focus Groups in Emancipatory and Feminist Work

Kamberelis, G. and Dimitriadis, G. (2005) 'Focus groups: Strategic articulations of pedagogy, politics, and inquiry', in N. Denzin and Y.S. Lincoln (eds), *The Sage Handbook of Qualitative Research*, 3rd edn. Thousand Oaks, CA: Sage. pp. 887–907.

Madriz, E. (2000) 'Focus groups in feminist research', in N. Denzin and Y.S. Lincoln (eds), *Handbook of Qualitative Research*, 2nd edn. Thousand Oaks, CA: Sage. pp. 835–50.

Salmon, A. (2007) 'Walking the talk: How participatory methods can democratize research', *Qualitative Health Research*, 17 (7): 982–93.

Wilkinson, S. (1999) 'How useful are focus groups in feminist research?', in R.S. Barbour and J. Kitzinger (eds), *Developing Focus Group Research: Politics, Theory, and Practice*. Thousand Oaks, CA: Sage. pp. 64–78.

Theoretical Issues in Focus Group Research

Barbour, R.S. and Kitzinger, J. (eds) (1999) *Developing Focus Group Research: Politics, Theory and Practice*. London: Sage.

Activity 2.1   Formulating questions for focus groups

Generate a topic for a focus group. Brain-storm for each kind of question listed below.

- Orienting questions or activities
- An opening question
- Focal questions
- Transition questions
- Closing/summarizing questions

Select questions you would use, and include a statement with each question that provides a rationale for why you would use the question, and the kinds of data you hope to generate.

Activity 2.2   Orienting activities

Select a topic about which you would like to know more. Locate a picture, text from a newspaper or magazine, or video-clip relevant to the topic that could be used to focus the participants' attention at the beginning of a focus group. Formulate a question or series of questions that could be used as an orienting activity.

Activity 2.3   Moderating a focus group

Moderate and video-tape a 45–60 minute focus group on a topic of your choice. After viewing the video of the focus group interaction, write a summary of the content of the focus group interaction, and a self critique of your skills as a moderator. Respond to the following questions:

- what kind of interactions were generated? (e.g., did participants express their opinions? were exchanges conversational?)
- what challenges did you face? (e.g., did you have individuals who were dominant speakers or who participated minimally?)
- what did you do well?
- would you change anything if you moderated another focus group? If so, what?

THREE

Theorizing the Qualitative Interview

This chapter introduces:

- Multiple conceptions of interviewing: neo-positivist, romantic, constructionist, postmodern, transformative, and decolonizing approaches.
- Theoretical assumptions underlying how knowledge is produced in these conceptualizations of interviews.
- Implications for asking questions and analysis and interpretation of data.

This chapter reviews six conceptualizations of qualitative research interviews that I have identified in qualitative research reports as well as methodological literature. No doubt there are more. The conceptualizations of interviews that I have selected to outline here reflect different theoretical orientations to social research that both overlap and conflict, and each responds in particular ways to various critiques of interview research. By considering the underlying assumptions of 'neo-positivist,' 'romantic,' 'constructionist,' 'postmodern,' 'transformative,' and 'decolonizing' conceptions of the qualitative interview, I argue that researchers will be better prepared to design research projects to use interviews in ways that are consistent with their epistemological and theoretical assumptions about knowledge production.

Labels that differentiate between different conceptions of interviewing are always limiting, and fail to capture the complexity represented in the field of qualitative methodology. Readers may well find that they identify with multiple conceptions of the interview. The categorization I present in this chapter, then, should be thought of as an heuristic device – a way of assisting qualitative interviewers in their initial explorations of interview practice. Readers might also consider how researchers concentrate on, for strategic purposes, certain kinds of theorizations of interviewing in their work, while relegating others to the background. Thinking theoretically about interviewing is one place to start in research design, and will assist researchers when making many of the decisions related to designing and carrying out a research project.

How we think about the qualitative interview has implications for how interviews are structured, the kinds of questions posed, and how data are analyzed and represented. On the one hand, the interviewer can take a detached or neutral position in relation to research participants, aiming for the generation of 'objective' knowledge;

while on the other hand, interviewers can see themselves as co-constructors of knowledge, and may strive to develop collaborative relationships with interviewees to initiate 'change.' These views represent dissimilar positions at opposite ends of a continuum of practice, and in this chapter I outline a range of variations and debates.

A Neo-positivist Conception of the Interview

Much of the advice literature on qualitative interviewing assumes that the interview subject has an 'inner' or 'authentic' self, not necessarily publicly visible, which may be revealed through careful questioning by an attentive and sensitive interviewer who contributes minimally to the talk. This interviewer–interviewee relation can be seen in the 'neo-positivist' conception of the interview proposed by Mats Alvesson (2003) (see Box 3.1).

Box 3.1   A neo-positivist conception of the interview

The 'skillful' interviewer ⇒ Asks 'good' questions ⇒ Minimizes 'bias' and 'researcher influences' through taking a 'neutral' role ⇒ Generates 'quality' data ⇒ Produces 'valid' findings.

- The data generated provide 'valid' and 'credible' knowledge concerning the beliefs, perceptions, experiences and opinions of the authentic self of interviewee.
- The interviewer generally refrains from participating in the data generation, other than asking questions.
- Data are commonly coded and categorized (for example, via ethnographic, phenomenological, or grounded theory procedures) to provide accounts of cultural groups, and substantive theory concerning the research topic.

The neo-positivist conception of interviewing draws on similar assumptions as to those used by researchers employing standardized surveys. William Foddy (1993: 13) presents a summary of these assumptions that may also be applied to qualitative interviewing. These are that:

- the researcher has a clearly defined topic about which participants have information that they are able to access within the research setting;
- interviewers and interviewees share a common understanding of the interview questions, and interviewees are willing and able to respond to these;
- interviewees' answers are deemed to be more valid if they do not know why the interviewer has asked the question, and if possible responses have not been suggested by the interviewer;
- the research context does not influence the production of the data, and the process of answering questions does not change participants' beliefs, opinions, and habits; and finally,
- the data produced from this kind of interview can then be meaningfully compared with that derived from other interviews.

Guidelines for effective data gathering taught to survey researchers are aimed at lessening or avoiding altogether the effects of the researcher on the 'validity' and 'reliability' of the interview data generated. Thus we see instructions such as 'ask the questions in the correct order,' or 'do not show approval or disapproval of any answer' (Brenner, 1985: 19). Researchers are provided explicit instructions for how to formulate and pose questions – for example, by focusing on 'brevity, simplicity and concreteness' (Foddy, 1993: 50).

One example of the impact on the production of data from *not* following these kinds of rules in a survey is drawn from the British television comedy series, *Yes, Prime Minister*. In this dig at the conduct of social surveys, we see Sir Humphrey Appleby, a plotting bureaucrat, teaching Bernard Woolley, the prime minister's principal private secretary, how to generate precisely the kind of 'findings' he needs to support an argument to present to the prime minister. Sir Humphrey demonstrates two different question–answer sequences with Bernard that result in radically different responses as a suggested means of intentionally producing findings that show public 'support' for a policy decision, in this case, the re-introduction of national service. Bernard Woolley describes the conversation in his memoirs:

> … the market researcher asks questions designed to elicit consistent answers.
> Humphrey demonstrated the system on me. 'Mr. Woolley, are you worried about the rise in crime among teenagers?'
> 'Yes,' I said.
> 'Do you think there is lack of discipline and vigorous training in our Comprehensive Schools?'
> 'Yes.'
> 'Do you think young people welcome some structure and leadership in their lives?'
> 'Yes.'
> 'Do they respond to a challenge?'
> 'Yes.'
> 'Might you be in favour of reintroducing National Service?'
> 'Yes.'
> Well naturally I said yes. One could hardly have said anything else without looking inconsistent. Then what happens is that the Opinion Poll publishes only the last question and answer.
> Of course, the reputable polls didn't conduct themselves like that. But there weren't too many of those. Humphrey suggested that we commission a new survey, not for the Party but for the Ministry of Defence. We did so. He invented the questions there and then:
> 'Mr. Woolley are you worried about the danger of war?'
> 'Yes,' I said, quite honestly.
> 'Are you unhappy about the growth of armaments?'
> 'Yes.'
> 'Do you think there's a danger in giving young people guns and teaching them how to kill?'
> 'Yes.'
> 'Do you think it's wrong to force people to take up arms against their will?'

'Yes.'
'Would you oppose the reintroduction of National Service?'
I'd said 'Yes' before I'd even realized it, d'you see?[1] (Lynn and Jay,
1989:106–7)

Nevertheless, prescriptions that rely on remarkably similar assumptions to those advising survey researchers appear in the advice literature concerning qualitative interviewing. For example, Robert Weiss counsels interviewers to avoid self-disclosure, since it 'complicates an interview situation by shifting the respondent's attention to the interviewer and altering the respondent's relationship with the interviewer' (1994: 79), and Daphne Keats (2000) provides recommendations to ensure that the researcher minimizes bias, and generates valid and reliable data.

Neo-positivist assumptions about interview data are clearly evident in much published research, particularly in research that uses mixed methods design (for examples of research reports using mixed methods, see Westheimer and Kahne [2004] and Zhao and Frank [2003]). In contrast to studies that have used standardized surveys, however, one is likely to see the inclusion of semi-structured interviews that have used open, rather than closed, questions. While researchers represent the results of standardized surveys numerically in the form of various statistical analyses, researchers using a neo-positivist conception of interviews are likely to represent findings in the form of themes supported by extracts from interview transcripts, sometimes complemented with models or diagrams. Let us take a closer look at a research report that relies on a neo-positivist conception of interviews.

A Research Example of a Neo-positivist Approach to Interviewing

Over a period of two years, Joel Westheimer and Joseph Kahne (2004) examined teachers' and students' beliefs about citizenship in 10 democratic education projects in the United States. Their report focuses on two of the programs, and findings from the study are drawn from their analyses of observational, interview, survey, and documentary data. Westheimer and Kahne report that 'the interviews and observations were designed to help us clarify students' beliefs regarding what it means to be a good citizen and the ways that features of the curriculum may have affected their perspectives' (2004: 247). Likewise, they wanted to understand teachers' conceptions and priorities concerning 'responsible and effective citizenship,' as well as their perspectives concerning teaching strategies and outcomes (2004: 247). The findings of the report are represented thematically, together with

---

[1]From THE COMPLETE YES PRIME MINISTER: THE DIARIES OF THE RIGHT HON. JAMES HACKER by Jonathan Lynn and Antony Jay, published by BBC Books. Reprinted by permission of The Random House Group Ltd.
Permission to reprint in the US and its dependencies has been provided by Jonathan Lynn and Antony Jay (6 August 2009 and 18 August 2009).

statistical analyses of changes from pre- and post-test surveys administered to students in the programs. The reporting of this study reflects underlying neo-positivist assumptions about the researchers (that they can generate objective findings) and also that research interviews can provide meaningful and stable data concerning interior states of minds (such as beliefs). Although these researchers provide a statement outlining their predispositions concerning the topic of 'citizenship,' this is not discussed in relation to either the generation or analysis of data. Westheimer and Kahne do, however, state that they asked teachers to 'reflect on our observations, not only to test the accuracy of statements but also to reexamine perceptions and conclusions' (2004: 248). This statement reflects the underlying concern for 'truth' and 'accuracy' in this conception of interviewing.

The use of standardized interviews as a method of generating knowledge about human experience has been widely critiqued by influential researchers such as Elliot Mishler (1986), who argues for an approach to interviews that recognizes and appreciates the co-production of narrative data; and Ann Oakley (1981), who has made the case for a 'feminist' approach to interviewing women that recognizes the experiences of both researcher and researched. These kinds of criticisms have also been applied to the neo-positivist conception of a qualitative interview. The chief problems that must be addressed by researchers with neo-positivist assumptions concerning interview data are that:

(1) research participants do not necessarily do what they say they do;
(2) research participants do not necessarily tell the truth;
(3) the researcher's subjectivities and beliefs may bias the data; and
(4) analyses and representations of interview data do not account for the researcher's part in the co-construction of data.

Responses to these criticisms have taken a variety of forms and primarily address the first two problems. Multiple methods of data collection are used for the purposes of methodological triangulation (for example, observations may provide opportunities to check the accuracy of what participants have said); longevity in the field allows researchers to verify the stability of participants' reports and subsequent analyses (data triangulation); and researchers frequently seek participants' responses and feedback on preliminary analyses and reports (member checking or member validation). All of these strategies are reported in Westheimer and Kahne's (2004) study. The third critique – that of how the researcher's subjectivities intersect with the research participants and topic – is frequently addressed in the next conception of interviewing that I discuss.

A Romantic Conception of Interviewing

Below is an excerpt from an interview promoted as 'a refreshingly honest no holds-barred-interview' in which pop singer Britney Spears 'took on the tabloids' in an interview with *Dateline* reporter Matt Lauer (broadcast on NBC, 15 June 2006).

Spears: I like to cook, try to cook, and I like to clean. I'm obsessive like that. If I watch TV, I like to watch the home-redoing-the-house shows – the whole thing – and I get into redoing the living room, the baby's room and all that stuff.

Lauer: So do you clean the house by yourself?

Spears: I have a maid that comes in once a week, but she slacks a little bit (makes face.)

Lauer: So if I were to come here and ring the doorbell by surprise, you'd be vacuuming, doing the toilets?

Spears: Doing the laundry, everything, mmm hmm.

Lauer: See, there's a side of you we didn't know ...

Spears: Oh honey, that is the real me, honey!

Lauer: I pictured there would be housekeepers around here.

Spears: This house is so big, I have to have some help. (Lauer, 2006)

We are well-acquainted with this style of interview, in which interviewees provide exposés about intimate personal details to interviewers who appear to be compassionate, sympathetic, and sensitive. Larry King, Oprah, Barbara Walters, and a host of other prime-time television hosts broadcast these kinds of interviews to global audiences. Yet while the authenticity of celebrities' self-revelations and interviewers' sincerity in interviews such as that quoted above are questionable – we are familiar with the machinations of publicity relations teams and the marketing of prime-time television slots – the conception of the romantic interview is well-established in the literature on qualitative research methodology (Alvesson, 2003). Elsewhere, this formulation of the interview is referred to as 'emotionalist' (see Silverman, 2001).

In contrast to the neo-positivist conception of the interview, when used for the purposes of social research, the interviewer–interviewee relationship in the romantic interview is one in which genuine rapport and trust[2] is established by the interviewer in order to generate the kind of conversation that is intimate and self-revealing (See Box 3.2).

Box 3.2   A romantic conception of the interview

The interviewer establishes rapport and empathic connection with the interviewee ⇒ Produces intimate conversation between interviewer and interviewee in which the interviewer plays an 'active' role ⇒ Generates interviewee's 'self revelation' and 'true confessions' ⇒ Produces in-depth interpretations of participants' life-worlds.

---

[2]A reading of the Lauer–Spears interview transcript shows in detail how Lauer works to distance himself from the 'paparazzi' who are shown to be Spears' enemies. Yet while asking questions that appear to be sympathetic and compassionate, the sequence of questions and voice-over text aggressively pursues Spears, and parallels the attacks by the 'paparazzi' that Spears attempts to counter. This interview shows how personal revelations are used in the public invention of self (see Atkinson and Silverman, 1997). These authors argue that social researchers' preoccupation with the use of the interview method reflects this kind of cultural preoccupation.

- The data generated provide in-depth knowledge and understanding concerning the beliefs, perceptions, experiences and opinions of the authentic self of the interview subject.
- The data are co-constructed by the interviewer and interviewee, and the interviewer may contribute his/her own views to the conversation in order to heighten rapport.
- Data may be coded and categorized to produce thematic accounts; or subject to various narrative analytic methods to produce evocative narrative accounts concerning the participants' life worlds.
- Research may draw on feminist, phenomenological, psychoanalytic, and psychosocial theories.

In this view, the interviewer is more apt to contribute to the interview interaction in order to prompt confessional detail from the interviewee (see also Douglas, 1985; McCracken, 1988).

One example of 'advice-giving' literature concerning the romantic conception of the interview is provided by sociologist, Joseph Hermanowicz (2002), who offers no fewer than 25 tips for novice interviewers in order to conduct an 'outstanding' interview. Using the metaphor of dating, Hermanowicz writes:

> Great interviewing is not pure sex; it's a romantic-like dialogue that progressively moves through stages (of revelation) and enacted rituals (greetings and introductions, questioning, explanation) culminating in the most intimate of exchanges ('intercourse'), even if all done within an hour's time. (2002: 482)

Embodied in Hermanowicz's approach to the interview is the notion of the skilled interviewer who, when able to successfully seduce his or her participant, will come away from the interview with descriptions of a person's 'essence or inner core' (2002: 481). The quotation above entails a common feature of methodological writing on qualitative interviewing that attempts to counter the notion of the 'neutral' and 'detached' researcher, seen earlier in the neo-positivist conception of the interview. That is, the interviewer must know how to work with participants to ask the right questions and sequence them in particular ways to generate good data. In fact, Hermanowicz provides specific instructions for posing the right question at the right time. For example, 9th and 10th on his list are:

(9) Word questions clearly.
(10) Sequence your moves:
    (a) first questions are introductory, easy to answer, nonthreatening;
    (b) difficult or threatening questions should be placed in the middle of the interview; and
    (c) an interview should always end on a positive note. (2002: 488–90)

Given that these kinds of prescriptions for good interviewing technique are similar to some of those we have seen in the description of the neo-positivist interview, what is different about the romantic interview? The aim of asking good questions in particular kinds of ways in the neo-positivist framework is to gain descriptions that are valid and reliable – that is, accurate and stable responses from the interviewee to unbiased questions from the objective interviewer concerning particular topics. In contrast, the object of the romantic interview is to ensure the development of a particular kind of researcher–researched relationship or rapport that will result in gaining data of an in-depth nature that is revelatory and revealing for both parties. For example, Jack Douglas writes:

> ... the self-disclosure and soul-communion involved in creative interviewing become a vital source of progressive self-understanding for both the informant friends and the handmaidenly researcher. (1985: 42)

In this approach the researcher must be intimately aware of his or her own subjectivities, and interview style, and makes no claim to being objective. I use the term subjectivities to refer to a researcher's personal assumptions and presuppositions, or as Alan Peshkin writes, that 'amalgam of the persuasions that stem from the circumstances of one's class, statuses, and values interacting with the particulars of one's object of investigation' (1988: 17). Like H.L. 'Bud' Goodall (2000), I take the stance that any exploration of subjectivities entails examination of one's personal experiences and biography as a researcher. This kind of advice is common in the literature on qualitative interviewing; for example both Douglas (1985) and Herbert Rubin and Irene Rubin (2005) include sections on researchers knowing themselves.

Qualitative researchers have paid close attention to the critiques of interviewing that seek to make explicit the interviewer's part in the research project. In fact, the inclusion of researchers' subjectivity statements and the possible impact of the researcher's race, status, gender, and perspectives on the data generation, analysis, and representation has become a common feature of research reports (see, for example, Duneier, 2000: 352–4; Ferguson, 2001: 12–16; Fordham, 1996: 36–7). Another feature of reports of studies relying on a romantic conception of interviewing – although by no means standard practice – is that of including the researcher's contribution to the interview talk in the final report. One example of this kind of work is found in Elliot Mishler's (1999) study of craftartists' narratives. Let us now turn to a research report that foregrounds a romantic conception of interview practice.

A Research Example of a Romantic Conception of Interviewing

The influence of romantic assumptions concerning interviewing may be seen in Sharon Chubbuck and Michalinos Zembylas' (2008) case study of the intersections of emotions and socially just teaching in a case study of one White novice teacher working in an urban school in the US whom they call Sara. The researchers conducted a micro-ethnographic study, audio-taping and writing observations of Sara's teaching and interviewing her six times over the period of a semester. These data were supplemented with interviews of the department chair, and 10 students; Sara's reflective journal, student work samples, and informal conversations between Sara and the first author who was the principal investigator. Chubbuck and Zembylas report that since Sara was a former student of the first author, a 'level of communication and trust' had already been established which provided the necessary 'level of openness' between the researcher and participant (2008: 290). The researchers also invited Sara to comment on the initial written report of findings from the study (2008: 292). In this study the authors document information concerning their subjectivities in relation to the research project; and stress the implications of their respective relationships with Sara for the generation and interpretation of data, which was informed by critical and feminist theories. While Chubbuck's relationship with Sara is described positively as a way to enhance data generation, the fact that she 'developed a strong affection for and confidence in Sara as a teacher' is also viewed as a limitation in that it could 'skew her observations and perceptions of the data' (2008: 292). Given that Zembylas had no prior experience with Sara, he was able to cross-check Chubbuck's interpretations with a 'critical outsider's eye' (2008: 292). In this study, multiple methods of data generation, clarification of researchers' subjectivities, researcher triangulation, and member checking throughout the research process are reported as methods to ensure the quality of the study.

In the research examples provided for neo-positivist and romantic conceptions of interviews, an underlying assumption is the notion that researchers are able to access the 'authentic self' of the interview subject via interview talk. This view has been seriously questioned by researchers taking constructionist and postmodernist perspectives to interviews. In the next section, I show how a constructionist conception of interviewing rejects access to the 'authentic' self via interview data in favor of a 'locally produced subject' in relation to a particular interviewer. Here, *how* the interaction unfolds becomes a topic of study in its own right, with researchers interested in the documentation of 'the way in which accounts "are part of the world they describe"' (Silverman, 2001: 95).

A Constructionist Conception of the Interview

IR: Interviewer
IE: Interviewee

IR: yeah .hhh u::m (.) next one is just <u>what</u> u:m is a good day for you w-
what kind of things would happen (1.0) on a good day
IE: u::m get a lunch time? no [heh heh heh um
IR: [heh heh heh .hhh
IE: o::h (.) it's a hard question
(3.0)
IE: can you give me an example? (Roulston, 2004: 156–7)[3]

---

[3]Transcription conventions are drawn from conversation analysis, and are found in Appendix 1.

The assumptions underlying a 'constructionist' perspective (Silverman, 2001) of the interview are outlined in Box 3.3.

Box 3.3   A constructionist conception of the interview

The interviewer and interviewee ⇒ Co-construct data in unstructured and semi-structured interviews ⇒ Generating situated accountings and possible ways of talking about research topics by the interviewer and interviewee ⇒ Researcher produces analyses of how the interviewer and interviewee made sense of the research topic and constructed narratives; researcher provides understandings of possible ways of discussing topics.

- The data generated provide talk-in-interaction produced within the social setting of the research interview as but one cultural event within the life-world of the participant.
- Data are not seen as reports – that is as directly reflective of either 'interior' states of mind, or 'exterior' states in the world. Instead, data are viewed as 'accounts' – or practical displays of the local organization of social order by the speaker/s (Baker, 2004).
- The data are co-constructed by the interviewer and interviewee, and any of the interviewer's contributions are subject to the same kind of analytic focus as that of the interviewee.
- In this approach 'it's all data' (pers. comm., Carolyn Baker). Interviewers use ordinary conversational skills to elicit data and do not necessarily need specialized skills or training. See, for example, Rapley (2004) and Hester and Francis (1994).
- Data may be analyzed through inspection of both structural and topical features. That is, 'how' talk is co-constructed (indexical features) is just as important as 'what' is said (referential features).
- Analytic methods may be drawn from conversation analysis, discourse analysis, narrative analysis, and sociolinguistics.

Alvesson (2003) uses the label 'localist' to describe this approach to interviewing, and it is likely that some researchers who describe their interviews as 'constructionist' define their work somewhat differently than I do. Nevertheless, the label 'constructionist' captures both the importance of social interaction for the co-construction of interview data, as well as the focus on examining the resources people use to describe their worlds to others.

There is a good deal of variation among researchers who rely on a 'constructionist' conception of interviews to how interviews might be transcribed. In the interview excerpt above, in which a first-year teacher is asked to describe a good day, details that are frequently omitted from transcriptions are included. For researchers more familiar with the carefully edited and punctuated versions of talk commonly included in the representations emanating from other conceptions of interviews, this kind of transcription is likely to be off-putting. Yet, researchers who draw on conversation analysis (Sacks, 1992) to examine social interaction do not claim to have captured the talk in its entirety by providing such detailed transcriptions, and are well aware that transcription is theoretically informed (Ochs, 1979) and necessarily always incomplete. Analytic approaches such as conversation analysis and some forms of discourse and narrative analysis rely on detailed transcriptions to capture the complexity of the ongoing construction of interview data. In this kind of work, pauses, silences, laughter, and even inhalations and exhalations provide rich detail for analysis concerning how interviewers and interviewees co-construct possible ways of talking about research topics.

In the constructionist conception of the interview, data provides situated accountings on research topics – that is, particular versions of affairs produced by particular interlocutors on specific occasions. Carolyn Baker explains that rather than analyzing interview talk as 'reports' corresponding to matters outside the interview – that is, what people actually believe, observe, or do – if treated as 'accounts,' we can investigate the 'sense-making work through which participants engage in explaining, attributing, justifying, describing, and otherwise finding possible sense or orderliness in the various events, people, places, and courses of action they talk about' (2002: 781).

From this perspective, 'how' interview data are co-constructed by speakers becomes a topic of study, rather than merely a transparent resource for discussing particular research questions. Some of the scholars working in this tradition draw on ethnomethodology, which teaches us that when people talk to one another, they are also performing actions (for example, clarifying, justifying, informing, arguing, disagreeing, praising, excusing, insulting, complaining, complimenting, and so forth). In interview talk, this means that in any sequence of utterances, speakers show how they have oriented to and made sense of other speakers' prior talk.

In the excerpt included at the beginning of this section, we see that the interviewee provides an assessment (see Appendix 2) of the interview question – 'o::h (.) it's a hard question' that indicates an initial inability to draw on knowledge and experience of what a 'good day' could be. Spoken directly after a tentative response to the interviewer's question, it indicates the interviewee understands that her candidate response ('get a lunch time?') is an incomplete description of a 'good day,' and she continues to search for a possible answer by asking the interviewer for an example of a 'good day.' In this short fragment of talk we learn something about this first-year teacher's cultural world as a teacher through her initial facetious response followed by further difficulties in formulating a reply. While some might argue that this teacher's inability to respond to the interviewer's question shows the question to be invalid, I propose that the trouble encountered by the interviewee in formulating a response (that is, 'how' the interviewee's responses are formulated) provides rich data concerning how the world of teaching is and could be organized (that is, 'what' the speakers are talking about, or the topic of talk) (see also Roulston, 2001).

While methodological issues may be highlighted in this approach to the examination of interview data, Baker has argued that the study of people's sense-making practices in interview talk – just as in any other social setting – provides access to how members of society assemble 'what comes to be seen as rationality, morality, or social order,' and locates culture in action (Baker, 2000: 792; see also Baker, 1983, 1984, 2004). Holstein and Gubrium (2004) have promoted the view that researchers can usefully study both 'how' interview interaction is constructed and 'what' is said (see also Holstein and Gubrium, 1995). A growing number of researchers have used a constructionist approach to the interview, and draw on analytic methods from ethnomethodology, conversation analysis, membership categorization analysis, discourse analysis, and narrative analysis (for a review, see Roulston, 2006a).

The chief criticisms of this approach to interviews is that the analytic focus is too 'narrow,' and that the aim of examining both 'how' data are constructed and 'what' the topic of talk concerns is inconsistent with the critiques of the romantic and neo-positivist models of interviewing posed by the constructionist perspective of interviews (see Silverman, 2001: 97–8). Before leaving this approach, however, let us look at an example of research that uses this approach.

A Research Example of a Constructionist Approach to Interviewing

Susan Walzer and Thomas Oles' (2003) study of 'uncoupling narratives' recounted to them in interviews by divorced men and women characterizes a constructionist conception of interviews. Their representation of findings draws on narrative analysis, and while sequences of talk include both questions and responses from the interviewer in relation to interviewees, they do not use the detailed transcription conventions used by some analysts (e.g., Mishler, 1986). Initially, the researchers wanted to study roles taken on by those identified as either 'initiators' or 'non-initiators' of divorce. After analyzing their data they discovered that the narratives were replete with discrepancies that they could not explain and reconcile. The researchers then analyzed discrepancies in the narratives, identifying instances in which speakers claimed to have initiated a divorce while providing narratives that suggested they had not, or vice versa. In their presentation of findings, Walzer and Oles recognize that the accounts that they studied do not provide a clear 'truth.' Drawing on Catherine Riessman's (1990) work that used narrative approaches to analyze people's accounts of divorce, their close examination of how speakers construct their narratives reveals the ways that speakers used 'gender' to justify and excuse their actions. In this report, the participants are seen as providing situated accountings that reveal 'interpretations that are generated in interaction with some kind of social audience' (Walzer and Oles, 2003: 341).

In the next conception of the interview, which I describe as 'postmodern,' the notion of interviewees enacting situated performances of various selves is frequently highlighted. Whereas in the constructionist conception of the interview, researchers show how interaction unfolds through in-depth, line-by-line analyses, in the postmodern conception of the interview, researchers have shown through artful analyses and representations possible ways of breaking from traditional research practices. Whereas the constructionist perspective seeks to interpret the moment-by-moment unfolding of co-constructed meaning in interview interaction, and how speakers orient to one another's talk, a postmodernist view argues that 'there is no stable "reality" or "meaning" that can be represented' (Scheurich, 1995: 249).

A Postmodern Conception of the Interview

Norman Denzin promotes a fourth version of the research interview, which I call here the 'postmodern' interview (see Box 3.4). Denzin, a scholar whose work spans the fields of media and communications studies, film criticism, and sociology, has conceptualized the interview as a 'vehicle for producing performance texts and performance ethnographies about self and society,' rather than a 'method for gathering information' (2001: 24). In contrast to an authentic self produced in an interview with the skilful interviewer as in the neo-positivist and romantic models, this interview subject has no essential self, but provides – in relationship with a particular interviewer – various non-unitary performances of selves (Denzin, 2001: 28–9). Indeed, Jim Scheurich writes that '[t]he indeterminate totality of the interview always exceeds and transgresses our attempts to capture and categorize' (1995: 249).

Researchers using a postmodern conceptualization of interviewing question the possibility of generating 'truthful' accounts by asking questions of others, and in their representations of data, question the method itself and trouble readers' assumptions about the findings represented. For example, Trinh T. Minh-ha in her film *Surname Viet, Given Name Nam* (1989), defines the interview as 'an antiquated device of documentary. Truth is selected, renewed, displaced and speech is always tactical' (Trinh, 1992: 73). She directly questions romantic assumptions about interview practices that aim to generate intimate portraits of a human subject's essence, and highlights the often unseen work of interviewers and authors in assembling texts that aim to represent others. Trinh continues:

The more intimate the tone, the more successful the interview. Every question she and I come up with is more or less a copy of the question we have heard before. Even if the statement is original, it sounds familiar, worn, threadbare. By choosing the most direct and spontaneous form of voicing and documenting, I find myself closer to fiction. (1992: 78)

While Trinh T. Minh-ha has used documentary film as one approach to representing and questioning interview data, other researchers have applied creative analytic practices (CAPs) (Richardson, 1994, 1999, 2002), such as ethnodrama (Mienczakowski, 2001), plays (Saldaña, 2003), fiction (Angrosino, 1998; Banks and Banks, 1998; Clough, 2002); performance ethnographies (Denzin, 2003a, 2003b), readers' theaters (Donmoyer and Yennie-Donmoyer, 1995) and poetry (Faulkner, 2005). This kind of work engages with audiences in new ways, often outside the academy. In Denzin's conception, a major aim for this 'new interpretive form, a new form of the interview, what I call the reflexive, dialogic, or performative interview', is to 'bring people together' and 'criticize the world the way it is, and offer suggestions about how it could be different' (2001: 24).

Box 3.4   A postmodern conception of the interview

The interviewer and interviewee ⇒ Co-construct data in unstructured and semi-structured interviews ⇒ Generating 'situated performances' ⇒ Producing data that may be subject to deconstructive analyses and/or fashioned by the researcher into performance texts in multiple genres, such as fiction, poetry, and performance texts.

- Data produced provides material for deconstructive readings and/or the construction of performance texts that are autoethnographic and/or critical.
- Both the interviewer's and interviewee's vulnerabilities are exposed to the audiences in texts and performances.
- Analytic methods may draw on critical, poststructural and postmodern theories, and represent multiple and fragmented 'selves', non-linear narratives, and use creative analytic practices (Richardson, 1994).
- Representations are partial and fragmented, and reject the notion of a unified self.

The application of postmodern theoretical lenses to interview data and the use of alternative modes of representation have invited both critique and applause (Gergen and Gergen, 2000). For example, in the US, the National Research Council's report *Scientific Research in Education* dismissed the work of 'extreme' postmodernists (2002: 25), and reinforced a particular perspective of science that was evidence-based, replicable, objective, and generalizable. Yet, such critiques have not dampened the enthusiasm of qualitative researchers across disciplines for alternative ways of doing and presenting research. For example, the journal *Qualitative Inquiry* has published numerous examples of this kind of work. One example of interviewing and representation that could be labeled postmodern is provided by anthropologist Michael Angrosino.

A Research Example of a Postmodern Approach to Interviewing

Angrosino's (1998) book, *Opportunity House: Ethnographic Stories of Mental Retardation*, is a series of fictional stories that he constructed from data generated in life history interviews with a group of men with cognitive disabilities. His interest in researching this group came from longstanding involvement as a volunteer worker at the house in which the men lived. Angrosino's treatment of interviews is multi-layered, and shows a deliberate recognition of the performative nature of the interview itself; as well as the performative potential of the researcher's re-presentation of the data. Angrosino writes:

> [T]he rendering of a life as a story – an artifact, a text – means that it has been filtered through at least two consciousnesses. It is no longer simply the internal memory of the

person who lived the life; it is also the narrative record of the question I asked about it and the directions in which I subtly or otherwise led the person to speak. There is also an implicit third consciousness – that of any potential audience for the story ... a life history may well provide us with nuggets of insight about the specifics of a culture, it is also, and most significantly, a document of interaction – primarily between the 'subject' and the researcher, and secondarily between both of them and their potential audience or reference group. (1998: 32)

Angrosino's reflections on the interviews he undertook with the men are instructive. He comments that 'while my [Opportunity House] friends might never be able to provide me with coherent, objective narratives of their life experiences, they were nonetheless communicating some very important information about how they construct and maintain relationship' (1998: 37). With the invention of settings, and the creation of composite and fictional characters, Angrosino's purpose was to convey 'truths' about adult experiences of cognitive disability, rather than 'facts.' Angrosino explains that as a non-therapist, he aimed to learn from the participants of his study, rather than advise them, or promote any kind of 'change' through interview dialogue. Unlike Angrosino, some researchers who take a postmodern conception of the interview align with critical perspectives and are change-oriented. In the next section, I consider an overtly 'transformative' conception of interviewing.

A Transformative Conception of Interviewing

In that Denzin's proposal of a 'new interpretive form' for the research interview challenges its audiences to reconsider the world in new and critical ways, and promotes a conception of a research interview as 'dialogical,' there is some overlap with the openly transformational intent in the next conception of the interview outlined in Box 3.5. Some might argue that any interview can facilitate some kind of transformation of parties to the talk (see for example, Wolgemuth and Donohue, 2006, pp. 1027–8). Indeed, in talking to other researchers about this topic I have found that many assert that as interviewers they have encountered transformational moments for both themselves and interviewees. Certainly, this may be the case. Here I use the term 'transformative' to denote work in which the researcher *intentionally* aims to challenge and change the understandings of participants, rather than 'transformation' that may be associated with new understandings on the part of either interviewer or interviewee. Jennifer Wolgemuth and Richard Donohue, for example, argue for conducting 'emancipatory narrative research with the explicit intent of transforming participants' lives by opening up new subjective possibilities' (2006: 1024). This work contributes to emancipatory and social justice work in that it assists in transformation of the parties to the talk, as well as generating data for research purposes.

Box 3.5   A transformative conception of the interview

The interviewer dialogues with the interviewee and may work in collaboration to design, conduct and present the research project ⇒ The interviewer and interviewee develop 'transformed' or 'enlightened' understandings as an outcome of dialogical interaction ⇒ Interpretations of data produce critical readings of cultural discourses that challenge normative discourses.

- Data produced changes both interviewer and interviewee; as each engages in dialogue that challenges former and current understandings.
- Impetus for this work is fostering social change for social justice.
- Analytic methods and representations draw on critical, emancipatory, and psychoanalytic theoretical perspectives (for example, critical theory, feminist theory, critical race theory, hermeneutics, and psychoanalysis).

The transformative interview has been discussed from two perspectives – in research emanating from an emancipatory or critical agenda (such as action research); and in work in which the 'therapeutic' interview has been applied to social research (Kvale, 1999). The distinction between these two perspectives of the transformative interview lies in the conception of the change made possible. In the first perspective, the transformative potential for participants cannot be pre-determined, 'since people's meanings and prejudices can only be brought forth at the time of articulation' (Melissa Freeman, pers. comm., 13 June 2006). In the therapeutic interview, change involves healing of the patient. According to Steinar Kvale, '[t]he purpose of the therapeutic interview is the facilitation of changes in the patient, and the knowledge acquired in the interview interaction is a means for instigating personality changes' (1999: 110). Kvale has advocated for the use of the psychoanalytic interview as a means of generating knowledge; and outlines a lengthy tradition in the field of psychology in which 'some of its most lasting and relevant knowledge of the human situation has been produced as a side effect of helping patients change' (1999: 110). A further distinction between these two strands of thought is that while in some incarnations the transformative interview is explicitly dialogic (and both interviewer and interviewee contribute to and are transformed by the interaction); in others it appears that the interviewers work to transform others.

While some feminist research may fit into the transformative conception of interviewing; not all does. For example, Terry Arendell's discussion of her interviews with men in her feminist study of divorced men discussed how she systematically avoided challenging interviewees who 'asserted their beliefs about male superiority, expressed other kinds of sexist and misogynist sentiments, and described behaviors hostile to women' (1997: 363). In Arendell's study, the interpretation produced in the final report produced feminist and critical readings of the data; however the interview itself could be characterized as romantic, in that the interviewer provided the kinds of responses necessary in order to elicit confessional detail from her informants; and withheld information when not directly asked that may have negatively impacted men's participation in the study (for example, that she was a feminist). Arendell's purpose was to generate *data* for her study; and her aim was not in any way to challenge or change participants of the study.

The key difference, then, between a 'transformative' interview and other models described earlier is found in the purpose of the interview. In this kind of interview, the relationship between the interviewer and interviewee aims for less asymmetry in talk, with 'transformative dialogue' enacted in the interview interaction. There are, however, few examples of what interaction that is truly 'dialogical' might look like, and how one might go about fostering that kind of talk in a research project. Kvale has discussed interviewer–interviewee relationships; in particular the problems associated with the asymmetrical power relation of the interview, arguing that 'a conception of research interviews as personal egalitarian dialogues masks the power asymmetry of hierarchical interview relationships' (2006: 496). A second issue that is not clear from the writing on this topic is how forthcoming interviewers are in working with interviewees about the aims of their research. While Adrianna Kezar (2003) has described some of the problems that arise in this kind of research interview, and Wolgemuth and Donohue propose an 'emancipatory narrative inquiry of discomfort [that] takes as its primary goal the transformation of individual into ambiguous selves' (2006: 1030), there is still much room for discussion of the place of research interviews in emancipatory and transformative research. This kind of methodological writing could show the range of talk produced by interviewers and interviewees in transformative interviews, and how such research might be facilitated with participants who may not share the interviewers' theoretical perspectives and aims.

A Research Example of a Transformative Approach to Interviewing

One example is provided by Melissa Freeman, who is theoretically informed by philosophical hermeneutics, which she describes as focusing on 'the event of understanding or interpretation as it occurs in the encounter' (2008: 386). Freeman (2006) describes a transformative conception of interviewing in her report on the use of focus group discussions with parents on the topic of state standardized testing. Although the purpose of the facilitation of focus groups was to gain data concerning parents' perceptions of the research topic, Freeman purposefully structured the talk to 'provide a space for people to engage critically and reflectively with issues that affect them daily' (2006: 84). Freeman provides some insight into the kinds of things that interviewers might do to facilitate dialogue. These include calling upon participants to 'think more deeply about the issues they bring to the discussion,' requesting examples of what participants mean; and use of alternative elicitation strategies such as the use of drawing, writing, or poetic transcriptions derived from prior data collection as a basis for group discussion (2006: 87). Another strategy that Freeman outlines is that the interviewer carefully consider what participants 'bring to the table,' and be less quick in judging talk as 'off topic' or 'irrelevant' (2006: 87).

One possible critique of this conception of the interview is the right and/or responsibility of the researcher in changing others' understandings. Further, researchers who frame their conception of interviewing using psychoanalytic theories are open to critique for blurring the lines between 'scientific research' and 'therapy.' For example, methods texts on qualitative interviewing frequently admonish researchers to clearly distinguish between doing 'therapy' and doing 'research' (see, for example, Seidman, 2006).

Writing on the transformative conception of interviewing is still sparse, and we have yet to see how this approach to data generation is taken up, adapted, and used for the purpose of doing social research. There are particular groups, however, who are likely to reject the notion that researchers might attempt to instigate dialogues of change with research participants in interviews. Some, perhaps, would reject direct involvement in research altogether. I speak specifically of indigenous groups with whom some researchers have worked to develop 'decolonizing' approaches to research.

A Decolonizing Conception of Interviewing

Research has long been a tool of colonization used by principalities and powers to explore, claim, divide, and vanquish peoples, cultures, and countries. Qualitative researchers are implicated in these explorations – for example, many methodological texts draw on advice provided in anthropological accounts authored by white researchers describing foreign lands and peoples and furnished with data extracted via interviews with key informants. Some argue that qualitative inquirers still participate in colonizing research. Thus, when Linda Tuhiwai Smith writes that decolonization of indigenous peoples 'is now recognized as a long-term process involving bureaucratic, cultural, linguistic and psychological divesting of colonial power' (1999: 98), she is also writing about research practices. In her influential book, *Decolonizing Methodologies: Research and Indigenous Peoples*, Smith shows how Western research practices that have objectified and endangered indigenous peoples throughout the world are an integral part of European colonialism. These practices, Smith asserts, have largely been experienced negatively by those who have been the objects (see also Stronach [2006], who addresses imperialism as a contemporary and continuing phenomenon in qualitative inquiry). Negative experiences with whites – research included – have led many indigenous people to mistrust non-indigenous peoples, researchers, and research itself (Smith, 1999).

Thus, before a researcher can conceptualize what a 'decolonizing' interview might look like, he or she must pay very close attention to indigenous research agendas. According to Smith (1999: 116–18), who is a Maori researcher in New Zealand, the indigenous research agenda involves the processes of decolonization, transformation, mobilization, and healing. She write that these 'are not goals or ends in themselves,' but 'processes which connect, inform and clarify the tensions between the local, the regional and the global ... that can be incorporated into practices and methodologies'

(1999: 116). Further, she asserts that indigenous peoples are moving through the conditions of survival, recovery, development, and self-determination (1999: 116). Thus any researcher planning to conduct research with indigenous peoples must thoroughly consider the issues outlined above, realizing that to be 'culturally sensitive' and to follow ethical codes of research conduct may be insufficient.

Smith writes that researchers with 'outsider' status are particularly problematic in indigenous communities, given that indigenous voices have often been silenced and marginalized by non-indigenous experts (1999: 139, see pp. 177–8 for models for culturally appropriate research by non-indigenous researchers). In some communities, research may only be conducted by indigenous researchers. Even so, indigenous researchers with 'insider' status in a community still face particular challenges in conducting research, given that often they are trained by and must meet standards for research required by academic communities that are in tension with those of indigenous communities.

Indigenous peoples have long relied on oral transmission of stories, yet interviewing as a method in some cases may not be appropriate. For example, Iseke-Barnes writes that:

> Often Elders decline to have their words recorded in print or on tape because when Elders' words are recorded the Elder loses the possibility of adjusting the lessons to the maturity of the learner and the ability to influence the ethical use of the knowledge. (2003: 214)

In settings in which interviewing as a method may be appropriate, what might a 'decolonizing interview' look like? Smith does not write specifically about a decolonizing conception of the interview, however, given the larger agenda that she articulates, together with the examples she provides, I draw pointers that must be considered in light of the particular issues relevant to different indigenous communities around the world (see Box 3.6).

Box 3.6   A decolonizing conception of the interview[4]

Prior to the interview, and throughout the research process

- The researcher observes culturally specific ethical protocols required by indigenous communities to gain entry to the community, as well as culturally specific protocols of respect, and practices of reciprocity with those involved in research (Smith, 1999: 118–20, 136).[5] Interviews as a form of data may only be used with permission of community members (Davis, 2004).

(Continued)

---

[4]This conception of the interview is framed using Smith's outline of an 'indigenous research agenda' (1999: 116–20).
[5]See also Smith (2005) and Bishop (2005) for suggestions concerning researcher conduct and models of decolonizing research in the Maori context.

(Continued)

- The interviewer has considered possible negative outcomes of the research, and worked to eliminate these (Smith, 1999: 173).
- The interviewer is aware of the potential for abuses of power in the researcher–researched relationship (Smith, 1999: 176).

The interview

The interviewer, with interviewee, generates the kind of talk that is deemed appropriate and valued in a particular indigenous community given the requirements of gender, status, and age of the interviewer/interviewee ⇒ Indigenous knowledge, practices and spirituality are taken into account by the interviewer in the design and conduct of the interview ⇒ Data analysis and interpretation is respectful of indigenous peoples and their knowledge and practices ⇒ Findings from research are shared by the researcher in respectful ways with and for the benefit of the communities studied, and in ways that may be understood by community members.

- Findings and interpretations from research studies are useful for indigenous communities and contribute to restorative justice.
- The impetus for this work is to contribute to the agendas of decolonization, transformation, mobilization and healing of indigenous peoples.
- Research follows the pathways of (1) community action research based around claims, and (2) advanced indigenous research and studies programs in academic institutions (Smith, 1999: 125).
- Analytic methods and representations draw on emancipatory and critical theoretical perspectives, and may involve community participation. Alternative representational strategies may include testimonies, story telling and oral histories, writing involving language revitalization, poetry, fiction, film, and art.

Indigenous ways of knowing may be seen as contradictory to Western ways of knowing, and doing research studies which aim to decolonize may involve different representational formats to traditional academic reports. For these reasons, one critique of this kind of work is that it is not sufficiently 'scientific' or 'academic.' Although issues outlined above represent substantial obstacles to the conduct of doing research with indigenous populations and the publication and dissemination of findings, there is a growing body of work from indigenous scholars from all over the world that 'talks back,' contradicts, and produces new understandings that counter the findings produced by non-indigenous researchers over many decades. The work of indigenous scholars is supplemented by that of non-indigenous researchers who have selected to work with indigenous communities. While there is a good deal of debate whether non-indigenous scholarly work can be decolonizing, or of value, there is a growing body of literature exemplifying decolonizing research.

A Research Example of a Decolonizing Approach to Interviewing

One example is Yoshitaka Iwasaki, Judith Bartlett, Benjamin Gottlieb and Darlene Hall's (2009) study that reports on leisure-like experiences of urban-dwelling Metis and First Nations people living with diabetes in Canada. The authors used a decolonizing methodology with the overarching aim of allowing the research process to be guided by Aboriginal world views. Specifically, the decisions concerning the project, which involved the use of in-depth interviews, involved collective discussions and consensus decision-making guided by Aboriginal researchers.

This article demonstrates some of the features of a decolonizing approach to research outlined by Smith (1999). First, the researchers purposefully avoided the use of Western-oriented academic language, such as 'stress,' 'coping' and 'leisure,' and pilot-tested questions that used culturally relevant terms approved by members of the Aboriginal community (Iwasaki et al., 2009: 162). The inclusion of input from community members with respect to question formulation recognizes the colonizing potential of research with indigenous peoples, and attempts to disrupt this. Second, the researchers paid specific attention to showing respect for Aboriginal people's knowledge throughout the research process. This is demonstrated in multiple ways.

Aboriginal researchers were included in discussions and decision-making concerning the research project; interviewers used broad, conversational probes in order to 'respectfully listen and honor the life stories' of participants in interviews; the research team did not assume that diabetes was central to participants' lived experiences (Iwasaki et al., 2009: 162); and the process of data analysis used a procedure called Collective Consensual Data Analytic Procedure (CCDAP), an approach to research adapted from facilitation and organization practices that have been used successfully with Aboriginal organizations in Canada (2009: 165). The research team also received input from three respected Aboriginal health and social service professionals in a two-day interpretive workshop that discussed the conclusions and verification of the findings. Finally, the authors report that those researchers who were not Aboriginal made specific attempts to bracket their 'conventional Western-oriented research paradigms and assumptions to become knowledgeable and immersed in an Indigenous way of doing research' (Iwasaki et al., 2009: 162). These researchers' emphasis on the development of a research project guided by Aboriginal researchers and knowledgeable Aboriginals within the community, as well as carefully considered procedures regarding collective decision-making, provides a useful guide to how a decolonizing methodology might be used by researchers seeking to advance knowledge about the lived experiences of Indigenous peoples.

Conclusion

In this chapter, I have outlined six conceptions of research interviews. In published accounts, readers may find that the distinctions outlined between these perspectives may blur. Yet it is useful for readers to examine how researchers foreground particular kinds of assumptions concerning their use of interviews. Locating these assumptions in research reports is helpful in clarifying the different theoretical positions that researchers take in their use of interview research. For example, do researchers emphasize their objectivity as interviewers or the sense of rapport and trust they have developed with participants? Do researchers foreground the researcher's co-production of interview data, or make explicit their rejection of a 'unitary truth' as an important feature in reports from qualitative interview studies? Or, perhaps, research reports feature dialogue that researchers assert shows how speakers have experienced transformational moments within the interview talk. Other accounts may foreground the need for culturally sensitive research practices that strive to avoid the denigration of indigenous ways of knowing. By asking these kinds of questions of research reports, readers can become more familiar with the different kinds of assumptions that researchers use in their work. Beginning researchers who familiarize themselves with a range of approaches to interviewing will be better able to situate themselves as researchers.

In the next chapter, I discuss how researchers might go about developing ideas into a topic for research, how research questions might be formulated, and the kinds of decision making that inform the design process. Finally, I discuss the issue of quality in relation to the design process.

Further Reading

A Neo-positivist Conception of Interviewing

Monte-Sano, C. (2008) 'Qualities of historical writing instruction: A comparative case study of two teachers' practices', *American Educational Research Journal*, 45 (4): 1045–79.

A Romantic Conception of Interviewing

Kouritzin, S.G. (1999) *Face[t]s of First Language Loss*. Mahwah, NJ: Lawrence Erlbaum Associates.

A Constructionist Conception of Interviewing

Baker, C.D. and Johnson, G. (1998) 'Interview talk as professional practice', *Language and Education*, 12 (4): 229–42.

Schubert, S.J., Hansen, S., Dyer, K.R. and Rapley, M. (2009) '"ADHD patient" or "illicit drug user"? Managing medico-moral membership categories in drug dependence services', *Discourse and Society*, 20 (4): 499–516.

A Postmodern Conception of Interviewing

Gale, K. and Wyatt, J. (2007) 'Writing the incalculable: A second interactive inquiry', *Qualitative Inquiry*, 13 (6): 878–907.

Gale, K. and Wyatt, J. (2006) 'Inquiring into writing: An interactive interview', *Qualitative Inquiry*, 12 (6): 1117–34.

A Transformative Conception of Interviewing

Stinson, D. (2008) 'Negotiating sociocultural discourses: The counter-storytelling of academically (and mathematically) successful African-American male students', *American Educational Research Journal*, 45 (4): 975–1010.

A Decolonizing Conception of Interviewing

Caracciolo, D. and Staikidis, K. (2009) '"Coming of age in methodology": Two collaborative inquiries with Shinnecock and Maya peoples', *Qualitative Inquiry*, 15 (8): 1395–415.

Kombo, E.M. (2009) 'Their words, actions, and meaning: A researcher's reflection on Rwandan women's experience of genocide', *Qualitative Inquiry*, 15 (2): 308–23.

Madison, D.S. (2008) 'Narrative poetics and performative intervention', in N.K. Denzin, Y.S. Lincoln and L.T. Smith (eds), *Handbook of Critical and Indigenous Methodologies*. Los Angeles, CA: Sage. pp. 391–405.

Activity 3.1   Reading research: Theoretical assumptions

Locate two reports of qualitative studies that have used interviews in a journal in your field of interest. Read each article, paying particular attention to the literature review and research design and methods section.

- What theoretical and conceptual frameworks are described by the author/s?
- What information is included about the researcher/s?
- How are the qualitative interviews characterized and described in the research design statement?
- If the interview questions are included, what do you notice about their formulation and sequence?
- How are interview data incorporated into the findings section?
- Are the interview questions and interviewer's interactions included in the report?
- What kinds of assumptions about qualitative interviews may be inferred from the research report?
- Which conception of the interview do the authors foreground in each report?
- How convincing did you find this report? Why?

FOUR

Designing Studies that Use Interviews

This chapter introduces:

- Approaches to *identifying a research topic*.
- *Research purposes* and formulation of *research questions*.
- Approaches to *selection* and *sampling* of participants.
- Considering *quality* in the use of qualitative interviews.

Designing a research project is a complex process in which the researcher identifies a research problem and topic, formulates research questions that examine different aspects of the topic, and outlines a plan of action, or research proposal, that explains the research design. The proposal allows readers – including funding agencies, institutional review boards, and thesis and dissertation committees – to understand the methods the researcher will use to examine the research questions, as well as the significance of the study to the field in which it is situated. The formulation of research questions, criteria used to identify the population to be studied, sampling strategies used to select participants, methods of data collection and generation, and analytic approaches and forms of representation employed are informed and guided by the researcher's epistemological and theoretical assumptions concerning how social knowledge is produced, as well as the theoretical and substantive literature in a specific field of study.

The design process entails a number of steps that do not necessarily unfold in the linear manner in which I present them here. In this chapter I focus on the tasks that researchers typically accomplish as they develop research topics and questions and select particular types of interviews for their research. I conclude Chapter 4 by discussing the issue of quality in relation to research design, focusing on how the theoretical conceptions of interviewing discussed in the previous chapter imply different design decisions.

Identifying a Topic

Researchers identify their research topics via an assortment of approaches. There is certainly no correct way to go about selecting a topic for research; however there are strategies that may be helpful for newcomers to research. First, researchers might consider the key problems identified by other researchers in a specific area of interest. These are frequently found in reviews of literature, essays presented by established researchers, as well as recommendations for further research found in published research as well as theses and dissertations. Reading in the key journals in a field of study will help beginning researchers learn more about directions for further research that have been identified by other scholars as well as important problems about which little is known. Second, researchers frequently come to an area of research interest via personal experience. For example, practitioners might begin with a problem that they identify in their everyday work. A next step is to explore how scholars in the field have studied this issue and identify what is already known about it. Researchers might then consider what kinds of questions have yet to be asked. Third, qualitative researchers are informed by research purposes that are informed by specific theoretical perspectives toward social research. These perspectives might be thought of as lenses through which the world might be viewed. Theoretical interests have significant import into how researchers examine a topic and how they formulate questions. For example, the topics and research questions examined by researchers using feminist theories are guided by an interest in forwarding feminist agendas. Fourth, research topics are frequently inspired by curiosity and observation concerning what is going on in the world around us. For example, 'unmotivated looking' is a guiding policy used by researchers taking an ethnomethodological perspective to research. This means that researchers consider the issues that arise in a social setting as a source of inspiration, rather than first formulating topics informed by theoretical advances in a field of study. Of course, a research proposal is likely to be informed by multiple facets of those mentioned above – findings from prior research, personal interest, research purpose and theoretical assumptions about how knowledge is produced, as well as observation of any particular social setting.

One way of thinking about the purpose of research has been outlined by Patti Lather (2004). Developing ideas posited by Jürgen Habermas concerning categories of human interest that underlie knowledge claims, Lather adds 'deconstruction' to those of 'prediction,' 'understanding,' and 'emancipation' as forms of postpositivist inquiry (Lather, 2004: 206). For Lather (2004), postpositivism encapsulates the idea that there are multiple approaches to doing science. Researchers might consider how their own assumptions about the production of knowledge in the social world can inform their selection of both the kinds of problems to examine, and how these might be studied. Thus, useful questions to ask of oneself as a researcher are, do I want to:

- Make predictions?
- Develop understanding?
- Promote transformation or social change?
- Make a long-term commitment to promoting decolonizing and social justice agendas?
- Deconstruct topics?

Researchers who aim to make predictions will need to use experimental methods in which hypothesis-testing is central. Broadly speaking, qualitative inquiry encompasses work that seeks to understand, promote change, or seeks to break apart and trouble – or deconstruct – current understandings of topics.

Once a research topic has been identified, a researcher must develop a rationale for studying the topic and formulate research questions. This typically entails developing an argument for the study that identifies both the research problem that will be addressed by the study as well as the significance of the study for the field of interest. For novice researchers, reading examples of research studies in the top-tier journals within a field of interest is helpful in learning how to situate one's argument in a scholarly field. What this means is that researchers must present the rationale for their research study in relation to prior scholarly work. Typically, researchers draw on multiple bodies of literature to inform their work, and in outlining the argument for their study they demonstrate knowledge of what is already known about a research topic, what questions have yet to be explored, what research problem they would like to address, how the study will examine the problem, and why it is important to examine these questions.

Table 4.1 uses Lather's framework to demonstrate how different research purposes and theoretical perspectives toward postpositivist research imply different kinds of research questions, which in turn require different research designs and methods of data generation. I have taken as a sample topic that of 'hip hop culture.' Omitted from Table 4.1 is an explanation of a *research problem* relevant to research questions posed, and discussion of the *significance* of studying the research questions for a particular substantive field.

Thus, the research questions posed should be read as demonstrations of research questions *made possible* by different theoretical perspectives toward social research. In order to design a study utilizing any of these research questions for a study that will contribute significant findings to the topic area of hip hop culture, a researcher would need to provide an argument outlining what is already known, and show how a study would contribute to knowledge in a specific area of research. It is critically important for researchers to show why a study is important, relate the proposed study to what is already known about a topic, show how the design of the study will generate data to respond to the research questions posed and how the study will potentially contribute to understanding the research problem outlined.

Formulating Research Questions

As discussed above, research questions must not only address a research problem that the researcher has identified, but they must be consistent with the theoretical assumptions underlying research. Below I consider some examples.

An Example of Research for Understanding

Kathy Charmaz has conducted multiple investigations of the topic of chronic illness using a grounded theory perspective. In a 1997 article drawing on data from a larger

Table 4.1   Examining a research topic from different theoretical perspectives

Research topic: hip hop culture

Theoretical perspective	Possible research questions	Research design	Methods of data generation
Research for understanding Symbolic interactionism	What do participants in hip hop culture identify as the key symbols and identifiers of hip hop culture? What were the circumstances, processes and contexts for the development of hip hop culture? What are high school teachers' perceptions of hip hop culture in x setting? What explains high school teachers' responses to students' demonstrations of and interests in hip hop culture?	Ethnography	Ethnographic interviews Observations Focus groups Documents (e.g., lyrics, newspaper reports etc.)
Phenomenology	What is the experience of being in hip hop culture as described by participants? What is it like for participants to experience hip hop culture?	Interview study	In depth phenomenological interviews
Hermeneutics	How do people interpret or understand hip hop culture? What cultural, linguistic and sensual resources do they draw on to make meaning of hip hop culture?	Interview study	Interviews Texts (e.g., lyrics, reports)
Ethnomethodology	How do peer groups who participate in hip hop culture make sense of each other's utterances and actions?	Naturally occurring interaction supplemented by interviews	Audio-recording and/or video-recording of hip hop performances, naturally occurring talk, interviews

(Continued)

Table 4.1   (Continued)

Theoretical perspective	Possible research questions	Research design	Methods of data generation
Research for emancipation Critical inquiry	How do students respond to an integrated-arts/literacy program in which hip hop artists work with students in schools? What contexts of learning that employ students' knowledge are necessary for educators to engage students in an integrated-arts/literacy program that incorporates elements of hip hop culture?	Participatory action research	Gather base line data (surveys, documents, interviews, observations, audio- and video-recordings of naturally occurring-data) Establish educational program for teachers Reflect → Modify educational program → Generate more data → Reflect →
Feminist theory	What are the experiences of women hip-hop artists? How are women portrayed in hip hop lyrics? What are the processes by which patriarchy is taken up, resisted and subverted in hip-hop music?	Collective case study	Interviews Texts Documents observations
Research for deconstruction Postmodern Poststructural	When and where did the discourse of hip hop emerge? How have discourses of hip hop culture been appropriated in popular culture? How have discourses of hip hop culture been appropriated in marketing and advertising? What explains the appropriation of hip hop culture in capitalist society?	Foucauldian text analysis • Archeology • Genealogy	Document analysis Interviews Texts, advertising, pictures, video images

study of people's experiences of chronic illness she reports on men's experiences of chronic illnesses. Charmaz outlines a number of research questions that she examined for this study, which involved semi-structured interviews with 40 men:

> What is it like to be an active, productive man one moment and a patient who faces death the next?
> What is it like to change one's view of oneself accordingly?
> Which identity dilemmas does living with continued uncertainty pose for men?
> How do they handle them?
> When do they make identity changes?
> When do they try to preserve a former self? (Charmaz, 1997: 38)

Charmaz's interest in studying 'identity' is reflective of the symbolic interactionist underpinnings of grounded theory (see Sandstrom et al., 2003). While Charmaz (1997) does not include a copy of the interview guide used for the study in this report, the kinds of questions that she asks in conducting this kind of research might be inferred from other writing (for example, Charmaz, 2002). As a grounded theorist, Charmaz has been interested in developing understanding of social and psychological processes entailed in people's experiences of chronic illness. As a result, her interview questions are aimed at eliciting data concerning the processes and conditions related to what people with chronic illnesses do, and what happens as a result (Charmaz, 2002: 678).

An Example of Research for Emancipation

In order to understand women's experiences of adventure recreation activities, Donna E. Little (2002) conducted a qualitative study that involved semi-structured interviews with 42 women about their experiences, and collecting activity diaries from them over a period of six months. Little's study examined questions related to women's experiences of adventure recreation, as well as the constraints related to their involvement and how they negotiated these. By understanding the experiences of women involved in adventure recreation, Little hoped to inform outdoor educators and facilitators about the options available to women as well as strategies to facilitate their involvement. Little includes a list of the interview questions used in the study, with questions responding to specific topical areas, including participation in adventure recreation, reasoning related to choices to participate, and how participants prioritized and negotiated their involvement. Little's description of the methods used for the study point to feminist interview strategies in that she allowed the women to explore the topics in individual ways. She also provided an analysis to participants so that they could provide input concerning the researcher's interpretations (Little, 2002: 162).

An Example of Research for Deconstruction

Patti Lather and Chris Smithies in their 1997 book, *Troubling the Angels: Women Living with AIDS*, used feminist poststructural theories to theorize and represent data concerning the lives of 25 women living with HIV/AIDS in Ohio, in the US. Rather than design and conduct a study in which they were disinterested observers, the researchers worked collaboratively with women within the context of support groups to discuss topics of interest to the women. In addition, they socialized with the women in informal settings, and joined with them in times of celebration, illness, and grief. The participants of the study were involved in the decision-making involved in representing their stories in the book and wrote their own introductions. This book deconstructs, takes apart, and exposes assumptions not only about public discourses surrounding HIV/AIDS that existed in the early 1990s and linger today, but also about research and how findings might be represented. The authors purposefully trouble readers with the women's unsettling stories, with the non-linear form of representation in which chapters are interspersed with statistics, comments, quotations, and images of angels, and with the authors' representation of their thinking processes throughout the study in a split text found across the bottom of each page. Unlike many research reports in which the interviewer's utterances are omitted in final reports, both Lather and Smithies' questions and comments are included in the excerpts of interactions from the unstructured conversations that took place in support groups. The authors pose several questions concerning the study at the outset: 'Are we talking *about* these women? *for* them? *with* them? We *should* be uncomfortable with these issues of telling other people's stories' (Lather and Smithies, 1997: 9). These kinds of questions reflect the deconstructive purposes represented by this kind of research, in that the researchers troubled their own assumptions about research. The book also challenges readers with explorations of uneasy answers to the research questions posed about how women live with HIV/AIDS in the US.

Using Research Interviews to Address Research Questions

Once researchers have formulated research questions, they must consider the kinds of methods that might be used most effectively to inform questions. First and foremost, researchers must consider their research purposes and whether other kinds of data will be needed in addition to interviews. For example, Little (2002) supplemented interview data with 'diaries' in which her participants documented their adventure activities over a six-month period. The diaries provided an additional data source concerning women's reports of actual participation in adventure recreation that supplemented the information gained from individuals concerning their perspectives, reasoning and experiences. Second, researchers may need to be flexible in response to the emergent design characteristic of qualitative studies. Lather and Smithies (1997), for example, reported that they had initially planned to conduct individual interviews for their study. Instead, they decided to pose questions within the free-flowing conversations involved in the women's support groups in which they participated, rather than conduct formal interviews. Thus, group interaction became an important part of the data used for the study, in that topics were discussed by groups of women, rather than in individual interviews.

Selection and Sampling

In conjunction with the development of a topic and research questions, researchers consider who might participate in a study, the criteria by which participants will be selected, and what approach to selecting a 'sample' from a population will be taken. LeCompte and Preissle (1993, ch. 3) distinguish between 'selection' and 'sampling.' In their view, *selection* involves making decisions concerning who or what is the focus of a study, and characterizing the potential population from which the study's participants might be drawn. Researchers define the criteria by which participants for a study will be selected and may employ a combination of characteristics in specifying these. For example, criteria could include the kinds of settings in which people live and work, as well as particular time frames in which specific kinds of activities are undertaken, among others. Researchers including participants in studies on the basis of ease of access or ready availability are using 'convenience sampling.' Strictly speaking, this is not a form of sampling, given that *sampling* is the process by which a *sub-set* of a population is identified and selected for the purpose of a particular study. Therefore, this is not generally viewed as a rigorous approach given that researchers are not sampling a sub-set from a larger population based on any specific criteria. LeCompte and Preissle (1993: 68–82) group the methods for selecting participants for a study into two general categories: *criterion-based selection* and *probabilistic sampling*. Table 4.2 describes approaches to criterion-based selection.

Criterion-based Selection

In criterion-based selection researchers specify characteristics and attributes of the population to be studied (see Table 4.2). As LeCompte and Preissle (1993: 69) point out, this is the 'starting point' to all research – whatever methods are used. Researchers seeking to select representative samples for their studies in order to generalize findings to larger populations are likely to use probabilistic sampling methods once the research population has been identified. That is, researchers want to define a sample that is 'representative' of the larger population and calculate the sample size in relation to the size of that population. Qualitative researchers are less likely to use probabilistic sampling methods, and frequently select from the sampling strategies listed in Table 4.2.

Probabilistic Sampling

This form of sampling requires that researchers use a mathematical formula to select a subset of participants from a larger population. *Random sampling* identifies participants through statistical procedures that ensure that any member of a population has an equal chance of being selected for a study. In contrast, *systematic sampling* employs an interval to select participants. For example, using a mailing list, a researcher might select every 10th name on the list as a potential subject.

Stratified sampling requires that researchers differentiate a population into specific subsets, from which they select a sample using random or systematic sampling

Table 4.2 Criterion-based approaches to selection

	Sampling strategies	Description
Forms typically used early in a study	**Forms aiming at representativeness**	
	Snowball or network sampling	• Participants are selected on the basis of successive referrals from participants recruited initially
	Comprehensive selection	• All possible participants in a research setting are included in the sample
	Maximum variation sampling or quota sampling	• A specific number of participants are identified via particular attributes outlined by the researcher
	Forms aiming at comparability	
	Extreme or deviant case sampling	• After researchers have identified the continuum of characteristics in a given population, participants are selected on the basis of 'extreme' or 'deviant' attributes
	Typical case sampling	• After researchers have identified the continuum of characteristics in a given population, participants are selected to 'typify' the norm for the population
	Unique case sampling	• Participants that are unusual or rare in comparison to the rest of the population are selected
	Reputational case sampling	• Participants are selected on the basis of recommendations from experts in a field
	Ideal-typical	• Researchers develop a profile for an 'ideal' type of some population and then use this as a guide to identify possible participants who fit the profile
	Comparable case	• Researchers select a group or site that shares attributes of other groups or sites studied; this may occur across a research career, or in a multi-site study
	Intensity sampling	• Information-rich cases are selected in order to examine the phenomenon of interest; however these do not necessarily represent 'extreme' cases; unique and reputational case sampling are forms of intensity sampling
Forms typically used later in a study	Negative and discrepant cases	• Researchers look for cases that contradict or refute emergent findings
	Theoretical sampling	• Researchers select participants, cases, instances, and/or settings in which a phenomenon of developing interest is evident in order to further explore theoretical concepts of interest; this approach is frequently associated with grounded theory approaches to research (Glaser and Strauss, 1967)
	Sequential sampling	• Sampling decisions are made on the basis of emergent findings; researchers use specific sampling strategies in order to pursue particular lines of inquiry (e.g., after preliminary research, strategies that aim to compare cases might be employed)

Source: Adapted from materials published in *Ethnography and Qualitative Design in Educational Research* (2nd edn), M.D. LeCompte and J. Preissle, Chapter 3, p. 71, Copyright Elsevier (1993).

techniques. For example, a population might be divided into sub-groups via a particular criterion (for example, age, ethnicity, gender, work experience), from which participants are sampled randomly from each group. *Cluster sampling*, in contrast, makes use of naturally occurring groups, and may also employ either random or systematic sampling. For example, a study of an elementary school setting might include a random sample of teachers, in addition to a systematic sampling of students from each grade level.

Additional strategies are used in longitudinal studies. LeCompte and Preissle (1993) discuss three forms: trend studies, cohort studies, and panel studies. In the first form, *trend studies*, participants are sampled from a particular population either systematically or randomly across time. For example, a researcher might return to a setting annually over a period of several years in order to interview a sample of the population. In *cohort studies*, a particular group of participants, or cohort, that has been selected either systematically or probabilistically, is followed over time. Both trend studies and cohort studies may entail loss of participants in successive rounds of data collection. Therefore, in *panel studies*, an attempt is made to follow specific participants over intervals of time.

Qualitative researchers can incorporate both criterion-based selection strategies and probabilistic sampling strategies in any single study. It is important, however, for researchers to document the attributes or characteristics that they have used to select participants for a study, as well as successive changes that have been made during the research process as a result of emergent findings. As mentioned earlier, if no clear approach to selection and sampling is used in a study, the research findings are likely to be open to critique with respect to quality. It is to the topic of quality that I now turn.

Demonstrating Quality in the Research Process

While the generation of information relevant to a research topic is an important criterion by which to judge the quality of interviews, many frequently used strategies to demonstrate quality related to the study as a whole, and take in decisions made during the design process, how interviewers report on the conduct of the study, and how researchers go about analyzing, interpreting, and representing their findings in publications.

I use the term 'quality' in the sense of demonstrating excellence, although many competing terms are used within the field of qualitative inquiry. These include, but are not limited to, *validity, reliability, rigor, trustworthiness, credibility, transferability* and *plausibility*. Although there is considerable debate concerning the standards by which qualitative research might be judged (see Freeman et. al., 2007), there are strategies that are frequently used to demonstrate quality in relation to qualitative studies generally, and interview studies specifically. I discuss these next.

One commonly-used strategy is that of *triangulation*. As Clive Seale notes (1999: 53), triangulation draws upon the strategy of taking bearings on multiple landmarks in navigation and surveying. Given that lines from two landmarks will intersect at the point of the observer, triangulation refers to the notion that it is possible to locate a single observable object. As Seale (1999: 53–6, citing Denzin, 1978) goes on to describe, there are four common approaches to triangulation, that of: (1) *data triangulation* in which multiple sources of data about a phenomenon across groups of people, settings, place and time are sought; (2) *investigator triangulation*, in which multiple researchers study a topic in concert; (3) *theoretical triangulation*, in which different theoretical perspectives of the data are compared; and (4) *methodological triangulation*, in which multiple forms of data are used (for example, individual interviews, focus groups, observations, and documents).

In interview studies, data triangulation in the form of multiple interviews over a period of time can be used to check the researcher's understandings of participants' views and compare these to preliminary analyses and findings gleaned from earlier interviews. Methodological triangulation is often used by researchers to show that they have not merely relied on claims made within interview settings to generate assertions. Thus, researchers collect other forms of data (for example, documents, photos, artifacts), and spend time in settings observing interactions among participants. By analyzing other kinds of data, portrayals of what is going on can be enhanced though the inclusion of details drawn from other sources. Sandra Mathison asserts that the 'convergence' on a point or object pursued in many applications of triangulation is a 'phantom image' (1988: 17), and proposes that by looking at the points where data, sources, theories and researchers' perspectives are inconsistent and contradictory, researchers can use various forms of triangulation as a way to construct 'plausible' explanations about the topics studied (for additional critiques of triangulation, see Seale, 1999: 56–61).

Another common feature of studies deemed to be of high quality is that the researcher has frequently spent a *lengthy period of time in the field setting*, generating data over a period of months, if not years. Again, the assumption here is that longer periods of time spent studying a topic will result in deeper and more complex understandings of phenomena on the part of the researcher.

In representing findings from qualitative interview studies, readers are frequently provided with *detailed subjectivity statements* from the author/s that outline the subject positions occupied by the researcher prior to and during the study. In addition, the decision making of the researcher is explained in reports, and challenges, problems, and ethical dilemmas that arose during the research process are frequently included in reports. These *explanations of decision making* provide a record of evidence to show what the researcher did to generate interpretations and conclusions from the study. Accounts such as these also provide readers with a way to retrace the steps of the researcher, as well as sufficient information to draw on aspects of the study's design in order to repeat it in other settings (for example, appendices might include in-depth descriptions of data sets, in addition to interview protocols used). Throughout the research process, qualitative researchers might keep a researcher journal to record the day-to-day decision-making entailed during the research process, and sometimes excerpts from these journals are included within reports of findings.

Another approach to this task is that of an *audit trail*, in which peers are invited to examine the evidence that researchers have generated and how data have been analyzed

(Seale, 1999: 141–2). This might be accomplished by reviewing transcriptions of interviews and comparing these with the assertions made in preliminary and ongoing analyses. *Data sessions* in which other researchers have access to the audio- and video-taped interactions and transcriptions, and compare their analyses[1] with those of the principal researcher(s) might also be used. Researchers must also provide sufficient information in design statements to show how data analysis was undertaken, and that the process was both systematic and thorough (for example, numerical counts of the number of instances that a phenomenon occurred in the data set might be included, in addition to provision of examples of coding and analytic decision-making).

How researchers go about representing findings to others is integral to the demonstration of quality. Strategies that researchers use include providing sufficient evidence to warrant the claims made (for example, multiple extracts of interview data are included); as well as including contextual information in narrative descriptions so that readers can readily discern the researchers' interpretations, and the data upon which these are based. Frequently, researchers mention that they have checked the findings with participants. This is known as *member checking* or *member validation* (Seale, 1999). This can be accomplished in a number of ways – for example, participants might be given transcriptions of interviews to check and/or add to; researchers might include a discussion of preliminary findings in another interview with participants (that is, conduct a *member check interview*); or participants might be given copies of reports from the study about which they are invited to comment. Where differences emerge between researchers' and interviewees' interpretations or ideas about representation of findings, these might be included in the final report (Howell, 1973; Lather and Smithies, 1997; Wolcott, 1973), or might lead to further fieldwork on the part of the researcher (Duneier, 2000).

For researchers with emancipatory, critical and decolonizing agendas, an important feature of research design is that of including participants in design decisions and allowing their input in the analysis and interpretation phases of the study. For researchers working from these approaches, participants might be invited to be part of planning meetings to decide what questions need to be studied (for example, Nyden et al., 1997). Researchers have also invited participants to be co-researchers, participating in the generation of data (for example, Kirby, 2004), as well as the analysis and interpretation phase (Bartlett et al., 2007).

For researchers working from transformative, postmodern, and decolonizing approaches to interviewing in which alternative modes of representation are used with the purpose of transforming, challenging, and/or complicating audience-members' understandings of research topics, the documentation of the process of learning from participants, audiences, and community members may become a strategy to establish the quality and effectiveness of the work itself in communicating with others (for an example, see Meyer, 2009). Finally, qualitative interviewers document how they have adhered to high standards of ethical behavior in providing details of how

---

[1]Where audio- and/or video-taped interactions are presented to other researchers, the principal researcher must have first gained permission to do so from the participants as part of the informed consent process that is documented within the human subjects' review process.

they have gained informed consent for their projects from participants, and how they have attended to ethical issues within the research process.

Aligning Methods with Theoretical Assumptions

Throughout this book I argue that by considering various conceptions of interviewing and articulating the assumptions about knowledge production underlying different viewpoints, researchers can make informed decisions about how to use interviews as a method of data generation in ways that are commensurate with their theoretical perspectives. At the most basic level, researchers must show in reports from their studies that the methods chosen to generate data for a study will provide data to address questions posed. For example, if a researcher is interested in asking questions about *how people do things*, then interviews are an insufficient method to study the topic, given that they provide a secondary source of data and will only provide reports of *what people say about what they do*.

In ethnographic interviews, however, an interviewer could possibly ask questions in relation to observing a participant's actions. For example, if there is a specific practice or space that the researcher would like to learn about, they might do so by observing while asking specific questions of a participant in informal ethnographic interviews.

Although there are multiple strategies that researchers use to demonstrate quality in their work, researchers working from different theoretical traditions tend to foreground particular practices over others. There are numerous critiques of work that fail to meet the criteria for establishing quality commonly invoked by a particular community of practice. Rather than apply criteria for the assessment of quality in generalized ways that do not align with different approaches, I argue that it is possible to detect particular approaches that are commonly used by researchers who adhere to particular stances. Below, I draw together the strategies that I have sketched above, and review how these are applied to each of the conceptions of interviews that were reviewed in Chapter 3. In reviewing reports from research studies, readers will quickly come to the conclusion that few research studies meet all of the criteria that I have outlined below. Thus, the practices and strategies outlined below should be seen as collections from which researchers routinely draw, rather than as prescriptions for the kinds of strategies that quality work must always encompass.

Addressing Quality in a Neo-positivist Conception of Interviewing

Triangulation

Researchers working from a neo-positivist approach to interviews frequently use multiple methods of data collection (for example, interviews are supplemented with observational data; naturally occurring data; documents and texts). By using multiple forms of data (methodological triangulation), and interviewing different groups of people within a social setting (data triangulation), researchers can check the accuracy of interviewees' statements, and evaluate the truth of claims made in interviews (such as by checking documentary data, eliciting views from representatives of different groups). Researchers might also undertake *multiple interviews* with participants (rather than one-shot interviews) in order to confirm the accuracy and stability of interviewees' reports (data triangulation). Multiple interviews allow researchers to trace the changes in views and perspectives reported by participants over time, rather than focusing on singular snapshots of particular points in time.

Audit Trail

The researcher makes his or her research process transparent to readers by documenting it in a detailed way that may be replicated by others (for example, inclusion of interview guides in final reports; documentation of the analytic process, including searches for discrepant data or negative cases; supporting assertions with sufficient data); and may invite other researchers to review materials at key points in the research process (such as a review of transcription, coding, and analysis processes).

Longevity in the Field

Researchers can also demonstrate that they have developed a deep understanding of their research topic and research participants' views through the length of time they have spent in the field, and through gathering data from different sources across different points in time (data triangulation). The *longevity* of fieldwork also may assist researchers in establishing the stability and/or truth of interviewees' reports, or showing how participants' viewpoints have varied over a period of time.

Neutrality of the Interviewer

The *bias* of the researcher is addressed by asking questions that do not lead the interviewee; open-ended questions are asked in particular sequences, usually from general to specific, with sensitive topics approached at a later stage in the interview after sufficient rapport has been developed between the interviewer and interviewee.

Member-checking

Researchers often use the process of member checking of transcriptions and interpretations with research participants to demonstrate that they have developed an adequate understanding of the phenomenon investigated. This strategy may entail sending copies of the completed transcriptions to interviewees that they may have invited to add to or edit, asking interviewees to assess and add to the preliminary findings developed by the researcher in a follow-up meeting or interview, or providing copies of preliminary reports and manuscripts for the participants to comment on. As a result of these kinds of strategies, researchers might conduct further fieldwork; or include participants' responses to the analyses and interpretations within the final report.

Addressing Quality in a Romantic Conception of Interviewing

Researchers who come from a romantic perspective also use the strategies of triangulation, audit trail, longevity in the field, and member checking as outlined above. The researcher might also demonstrate that by spending a long time in the field, sometimes as a participant within the setting, they have established their credibility to understand and interpret insider perspectives, and have established sufficient rapport with participants to generate quality data (that is, rich, detailed descriptions of authentic selves of the participants).

Subjectivity Statements and Researcher Reflexivity

The researcher is self-consciously aware of his/her *subjectivities* in relation to the research participants and the research topic over the course of the project, and explores how these relate to the research findings in representations of research, thereby demonstrating researcher reflexivity. These statements might also include accounts concerning challenges and ethical dilemmas faced by researchers in the research process in final reports.

Researchers from this tradition are more likely to report on the part they played in the research process, and given that they are likely to be sensitive to how the sequencing of questions impacts data generation, might report how that has played out within interview interaction, as well as including their questions, and contributions to the interview talk in final reports.

Addressing Quality in a Constructionist Conception of Interviewing

For researchers working with a constructionist perspective of interviewing, *audio- and video-tapes of transcriptions* may be made available to audiences for inspection and analysis in group data sessions. Thus, although transcriptions are seen as theoretical constructs rather than holistic representations of data, they provide considerable detail concerning interactions, and what features of talk may be analyzable. Both transcriptions and analyses may be challenged by other researchers who have access to the audio- and/or video-recordings. Detailed transcriptions show how interviewers contribute to the generation of the talk, and researchers generally refrain from separating particular sequences of talk from the conversational environment in which they were generated by speakers. Thus, speakers' utterances are not viewed as expressions of 'interior perspectives,' but rather as co-produced with a particular interlocutor in response to whatever he or she has said. Thus, the interviewer's participation in the interview talk is subject to the same kind of analytic focus as talk generated by the interviewer and the interviewer's talk is included in the final report. Such sequential analysis also shows how interviewers and interviewees handle misunderstandings about the topic of the talk within the interactions, as well as the assumptions about research topics that are embedded within the interview questions.

Naturally occurring data are considered to be a valuable source of information in order to understand how participants make sense of topics of research in situ, and recordings of naturally occurring events might supplement interviews as a source of data (for example, Potter and Hepburn, 2005; Silverman, 2007).

Addressing Quality in a Postmodern Conception of Interviewing

Those researchers with a postmodern conception of interviewing are acutely and self-consciously aware of their *subjectivities* in relation to the research participants and the research topic, and explore how these relate to the research findings in representations of research through *subjectivity statements*. Such statements might include accounts of challenges and ethical dilemmas faced by researchers in the research process in reports of studies, and demonstrate 'uncomfortable reflexivities' (Pillow, 2003). Researchers working from this perspective may aim to engage with audiences beyond academic settings in ways that are challenging and provocative. Thus, they may call upon readers/listeners/participants to consider topics in different ways, and do so via creative analytic practices (Richardson, 1999). These presentations often use non-linear and fragmented texts, and arts-based inquiry methods to emphasize reflexive, dialogic, deconstructive, and multiple readings of data. These kinds of representations aim to complicate and trouble audience members' understandings of topics, and may use aesthetic criteria such as artistic merit to judge the quality of performance (Eisner, 1997; Faulkner, 2007).

Addressing Quality in a Transformative Conception of Interviewing

Researchers, who view the interview as a space for the transformation of themselves and others, work towards ensuring authentic input and access to full participation for participants in multiple aspects of the research process and representation of findings. This calls for a sensitivity to the participants' understandings of issues: what they see as relevant topics for research, and what is helpful for communities engaged in research projects. Again, researchers taking this approach are self-consciously aware of their *subjectivities* in relation to the research participants and the research topic (*reflexivity*), and explore how these relate to the research findings in representations of research (*subjectivity statements*, inclusion of challenges and ethical dilemmas faced by researchers in the research process in reports of studies).

The concepts of *communicative* and *pragmatic validation* proposed by Kvale (1996) provide possible ways to consider how quality is assessed in this type of work. Kvale argues that the validity of knowledge may be 'constituted when conflicting knowledge claims are argued in a dialogue' (1996: 245). Kvale (1996: 246–7) discusses three different kinds of audiences that might be involved in these kinds of discussions, including interview subjects, the general public, and the scientific community. Pragmatic validation (Kvale, 1996: 248–51) refers to testing of the work in action, that is – do the resulting actions produce desired results? Pragmatic validation is particularly applicable in various forms of action research, as well as research that aims to include participants in collaborative roles.

Addressing Quality in a Decolonizing Conception of Interviewing

Researchers working from a decolonizing perspective might also use *subjectivity statements* to record their stake in projects, and might also report on the challenges and ethical dilemmas faced by researchers in the research process in reports of studies. Researchers from this perspective are also self-consciously aware of their relationships to the indigenous community that is being studied, and the impact of their social locations and positionalities for the conduct of research, their relationships to participants, and the representation of findings. These are ethical matters of ongoing concern for the researcher, and are inextricably entwined with the motivating force for the research itself – that of working towards social justice for indigenous peoples. Findings from research are shared by the researcher in respectful ways with participants for the benefit of the communities studied, and in ways that may be understood by community members. For example, Yvonna Lincoln and Elsa González y González (2008) outline various ways of representing bilingual texts that contribute to decolonizing methodologies. Researchers working from this perspective are aware that release of some research findings may have negative impacts for the community studied, and work actively to ensure that this does not take place. From this perspective, the well-being of the community is deemed more important than the publication of research findings, and researchers might select to withhold findings that might be used in ways that are detrimental to a community (see Guterman, 2006).

Designing Research Studies Using Interviews

Above I have sketched some strategies that researchers working from a variety of theoretical perspectives might consider to establish the quality of their work. How these strategies might be employed within a study is part of the decision-making that takes place in the design phase. To review this decision-making, I summarize the key ideas in Table 4.3, which includes a series of questions that researchers might consider as they formulate their research questions and research designs.

Table 4.3 Designing a quality research study using interviews

What is the purpose of the research?[1]	Which conception of the interview attracts you?	What are the implications for the following choices?	Who are you in relation to your participants?	What analytic methods and representational strategies will you use?
Do you want to:		*Method of interviewing*	Race/national origin/ ethnicity/cultural background	Thematic analysis
Develop understanding?	Neo-positivist	Conversational/unstructured	Education	
	Romantic	Semi-structured	Professional status	Grounded theory
		Structured	Religion	
		Which of the following interview formats will best serve your purposes?	Gender	Ethnographic analysis
		Phenomenological	Age	
		Ethnographic	Sexual orientation	Narrative analysis
Promote transformation or social change?	Constructionist	Feminist	What other subject positions are relevant for this topic, and the population you plan to interview?	Phenomenological analysis
		Life history/oral history		
Deconstruct topics?	Postmodern	Dialogic		Ethnomethodological
		Use of stimulus texts to generate data (e.g., photos, films)		• conversation analysis
		Group interviews/Focus groups	What is your prior knowledge of this topic, and what position do you occupy in relation to the topic of the study? (e.g., are you a novice to this topic, are you a participant in the setting studied?)	• membership categorization analysis
		Participant selection, Sampling and recruitment		
		By what criteria will participants be selected?		
		What sampling strategy will be used?		
Make a long-term commitment to promoting decolonizing and social justice agendas?	Transformative	How many participants will you need? How will they be recruited?		Deconstructive methods
		How many times will each participant be interviewed?		• poststructural methods
		What is the duration of interviews?		• postmodern approaches
	Decolonizing	Do you want the participants to participate in the research process? In what ways? E.g. contributing to the development of research questions; conducting interviews; analyzing data; reading reports; contributing to writing the report?		

(Continued)

Table 4.3   (Continued)

What is the purpose of the research?[1]	Which conception of the interview attracts you?	What are the implications for the following choices?	Who are you in relation to your participants?	What analytic methods and representational strategies will you use?
		Ethics How will participants conceptualize the topic of your study? Will your topic be seen by participants as sensitive? (e.g., will access to counseling services in the event participants experience discomfort as a result of interviews be needed?) Are there ethical issues to be considered? What are the implications for questions posed for maintaining confidentiality? *Assessment of quality* • Do you need other kinds of data in addition to interviews in order to inform your research questions? • What methods do you intend to use to demonstrate quality?		

Source: [1] 'What is the purpose of the research?' is adapted from Lather (2004). Reprinted with permission of Taylor & Francis Group LLC – Books.

Conclusion

While there are some commonalities visible in strategies used by researchers to demonstrate quality, each conception of interviewing relies on different assumptions about interviewing and the production of knowledge about social worlds. In order to demonstrate that a research study is one of quality, researchers who use interviews must answer the following questions:

- To what community of practice will reports from the study be directed?
- What are the norms for decisions for judging quality in this community of practice?
- Given the researcher's epistemological and theoretical perspectives, what assumptions are implied about the production of knowledge and conceptualization of interviewing?
- From this perspective, what evidence is needed to warrant claims?

In this chapter, I have shown how different theoretical perspectives toward knowledge production imply different types of research question. These research questions, in turn, imply different research methods, forms of interview, and strategies to demonstrate the quality of research.

As outlined in Chapter 3, a concern of researchers using a neo-positivist conception of interviews is to establish the truth and accuracy of the evidence by showing how research participants and the researcher are reliable witnesses. In the romantic perspective to interviewing, the focus for establishing quality shifts to showing how the researcher's articulation of his or her relationship to the research participants and research process has generated plausible interpretations. From a constructionist perspective, researchers must show how data were generated in specific research settings by particular speakers, and how their analyses and interpretations can also account for how data were generated. Postmodern and transformative interviews move the assessment of quality from the researcher to audience members. In the postmodern interview, relevant questions to ask are:

- Do representations of research findings provoke dialogue, interaction and communication among audiences?
- Do representations have artistic merit?

Similarly, in order to judge the quality of research using transformative interviews, audience responses are taken seriously. Relevant questions include:

- Have authentic dialogue and change among participants and researchers been facilitated by the research?
- Have the findings from the research achieved the desired results in terms of change for the participants and researchers?

Finally, from a decolonizing perspective, the interview is a research tool to be used to advance restorative justice for indigenous communities. Thus, researchers must seriously consider whether the research has been conducted respectfully, has done no harm, and has contributed to decolonizing agendas for the community served.

How we think about the qualitative interview has implications for how research projects are designed, how interviews are structured, the kinds of questions we pose, and how data are analyzed and represented. While there is much debate with respect to the limitations and merits of each of the perspectives to interviewing outlined in this book, by seriously considering how different theoretical stances on qualitative interviewing treat the issue of quality, qualitative researchers can make more informed decisions concerning research design and methods, the formulation of interview questions, and appropriate ways to analyze and represent interview data. Whatever one's stance on the qualitative interview – to quote Clive Seale (1999), quality *does* matter.

In Chapter 5, I review steps to prepare for interview studies, including gaining approval for the study, recruiting participants, scheduling interviews, issues to consider in recording interviews, and options for transcribing recorded interviews and preparing data for analysis.

Further Reading

Theoretical Perspectives and Qualitative Research

Crotty, M. (1998) *The Foundations of Social Research: Meaning and Perspective in the Research Process*. Thousand Oaks, CA: Sage.
Prasad, P. (2005) *Crafting Qualitative Research: Working in the Postpositivist Traditions*. Armonk, NY: M. E. Sharpe.

Qualitative Research Design and Methods

DeMarrais, K. and Lapan S. (eds) (2004) *Foundations for Research: Methods of Inquiry in Education and the Social Sciences*. Mahwah, NJ: Lawrence Erlbaum Associates.
LeCompte, M.D. and Preissle, J. (1993) *Ethnography and Qualitative Design in Educational Research*, 2nd edn. San Diego, CA: Academic Press.
Mason, J. (2002) *Qualitative Researching*, 2nd edn. London: Sage.
Maxwell, J.A. (2005) *Qualitative Research Design: An Interactive Approach*. Thousand Oaks, CA: Sage.

Activity 4.1   Designing a qualitative interview study

Complete the following questions with respect to your study:

- The following problem is in need of further research ...
- The purpose of this study is to ...
- Research questions that inform the study of this topic include ...
- Theoretical perspectives and theories that inform this research study include ...
- The research design for this study involves the following methods of data generation/collection ...
- Participants will be recruited using the following methods ...

- The following criteria for selection will be used to recruit participants for this study ...
- The targeted number of participants for this study is ...
- The research setting and context for the study is ...

Activity 4.2   Constructing an interview guide

What is the research topic?
What are the research questions?

What are possible topics that relate to each research question?	What do you want to know about this topic?	What are possible questions that would generate talk about this topic?
1.		
2.		
3.		

FIVE

Doing Interview Research

This chapter introduces:

- Steps to prepare for interviews, including *gaining consent* for the study, *recruitment* of participants, *scheduling* interviews and *background research*.
- *Recording* and *transcription* options.
- Approaches to working with *translated data*.
- Resources for working with specific populations.

Preparatory steps for any research study include gaining consent and securing entry to the research context, recruiting participants, and scheduling interviews. Prior to interviewing, researchers need to conduct relevant background research, in addition to considering the recording options available, along with how recordings will be transcribed. Whether a researcher will provide participants opportunities to comment on the transcriptions, analyses or interpretations of interview data generated for the study must also be considered during the design phase, given that this information is provided to participants as part of the informed consent process and needs to be included in applications for research with human subjects. Although much is written about each of these procedures, there are no simple recipes that can be used across qualitative studies. Therefore researchers need to thoughtfully consider the contexts of their studies, provide rationales for their decision-making, and make available to readers of research reports a record of what they did throughout their projects.

Consent for the Study

Review boards for research with human subjects have been institutionalized to avoid research involving deception and experimentation involving participants, which have in the past resulted in public scandals and critiques of scientific research (for two notorious examples, see Laud Humphreys' [1970] *Tearoom Trade: Impersonal Sex in Public Places*, and reports concerning the Public Health Service Syphilis study which took place in Tuskegee, Alabama from 1932–1971). Both of these studies involved participants in research in ways that were deceptive, and in the second study, people were not provided treatment for life-threatening illness. Thus, in recent years the implementation of guidelines for the conduct of research has become increasingly rigorous, and social scientists using qualitative methods must submit their research proposals for review to institutional review boards that in the past have formerly focused their attention on bio-medical research.

There has been a good deal of debate in the US in recent years as to whether research – in particular qualitative research – has been stifled as a result of overly cumbersome requirements of institutional review boards (IRBs) (see for example, Gunsalus et al., 2007; Johnson, 2008; Lincoln and Tierney, 2004), and whether the review requirements are even applicable to qualitative interview research. Nevertheless, in order to conduct qualitative interview research, all researchers must fulfill the requirements mandated by the institution in which they work, as well as those required in the settings where they seek to conduct research.

Depending on the research setting that researchers intend to investigate, there may be multiple levels of consent to negotiate. These include university human subjects review boards as well as ethical review committees associated with other institutions such as hospitals and schools. Permission for studies must also be sought from managers in the case of research in business and other institutional settings. Depending on the country in which the study is conducted, authorization for research may be needed from state or provincial authorities and local community groups (for an account of the process of gaining access negotiated by a researcher in Botswana, see Koosimile [2002]). Researchers must familiarize themselves with procedures that are relevant to the social contexts in which they plan to conduct their research. For example, in order to interview teachers and students in a school, a researcher must gain permission from their university and school district review board, as well as the local principal. With consent gained from each of these authorities, the researcher may invite teachers to participate. To interview students, researchers must seek permission from parents or guardians, before gaining independent consent, or assent, from students. In some institutional settings – such as prisons – researchers may only conduct research that relates to topics defined and authorized by the governing authorities.

Gaining formal consent from ethical review boards and those in authority does not necessarily mean that access to settings will be secured. For example, Carolyn Wanat (2008) describes how gaining access is different to gaining cooperation, and explains that gatekeepers' cooperation in studies in which she was involved was influenced by their perception of the possible outcomes of the study, and how they could be impacted by these. These involved three issues: *public relations*, or the possibility of the exposure of negative or positive findings from the study; *power issues*, in that if participants felt that they were required by those in authority to participate, they expressed resentment; and *accountability* – some participants believed that there were unstated reasons for the research projects which related to evaluation and accountability. Wanat (2008: 203–4) suggests that researchers need to be aware of the differences between 'formal' and 'informal' power, as it operates in particular contexts in order to identify particular individuals who will be able to assist researchers with gaining entry to organizations, as well as encourage people to participate in research studies. As Wanat (2008) shows, recruiting participants for studies is a complex task that may be hindered or helped by the gatekeepers involved.

Recruiting Participants

Recruitment means that researchers ask people to participate in interviews for the purpose of research. This task is sometimes more easily described than accomplished, and some research simply is not possible because people do not want to participate. Recruiting, then, can involve a number of tactics on the part of the researcher. These include accessing possible participants via personal networks or ethnographic fieldwork, and advertising in public spaces.

Use of *personal networks* involves researchers relying on family members, friends, work colleagues, and acquaintances to recommend people who fit the criteria for the population identified for the study. Once possible participants have been identified, the researcher can invite a sample to participate. Researchers can use snowball or network sampling to locate further participants (see Chapter 4).

Ethnographic fieldwork involves spending lengthy periods of time in a social setting: hanging out, participating, and generally getting to know people and becoming familiar with the research context. Over time, the researcher hopes to gain the trust of an informant, or gatekeeper that can provide access to key people in a specific setting (see, for example, Duneier, 2000; Hecht, 2006). Likewise, the kinds of people recommended or introduced by the gatekeeper may vary over a lengthy period of time due to the particular motivations and internal politics of a given setting (see, for example, Rymes, 2001). Although Melissa Freeman's (2000) interview study did not include ethnographic fieldwork, recruiting participants for her study of parents' perspectives of home–school relationships entailed a number of strategies common to ethnography. These included visiting play groups in the community in which she was studying in order to meet parents, and walking from door to door to recruit participants.

For researchers recruiting from populations who are not already known to them, access may be gained via *mailing lists, listservs,* or *websites.* Here, researchers can send letters or emails asking for interested people to participate in the study. The drawback of this approach is that the response rate may be low, unless the researcher is already known to the population, or if a gatekeeper within the community study recommends the study to members. Another approach is to distribute *fliers* or use *advertisements* in newspapers – these techniques are commonly used on university campuses, and are often used in combination with some form of incentive (for example, money, gift cards, etc.).

For researchers using personal connections to informants as a means to recruit participants, relative intimacy and rapport with participants may enhance the generation of data in interview settings in ways not possible for 'outsider' researchers. Yet, researchers who use personal networks for research need to be aware of the implications of studying those close to them. Working with participants who are already known may engender other challenges. For example, prior relationships with participants – while in some respects facilitating rapport – may also set boundaries on the kinds of topics that can be explored and represented. When a researcher knows a particular research participant well, it may be difficult to discuss research topics and ask questions – since both interviewer and interviewee rely on shared knowledge and understandings. Pierre Bourdieu discusses the problems of the interview method associated with the extremes of knowing one's participants or topic too well and having no commonalities upon which to develop a productive interview relationship:

> Every investigation is therefore situated between two extremes doubtless never completely attained: total overlap between investigator and respondent, where nothing can be said because, since nothing can be questioned, everything goes without saying; and total divergence, where understanding and trust would become impossible. (Bourdieu et al., 1999: 612)

Researchers who are examining topics related to groups of which they are members, or to which they have close personal ties need to consider the possible ethical issues concerning representation of participants that may arise during the reporting and publication phases of a study. Again, there is neither one way to go about recruiting participants, nor a right way; however, researchers need to practice patience and ingenuity, and consider the ethical implications of their decision-making, since often attempts to access communities and specific people can falter unexpectedly.

Scheduling Interviews

Interviews are usually scheduled at the convenience of both interviewer and interviewee. Of course, for researchers in the midst of ethnographic field work, interviews may resemble spontaneous conversations, and the topics of talk may be jotted down in field notes, rather than recorded in a more formal setting. Sometimes, researchers are able to secure interviews spontaneously. For example, Derrick Alridge, an oral historian studying hip-hop described one interview that he conducted:[1]

DA: I went to a club, a few years ago, here in Athens [Georgia], because a member of the Dungeon Family rap group – his name was the Witchdoctor – I had found out that he was going to be playing in a local club here, and I wanted to interview him. So I walk[ed] up to him and [said], 'Witchdoctor, I would love to interview you.' He said, 'Alright. Let's do it right now.' And so I interviewed him while he was backstage before he went on stage, and I did a 30-minute interview with him. And there was

[1]Interview excerpts with researchers throughout the text were conducted in 2007–2008 by the author in a study entitled 'Qualitative researchers' accounts of their use of research interviews.' Researchers gave their consent to be named in publications, and all were provided with draft copies of the manuscript in which excerpts from their interviews were used, and invited to provide comments.

no opportunity for me to try to be formal or anything like that, I just had to do the interview on the spot. So that's my most memorable interview, was with the Witchdoctor behind stage before he was to go on stage.

KR: Did you have to the chance to record that one?

DA: Yes, I just, I always take, whenever I go to see rap concerts, I always take a portable tape recorder

K: uh huh

DA: with me, a small hand held and I was able to interview him. (Interview conducted 4 September, 2007, by author)[2]

This example shows that depending on where our research leads us qualitative researchers may need to conduct interviews at any time and place.

More commonly, a researcher will get in touch with a potential participant by letter, telephone, or email, and arrange a time and place for an interview that is mutually agreeable. Researchers report that they have interviewed in private homes, in their offices, their participants' workplace settings, or in other public spaces, such as restaurants, or cafés. For particular topics such as interview studies of violence, or domestic abuse, it may be inappropriate to interview participants in private homes. For example, Terry Arendell (1997) reports on some of the complexities that women researchers may encounter when scheduling interviews with men, while some elderly people have reported discomfort with young researchers (see, for example, Wenger, 2002). A general guideline for practice is to find a place and time to conduct an interview in which both the interviewer and interviewee feel safe and comfortable, and that provides sufficient privacy to audio-record interviews without interruption. Even then, this may not always be possible.

Sharan Merriam, an adult education researcher, for example, reports that in her cross-cultural research with co-researchers in both Botswana and Malaysia, she has had to be flexible with some of the norms of research practice familiar to researchers in Western countries. For example, in one interview study conducted in Malaysia, in order to interview one participant, she and her colleague needed to interview his boss:

SM: There's all these protocols and things. We interviewed some person in his office in Kuala Lumpur, the capital city, [an] educated man in his office and he said, 'Before we start the interview, I really have to take you to meet my superior,' his boss. So we said 'Fine.' We went up to meet his boss. Well the boss says, 'Oh, this sounds like fun, I want to be interviewed.' And there was nothing that we could do ....

KR: So you [had] to do that one first?

SM: So we had to do that interview first. (laughter). (Interview, conducted 3 April 2007 by author)

Interviewees may select venues for interviews that are problematic for the researcher. Restaurants, for example, although open and public spaces, are frequently noisy. Further, the interviewer and interviewee may be interrupted by other speakers in the setting, making transcription of audiotapes or digital files difficult. Yet there are times when this may be the only workable setting for an interview.

---

[2]Square brackets indicate researcher's insertion for clarity.

Another issue to be dealt with is that of overhearing audiences. This may be problematic for researchers conducting research on sensitive topics. In cases in which the interviewer is interviewing in a home setting, this may entail conducting an interview in the company of children, pets, family members, and friends. Describing interviews that she had jointly conducted with a colleague in Malaysia, Sharan Merriam spoke about the overhearing audiences present at the time:

> SM: Well they [family members in the room] would have little sidebar conversations. Or in one case, this woman in the village we interviewed ... and her sister, sat on the step with her back to us. And ... every once in a while, she would laugh and chuckle and she was thoroughly enjoying this conversation (laughter) ... Another time we interviewed a woman who had a small business in another part of the country and her ... husband sat in the shop, way over on the other side and every once in a while he'd say 'Oh yeah I remember that' or something. It was ... an interesting experience for them. (Interview conducted 3 April 2007 by author)

While in these descriptions, overhearing audiences are described as simply listening to the narratives told by family members being interviewed, in other cases, family members may want to conduct their own investigations of a researcher on behalf of the interviewee. For example, Juanita Johnson-Bailey described an interview with one woman whose husband wanted to meet the researcher:

> JJB: Her husband insisted on being there ... when I had told her [the participant] that I was getting my degree in Adult Ed and Women's Studies, he said 'Those Women's Studies women.' So he wanted to be there to be sure I wasn't one of those radical feminists or that I wasn't some kind of lesbian hitting on [his wife] (laughter). I mean he said this and he stood there during the first part of the interview to make sure, because I was picking his wife up to take her to another location for the interview, so he wanted to check me out. And I thought ... 'Now how's he going to tell by looking at me?' (laughter) But anyway, we did the interview and it turned out to be a very good interview. (Interview conducted May 10, 2007 by author)

What we might learn from these first-hand accounts from experienced researchers is the need for flexibility on the part of interviewers to accommodate the needs and wishes of interviewees, as well as abiding by the cultural norms within a specific community. For researchers conducting cross cultural research, interviewing in front of others may well be the *only* way to generate data. Rather than provide a set of prescriptions that should be followed in all cases, the following questions need to be considered by the interviewer in preparation for an interview:

- Is the location for the interview a convenient, safe and comfortable location for both interviewer and interviewee/s?
- What are appropriate behaviors and deportment for the interviewer in the cultural setting in which the interview will be conducted?
- Will other people be present for the interview? If so, what are the implications for the questions asked and data generated?
- Is the location selected for the interview one in which audible recordings may be generated?

- How will the interview be recorded? (e.g. notes during and after the interview, audio-recording, video-recording)
- Do both interviewer and interviewee have sufficient time in which to discuss the topic of the interview?

In order to take into account needs of particular participants in each and every interview context, researchers must consider their own subject positions in relation to those of interviewees. This includes the researcher's age, ethnicity, race, class, status, education, and gender, among other social locations, in relation to participants. Rather than discuss specific population groups here, at the end of the chapter, I include suggested readings on interviewing children, women, men, older people, people with illnesses, and elites, as well as interviews in which race, culture and sexual orientation are relevant.

Getting Ready to Interview

Preparation for interviews may take multiple forms. For example, the interviewer might need to learn as much about the participants as possible prior to the interview. This is especially the case when interviewing elites. Here, the researcher might review publicly available information available about the interviewee (for example, websites, newspaper reports, other documents, publications, etc.). Juanita Johnson-Bailey, for example, described the work that was involved in preparing to interview the poet Sonia Sanchez (Bell-Scott and Johnson-Bailey, 1998).

KR: Can you talk about how you actually got to arrange that interview and what you went through?

JJB: Yes. It took a lot. You know, contacting her agent, contacting people that knew her to get it set up and the background work was probably the most extensive work I've ever done to interview a subject. I read all [of] her books of poetry. I read every interview that I could find that had ever been done on her. And I think perhaps that's one of the things that relaxed her a bit, is because I knew her work and appreciated her work. And so when she would refer to a poem I knew it instantly. And actually I remember she was trying to get the line of this poem and I just pulled the book out of my briefcase, [because] I happened to have it there. I have all of them. But ... it was just a matter of flying up, and renting a car, and stumbling around to find where she lived and actually I think I arrived an hour early and just sat outside of her house in the car. But ... it's often quite a process to get to interview people who are elite subjects. And I think that that is a different kind of interviewing because you have a special responsibility because there is no anonymity, there is no confidentiality. People know who they are, there's already a representation of them out there, and so I think it adds an extra layer of responsibility. (Interview conducted 10 May 2007 by author)

This excerpt illustrates the kind of extensive background research that qualitative interviewers may need to do in order to prepare for an interview.

Even if a researcher speaks the participant's language fluently, he or she also may need to learn something of the local language and expressions used by participants of the study. This might include studying relevant contexts prior to conducting interviews in order to generate usable data. For example, anthropologist Charles Briggs (1986) advocates that researchers must 'learn how to ask' before conducting interviews for the purpose of social research. His recommendations, drawing on linguistics and theories of communication (Briggs, 1986: ch. 5) include a number of strategies for more effective interview research, including studying how participants routinely speak within a given setting, learning what kinds of questions might be asked in that setting, examining one's own interview interaction, and analyzing both the structure of the interview as well as individual utterances (see Pollock [2004] for an example of extended ethnographic work that in some ways characterizes this approach).

Elizabeth Hoffman (2007) describes the emotional labor involved in conducting research interviews in her study of workplace grievances. Prior to research interviews with coal miners, who were one group of participants of her study, Hoffman talks of learning about:

> the equipment, terminology, and challenges of this industry; I read several books about coal mining, the industry's culture, and the economic impact of this industry shrinking; I skimmed many newspaper articles that addressed current issues in the coal-mining industry. Without these efforts to educate myself, I would have been forced to ask basic informational questions of my coal miner interviewees. This would both waste time during the interview, taking time away from the focus of the study, and also would have demonstrated my ignorance in not understanding key aspects of the coal miners' work experiences. (2007: 336)

Preparing for the interview, then, may include background research on participants and the contexts in which they live and work, becoming familiar with the expressions and terms that they routinely use, and learning about the local norms for the kinds of questions that might be asked and topics that might be discussed.

Recording the Interview

In the early part of the 20th century, interviews were recorded by taking notes. There is evidence to suggest that tape recorders began to be used by sociologists to record research interviews in the late 1940s (Lee, 2004). While in ethnographic work, there may still be a need to record interviews by taking notes – for example, when a researcher asks questions in spontaneous and unplanned conversations – audio- and video-recording of qualitative interviews are now standard practice. An essential preparatory step is to have the right kind of equipment. The most common forms of recording devices include audio-cassette recorders (both standard and micro-cassette recorders), and digital audio- and video-recorders. With the increase in digital technologies, the digital recording device is rapidly overtaking the analog audio- and video-cassette as the method of choice used by social science researchers. Digital recording devices are compact, easily carried, and have lengthy recording times. Files can be downloaded to computers and copied to storage devices. Researchers who wish to purchase digital recorders need to be aware that some devices do not allow for downloading of files, so files cannot be copied to other devices. Some brands of digital recorders use proprietary software, and the file formats may not be exportable into particular programs for transcription purposes (e.g., two software programs include Express Scribe and Transana™). Therefore, time is well spent in researching the kinds of file formats supported by a device, how these might be downloaded, and how transcription will be undertaken prior to conducting any interviews.

Whether one uses an analog-cassette recorder or a digital recorder, there are several other things that all researchers must attend to – whatever one's level of expertise. Close attention to these issues will avoid the problem of generating recordings that are difficult, if not impossible, to transcribe.

- If possible, schedule interviews in settings in which audible recordings can be made. In some research projects, this will not be possible; therefore, researchers can use strategies such as writing field notes about the interview as soon as possible after concluding the interview, or audio-recording reflections that are later transcribed.
- To enhance the quality of recorded interviews, researchers should use the best equipment available to them. External microphones improve sound quality. Interviewers need to allow time to conduct a sound check with their equipment prior to *every* interview; use fresh batteries if an external power source is not being used, and have extra tapes, batteries, or storage devices on hand should they be needed. Occasionally, interviews anticipated to take one to two hours may actually take three or four. Many external microphones are battery-powered, and batteries should also be checked and changed regularly.

Many recording mishaps occur simply because researchers did not know their equipment sufficiently, or failed to check it prior to the interview. When scheduling interviews, researchers must allow sufficient preparation time prior to the interview to check the equipment and recording devices.

Conducting Interviews

During research interviews interviewers must judge on a moment by moment basis whether they are generating the kinds of data that will be useful to examine their research questions and prompt participants to provide the kinds of descriptions that will provide in-depth details of the phenomenon of interest. For researchers using a constructionist conception of interviewing, 'all is data,' and both interviewers' and interviewees' interactions may be subject to analysis of how and what was said. For researchers taking a romantic or neo-positivist approach to interviewing, there are commonly accepted standards of practice with respect to effective ways of generating data, as explained in Chapter 3. Likewise, researchers who intend to conduct interviews for the purpose of generating transformative dialogue, or who aim to contribute to research agendas that are deconstructive or decolonizing, must give serious consideration to how interviews might be facilitated and questions asked to meet those aims.

As I have argued throughout this book, if researchers consider the theoretical conceptions they have of interviewing and understand how interaction functions, they will be better prepared to elicit the kinds of data that will be useful for examining their research questions. In Chapter 7 I will demonstrate how one might go about analyzing interview data in order to examine whether the ways in which questions are asked and answered meet the needs of a project.

Transcribing Interviews

Just as mishaps can occur during audio-taping, researchers can take precautions prior to the transcription phase of the study. This includes making copies of tapes or audiofiles that will be transcribed in case the audiotapes or digital files are lost or erased; and accurately labeling tapes and storage devices to avoid loss of recordings. Transcribing interviews is a time-consuming and physically demanding task. Yet, transcription is not merely a technical endeavor. As many researchers have argued, how one chooses to represent audio- or video-recorded data is embedded in our theoretical assumptions about research, reflects ethical decision-making about how we represent others, and is a political act (Bucholtz, 2000; Davidson, 2009; Green et al., 1997; Ochs, 1979). Mary Bucholtz argues that:

> All transcripts take sides, enabling certain interpretations, advancing particular interests, favoring specific speakers, and so on. The choices made in transcription link the transcript to the context in which it is intended to be read. Embedded in the details of transcription are indications of purpose, audience, and the position of the transcriber toward the text. Transcripts thus testify to the circumstances of their creation and intended use. (2000: 1440)

During transcription, interviewers re-listen to their interviews, review the topics discussed, and begin the process of interpreting interview data and generating preliminary analyses. Just as asking a follow-up question within an interview demonstrates the interviewer's analysis of what has been said, how one chooses to transcribe talk involves analytic decisions.

Although researchers working on large funded projects frequently sub-contract transcription to others – some of whom may not be directly involved in the project – it is valuable for interviewers to re-listen to audio-recordings, especially if they have been transcribed by others. Blake Poland (2002), for example, describes how paid transcribers may intentionally edit transcriptions, or unwittingly change what was originally said.

There are many possible ways of transcribing interviews – the simplest of which is including words spoken. An example of this is seen in Excerpt 5.1.

Excerpt 5.1

Interviewee (IE)   Well I'm really just doing that because I had to. I really don't like this part of the medicine. I think there is no way we can apply that when we just have 15 minutes to see a patient with hypertension. It's like OK, I have a patient with five different problems, and he has some other issues. So how can I use that knowledge to help the patient. I can't see a way to. And so far I don't think the classes we have, the conferences will help us with that.

Here, the participant's words have been notated and transformed into punctuated sentences. Yet, as conversationalists, we know that much is conveyed by non-verbal mannerisms, tone of voice, gestures, and other paralinguistic features of talk. Excerpt 5.2 uses Jeffersonian conventions to convey some of these features of talk (see Appendix 1 for details).

Excerpt 5.2

```
 1.  IE  we:ll (.) I really (.) just doing that because I had to I I I really don't like
 2.      this=
 3.  IR  =uh huh=
 4.  IE  =this part of the medicine I think there is no way we can apply that
 5.      when we just have fifteen minutes to see a patient=
 6.  IR  =uh huh=
 7.  IE  =with hypertension it's like OK I have the patient with five different
 8.      problems  and he has some (.) other (.) issues so how can I use that
 9.      knowledge to:: (.) to help the patient I can't I can't see a way to do
10.      that=
11.  IR  =uh huh=
12.  IE  =and so far I don't think the classes we have the conferences will
13.      help us with that uh=
```

This excerpt provides detail of some of what has been omitted in the previous transcription – including the researcher's utterances ('uh-huh'), pauses, and stressed words. This transcription also provides insight into the close coordination of talk between speakers in which there are no pauses between speakers' utterances (this is known as 'latching'). Although this transcription provides a level of detail that may be used to analyze turn-taking features and the sequential structure of the talk, it is an inappropriate way to present the sequence for readers interested in the topic of the talk. Thus, Excerpt 5.3 shows how this particular excerpt was represented in an evaluation report to the administrators at the Family Medicine residency in which this interview was conducted. In Excerpt 5.3, the speaker's utterances have also been edited to omit slips and *repairs* in the talk, and the researcher has inserted words using square brackets to clarify the meaning of what was said by the interviewee.

Excerpt 5.3

R18 began the interview with the following statement in response to the question: 'What do you think of when you hear the term mind–body interventions?'

R18: Well I'm really just doing that because I had to. I really don't like this part of ... medicine. I think there is no way we can apply that when we just have 15 minutes to see a patient with hypertension. It's like, OK, I have a patient with five different problems, and he has some other issues. So how can I use that knowledge to help the patient? I can't see a way to [do it]. And so far I don't think the classes we have [had], the conferences will help us with that. (Individual interview, first-year resident, October 2007)

In the report, the following note was added to let readers know how the transcriptions had been edited:

> For the purpose of clarity and readability, transcriptions have been edited. For example, expressions such as 'like,' 'I mean,' 'you know,' and 'sort of' have been omitted.
> Transcription conventions used:
> ... one omitted word
> .... several omitted words
> [ ] author's insertion for clarity
> ( ) utterances are best guess

While there is much to be learned from transcriptions that include features of talk such as word stress, pauses, silences, speed of talk, how speakers take turns, and so forth, researchers must be clear on what they want to accomplish in their analysis, and the audiences to whom they will present their work. For researchers interested in analyzing how talk is co-constructed, and how speakers formulate their descriptions, this information provides critical data for analysis. Not all studies will require this level of transcription, however.

Videos of interaction will provide even more information that is analyzable – for example, gaze, gesture, and posture. These features of interview talk have been frequently omitted in transcriptions for a variety of reasons, not least of which is social researchers' reliance on audio- rather than video-recording of research interviews. Increased access to video-recording is leading to a proliferation of research that investigates non-verbal features of talk. Researchers choosing to use this means of recording interaction need to consider whether the kinds of questions that they seek to examine necessitate the use of video-interaction, and how the data will be presented (for example in documentary, rather than written formats).

Novice researchers are often surprised at the subjective choices they must make in transcription – for example, how to convey what has been spoken in grammatical and punctuated sentences, whether to notate dropped letters (goin') or include swear words, or even if they should include utterances commonly used in everyday talk ('umm,' 'uh huh,' 'you know,' 'like,' and 'do you know what I mean?'). If the transcription is to be reviewed by the participant, what to include in the transcription is an important question to consider, as many interviewees and interviewers are shocked to read what they have said when notated in detail, and may request that researchers edit transcriptions prior to presentation and publication.

Translated Data

Some researchers conduct interviews with participants who speak a language that differs from the language of representation. In these instances, researchers will need to explain their decision-making in relation to translation. Researchers have handled translated data in a variety of ways. They may transcribe the interview in the original language, generate findings, and then translate these to the language of representation. Another alternative is to translate the data at the point of transcription, and conduct the analysis and interpretation in the language of representation. There are a variety of ways to represent translations in publications. These include presentation of the translated data only; line-by-line translations underneath the original language, sometimes with morphemic translations included; translated data in block text next to the original language; or translated data in the language of publication in the text, with the original transcription included in an appendix (see Duranti, 1997: 154–60; Have, 2007: 109–10; Nikander, 2008). William Corsaro and Luisa Molinari (1990) and Isabella Paoletti (2001) provide two examples of reports that include both the original language and translation within the text. In some instances, researchers have handled expressions that are impossible to translate accurately by including the original words in the final text (see, for example, Behar, 1993; Lincoln and González y González, 2008). For interviewers conducting interviews in a language different to that in which they will present their reports, it is useful to let readers know the point at which translation and analyses were undertaken, and provide readers with enough information to understand the texts represented – especially in cases in which colloquial expressions were used by speakers and are not translated in the text.

A number of researchers have addressed the issue of translation in research (Esposito, 2001; Temple, 1997; Temple and Edwards, 2002; Temple and Young, 2004). All agree that identifying the steps that researchers have taken in relation to translation is a central issue in the representation of findings. Bogusia Temple (1997) proposes that researchers using translated data include 'intellectual biographies' of the researcher and others involved in research (for example, translator, interpreter, transcriber) in reports from studies. In her view, an intellectual biography has been helpful in her work in the following ways:

(1) It alerts the researcher to the ways in which other people define concepts relevant to the research differently, and assists the researcher to value and acknowledge these differences.
(2) It assists the researcher to consider the relationship between him or herself, and the participants of a study.
(3) It enables the researcher to discuss differences in 'conceptualizations due to the influences of time and place.'
(4) It assists the researcher in discussing the links between 'the individual and the social ... via the examination of how the researcher and translator come to know what they know.'
(5) It aids the researcher in demonstrating 'the complexity and diversity of ways of experiencing .... without denying that categorizations are valuable.' (1997: 616, 617)

Temple's 'intellectual biography parallels the 'subjectivity statement' described in Chapter 6, and the issues listed above may provide points of focus for researchers using translated data as they write subjectivity statements in relation to their research.

Decision Making in Transcription Practice

Researchers might ask a number of questions to guide their decision making concerning transcription practice. First, given the range of possibilities for what elements might be included in transcriptions, an important question to answer is: what are the implications of one's theoretical view of interviews for how interaction might be transcribed? How researchers conceptualize interviews, how they anticipate analyzing and representing data, and the decisions that they have made in relation to participants' access to the transcriptions and reports from the study are all issues that will factor into how transcriptions are constructed. If, for example, the interview transcription will be made publicly accessible (as in oral history projects), the transcription conventions used will likely be very different to those used by a linguist studying phonetic variation. Daniel Oliver, Julianne Serovich, and Tina Mason (2005) provide insights into one research team's process of decision-making concerning transcription practice, and suggest that researchers reflect carefully on the implications of their transcription processes for the study's participants, analytic processes, and research outcomes.

Second, are there relevant transcription conventions required by the analytic methods to be applied? For example, James Gee's (1999) approach to discourse analysis transcribes talk in a series of stanzas, while conversation analysis uses conventions developed by Gail Jefferson (Psathas and Anderson, 1990). Mary Bucholtz and John DuBois (n.d.) have developed a hierarchy of 'transcription delicacy' that includes seven features of interaction that may be included in transcriptions (this may be accessed at: http://www.linguistics.ucsb.edu/projects/transcription/index.html).

Such fine detail achieved by these transcription practices allows for close analysis of utterances via a variety of linguistic methods less commonly used by qualitative researchers.

Many researchers intend to use inductive methods of analysis to generate themes, or narrative analysis in which participants' stories are re-presented by the researcher. A useful guide to transcription for these approaches is provided by Willow Powers (2005), who gives suggestions for dealing with speech and spelling, punctuation, incomplete and faltering speech, 'fillers' (such as 'like' and 'you know'), continuers (such as 'mm-hmm' and 'uh-huh') and nonverbal sounds. Powers (2005) also provides sample forms for formatting transcriptions that might be used by researchers when this work is sub-contracted to others. While Powers' recommendations for what to include in transcriptions includes less detail than that commonly used by linguists, the practices suggested include more detail than what has been traditionally used in reports from qualitative studies.

Third, and finally, when presenting data in research reports, authors can clarify their transcription and editing practices for readers. Research studies that utilize qualitative interviews are likely to generate many hundreds of pages of text for analysis. Authors will select only a minute fragment from that text to re-present in reports. Questions that researchers might consider for clarification in their reports include:

- What choices were made by researchers during the transcription process – what kinds of utterances and details were omitted? What was included? How were transcript excerpts edited prior to inclusion in reports?
- Will readers have access to the questions that generated the accounts and descriptions included in reports?
- Will researchers include their own participation in the co-construction of talk?

Again, how researchers respond to each of these questions will differ according to the theoretical commitments and purposes of a particular study, and authors may be called upon by editors of journals to justify their decisions with respect to transcription.

Conclusion

In this chapter I have reviewed steps to prepare for an interview study. I then outlined considerations for transcription of interview data and how translated data might be dealt with. In the next chapter, I discuss practical strategies that novice researchers might use to theorize their roles as researchers.

Further Reading

Interviewing Children

Cappello, M. (2005) 'Photo interviews: Eliciting data through conversations with children', *Field Methods*, 17 (2): 170–82.

Clark-Ibáñez, M. (2004) 'Framing the social world with photo-elicitation interviews', *American Behavioral Scientist*, 47 (12): 1507–27.

Darbyshire, P., MacDougall, C. and Schiller, W. (2005) 'Multiple methods in qualitative research with children: More insight or just more?', *Qualitative Research*, 5 (4): 417–36.

Eder, D., and Fingerson, L. (2002) 'Interviewing children and adolescents', in J. Gubrium and J.A. Holstein (eds), *Handbook of Interview Research: Context and Method*. Thousand Oaks, CA: Sage. pp. 181–201.

Freeman, M. and Mathison, S. (2009) *Researching Children's Experiences*. New York: Guilford Press.

Nespor, J. (1998) 'The meaning of research: Kids as subjects and kids as inquirers', *Qualitative Inquiry*, 4 (3): 369–88.

Interviewing Women

Cotterill, P. (1992) 'Interviewing women: Issues of friendship, vulnerability, and power', *Women's Studies International Forum*, 15 (5–6): 593–606.

Finch, J. (1984) '"It's great to have someone to talk to": The ethics and politics of interviewing women', in C. Bell and H. Roberts (eds), *Social Researching: Politics, Problems, Practice*. London: Routledge and Kegan Paul. pp. 70–87.

Oakley, A. (1981) 'Interviewing women: A contradiction in terms', in H. Roberts (ed.), *Doing Feminist Research.* London: Routledge. pp. 30–61.

Reinharz, S., and Chase, S.E. (2002) 'Interviewing women', in J. Gubrium and J.A. Holstein (eds), *Handbook of Interviewing: Context and Method.* Thousand Oaks, CA: Sage. pp. 221–38.

Riessman, C.K. (1987) 'When gender is not enough: Women interviewing women', *Gender and Society*, 1 (2): 172–207.

Tang, N. (2002) 'Interviewer and interviewee relationships between women', *Sociology*, 36 (3): 703–21.

Interviewing Men

Arendell, T. (1997) 'Reflections on the researcher–researched relationship: A woman interviewing men', *Qualitative Sociology*, 20 (3): 341–68.

Lareau, A. (2000) 'My wife can tell me who I know: Methodological and conceptual problems in studying fathers', *Qualitative Sociology*, 23 (4): 407–33.

Schwalbe, M.L. and Wolkomir, M. (2002) 'Interviewing men', in J. Gubrium and J.A. Holstein (eds), *Handbook of Interviewing: Context and Method.* Thousand Oaks, CA: Sage. pp. 203–19.

Sexual Orientation in Interviews

Kong, T.S.K., Mahoney, D. and Plummer, K. (2002) 'Queering the interview', in J. Gubrium and J.A. Holstein (eds), *Handbook of Interviewing: Context and Method.* Thousand Oaks, CA: Sage. pp. 239–58.

Interviewing the Ill

Frith, H. and Harcourt, D. (2007) 'Using photographs to capture women's experiences of chemotherapy: Reflecting on the method', *Qualitative Health Research*, 17 (10): 1340–50.

Morse, J.M. (2002) 'Interviewing the ill', in J. Gubrium and J.A. Holstein (eds), *Handbook of Interview Research: Context and Method.* Thousand Oaks, CA: Sage. pp. 317–28.

Radley, A. and Taylor, D. (2003) 'Remembering one's stay in hospital: A study in photography, recovery and forgetting', *Health*, 7(2): 129–59.

Interviewing Elites

Dexter, L. (1970) *Elite and Specialized Interviewing.* Evanston, IL: Northwestern University Press.

Hertz, R. and Imber, J. (eds) (1995) *Studying Elites Using Qualitative Methods.* Thousand Oaks, CA: Sage.

Kezar, A. (2003) 'Transformational elite interviews: Principles and problems', *Qualitative Inquiry*, 9 (3): 395–415.

Odendahl, T. and Shaw, A.M. (2002) 'Interviewing elites', in J. Gubrium and J.A. Holstein (eds), *Handbook of Interviewing: Context and Method.* Thousand Oaks, CA: Sage. pp. 299–316.

Interviewing Older People

Wenger, G.C. (2002) 'Interviewing older people', in J. Gubrium and J.A. Holstein (eds), *Handbook of Interviewing: Context and Method.* Thousand Oaks, CA: Sage. pp. 259–78.

Race and Culture in Interview Research

Best, A.L. (2003) 'Doing race in the context of feminist interviewing: Constructing whiteness through talk', *Qualitative Inquiry*, 9 (6): 895–914.

Bhopal, K. (2001) 'Researching South Asian women: Issues of sameness and difference in the research process', *Journal of Gender Studies*, 10 (3): 279–86.

Dunbar, C., Rodriguez, D. and Parker, L. (2002) 'Race, subjectivity, and the interview process', in J. Gubrium and J.A. Holstein (eds), *Handbook of Interview Research: Context and Method*. Thousand Oaks, CA: Sage. pp. 279–98.

Johnson-Bailey, J. (1999) 'The ties that bind and the shackles that separate: Race, gender, class and color in a research process', *International Journal of Qualitative Studies in Education*, 12 (6): 659–70.

Merriam, S., Johnson-Bailey, J., Lee, M.-Y., Ntseane, G. and Muhamad, M. (2001) 'Power and positionality: Negotiating insider/outsider status within and across cultures', *International Journal of Lifelong Education*, 20 (5): 405–16.

Song, M. and Parker, D. (1995) 'Commonality, difference and the dynamics of disclosure in in-depth interviewing', *Sociology*, 29 (2): 241–56.

Activity 5.1   Planning interviews

Consider the following questions in relation to the research topic that you would like to examine:

(1) Who would you like to recruit for the study?
(2) What are the criteria for selection of participants?
(3) How many participants will be involved?
(4) How will you go about recruiting them?
(5) Are there gatekeepers involved in recruitment? If so, who? How will you gain gatekeepers' assistance?
(6) What background information do you need in order to interview participants?
(7) How will the interview be recorded?
(8) Will the participants have access to the transcripts and/or final reports?
(9) What transcription conventions will be used for interviews?
(10) What analytic methods are implied by the conventions you intend to use?

Activity 5.2   Handling problematic interview encounters

Practice conducting an interview of 15–20 minutes with a classmate in which he/she has taken on one of the roles listed below. De-brief what happened, and how the interviewer handled the interviewee's interactions. Swap roles as interviewer and interviewee.

Interviewee's role: 'The busy person'

You are a very busy person and accepted the researcher's request for an interview because you are prominent in the community and have political aspirations.

You are willing to have your real name published in the report from the study. The interview is scheduled between meetings – and you're late. You don't have much time to talk...

Interviewee's role: 'The talker'

You are an invalid who does not get many visitors to your home. You are excited that a researcher has asked you to be involved in a study. You'd like to tell them about your family, your pets, and show them your photo album. You've set aside the whole afternoon for this interview. You invite the interviewer in for a cold drink and snack...

Interviewee's role: 'The short answerer'

You have never participated in a research interview before, and have a shy, retiring personality. You aren't given to lengthy descriptions or elaborations, and aren't really clear on why the interviewer would even want to speak with you. You ask a lot of clarification questions of the interviewer, so you can be sure that you know what the researcher wants from you.

Interviewee's role: 'The wanderer'

You have had a long and interesting career and love talking to other people about your experiences. You often interrupt yourself to diverge to other interesting topics, giving lots of descriptive detail as you go. Yes, this researcher may want to find out about how you came to your present career, but you'd really rather talk to them about the short courses you take as a recreational interest – and there's so much to talk about, your wine tasting weekend; the golf course you've recently enrolled in. Then there's the hiking vacation you've planned for the Summer!

Interviewee's role: 'The teacher'

You are an experienced researcher and you participated in this interview because you like to help beginning researchers. In fact, you are an experienced interviewer yourself, and are generous in giving suggestions to other researchers about how they should do things. In fact, the interview guide that the researcher has with them needs to be revised. This researcher needs some help ....

Interviewee's role: 'The player'

You enjoy being a research participant, and particularly like to choose projects in which there is some benefit to you – cash payments are your preferred option. You see it as your duty to provide data that won't 'fit' – you've taken research courses yourself, and think that it's fun to see what kind of reaction you can arouse in your interviewer. You've had some pretty enjoyable moments that make great stories at parties.

(Continued)

(Continued)

Interviewee's role: 'Distracted'

You are due to be in a wedding party next weekend, and unfortunately said you'd help out a friend to be in this study. You've got a lot of responsibility in helping out the happy couple, and can't really afford the time to do this inter-view. You've also not ever been this involved in a wedding before, and need some help with etiquette. Maybe the researcher could help you?

Interviewee's role: 'Questioner'

You've agreed to be part of this interview because you want to go to graduate school. You know that the interviewer is doing a graduate degree. You are really curious to know how the researcher got into graduate school and what they're doing. It could help you decide what school to apply to, and what professors you could talk to. Perhaps they could give you some advice?

SIX

Theorizing the Researcher:
The Reflective Interviewer

This chapter introduces:

- *Reflexivity* and *subjectivity* in qualitative research.
- Approaches to examining the researcher's subject positions: *being interviewed*, writing *subjectivity statements* and *research journals*, and *examining interview data*.

Qualitative researchers and interviewers are inevitably part of the studies that they conduct, whether or not they make explicit the connections between their subject positions and the ways in which these impact the outcomes of their studies in their reports. As Chiseri-Strater has commented:

> [a]ll researchers are positioned....by age, gender, race, class, nationality, institutional affiliation, historical-personal circumstance, and intellectual predisposition. The extent to which influences are revealed or concealed when reporting data is circumscribed by the paradigms and disciplines under which we train, work, and publish. (1996: 115)

How might researchers learn more about the assumptions they bring to their study, and how researchers' selves are infused throughout the research process? In this chapter, I review practical ways for inexperienced researchers to think about these issues in relation to the research projects they design and conduct, and discuss how researchers have addressed these issues in their work.

Interviewers bring different conversational styles to the task of interviewing unique participants on diverse topics, and approach their work from a variety of theoretical perspectives. Although there are some commonalities in the kinds of things researchers routinely do in order to generate interview data, settling on common standards for what qualitative interviewers should do is complicated by the uniqueness of each and every interviewer–interviewee encounter. Interviewers work in local contexts and are informed by their own and others' racial, ethnic, cultural, and national origins. Combined with the specificities of the class, gender, language abilities, status, age, and education – in addition to any number of other social locations – of both participant and researcher, and the extent and nature of their prior relationship, qualitative research projects each bear the unique imprints of the particular set of complex relationships and interactions that unfold. Thus, it is a useful move for qualitative researchers to critically consider their subject positions in relation to their research topic and those involved in their studies.

There are a number of terms that are frequently used by qualitative researchers when discussing the topics of knowing oneself as a researcher, and articulating one's place and involvement in research. Principal among these are 'reflexivity' and 'subjectivity.' Discussions of these topics are frequently implicated in debates concerning what it means to be an 'insider' and/or 'outsider,' and representational issues – that is, how others are represented in research findings and the 'voices' made visible in the text. I begin my discussion of the ways in which researchers can theorize their roles as researchers by first examining the concept of reflexivity.

Reflexivity in Qualitative Research

The *Oxford English Dictionary* indicates that one meaning of reflexive is to be 'capable of turning, or bending back.' Encapsulated in this definition is the property of self-reference. With respect to research, reflexivity refers to the researcher's ability to be able to self-consciously refer to him or herself in relation to the production of knowledge about research topics. Linda Finlay and Brendon Gough comment that reflexivity involves:

> thoughtful, self-aware analysis of the intersubjective dynamics between researcher and the researched. Reflexivity requires critical self-reflection of the ways in which researchers' social background, assumptions, positioning and behaviour impact on the research process. (2003: ix)

Reflexivity should not be confused with 'reflection,' although the former may involve the latter. While reflection demands thinking about something (Finlay and Gough, 2003: ix), it does not require an 'other' (Chiseri-Strater, 1996: 130).

Reflexivity has long been explored from a range of theoretical positions, and there is a wide array of views as to its usefulness in social research. For some researchers, reflexivity is an intricately peculiar problem (see for example, Ashmore, 1989; Woolgar, 1988a). Envision an image of endless mirrors within which one's face is reflected repeatedly, and you will begin to picture the 'infinite regress' intrinsic to the folding back involved in reflexive actions (Lynch, 2000). In ethnography, for example, Steve Woolgar (1988b) considers the problem of observing the observer being observed.

Michael Lynch (2000) outlines an inventory of no less than six forms of reflexivity, settling on ethnomethodological reflexivity as the preferred kind. For Lynch and other ethnomethodologists (for example, Macbeth, 2001), reflexivity is a ubiquitous and unremarkable property of everyday life and human action, and there is no particular advantage in demonstrations of reflexivity by social science researchers as exemplified in biographical position statements, or textual deconstructions. Indeed,

Lynch critiques the kinds of reflexivity that aim for 'methodological virtue,' asserting that the 'light' shed by the epistemological achievement of reflexivity is 'dubious' (2000: 46–8). Yet, an ethnomethodological viewpoint of reflexivity has many competitors within the field of qualitative inquiry.

For other social scientists, reflexivity opens up possibilities to provide more complicated representations of research data and multi-layered accounts incorporating the researcher's voice as an alternative to un-situated accounts from 'neutral' researchers who absent themselves from their texts through the use of third person and passive voicing. Linda Finlay (2002), a researcher in the health sciences, argues for the use of reflexivity as a methodological tool, while also urging researchers to be aware of various pitfalls. It is instructive to examine the variants of reflexivity that Finlay outlines in more detail, along with problems she associates with each, since these are views espoused frequently by qualitative inquirers.

Finlay's (2002) typology of five pathways to reflexivity broadly encompasses critical self-reflection on the researcher's inner thoughts, actions and interpersonal interactions, and the textual deconstruction involved in 'messy texts.' The first form, 'reflexive introspection,' is a form of self-discovery that is accomplished through reflection and intuition (2002: 213–15). A possible problem of this form of reflexivity is that it privileges the researcher's perspective over participants' voices, and can be written off as academic 'navel-gazing' (2002: 215). The second form, 'intersubjective reflection,' examines meanings as they emerge in interactions with others during a research relationship, and may involve psychoanalytic interpretations (2002: 215–18). Based on realist assumptions, researchers using this approach to reflexivity may encounter problems of gaining access to 'unconscious motivations' and must also carefully weigh the use of therapeutic techniques in doing social research (2002: 218). Given the decidedly different projects involved in doing therapy and doing social research, this kind of reflexivity seems to be reserved for use by those social scientists that are professionally licensed as therapists. 'Mutual collaboration,' an approach frequently used by feminist researchers, involves the use of co-operative approaches to inquiry that involve participants in reflexive dialogues that may include data analysis and interpretation during the research process as well as co-authorship (2002: 218). Critiques of the outcomes of this kind of research include the charge that compromise and negotiation during the research process can lead to 'watered down' findings, and concerns that the collaboration is authentically represented in reports and that research collaborations merely disguise unequal power relationships between researchers and participants (2002: 219–20). Forms of reflexivity that focus on 'social critique' acknowledge power imbalances inherent in research relationships, attend to the tensions arising in the research process, and are aware of the shifting and multiple positions held by stakeholders (2002: 220–2). This kind of reflexivity, according to Finlay, can lead to endless examinations of one's actions as a researcher. The identification of the shifting positions of those involved in research relationships is complex and difficult, and may inevitably result in claims to greater authority in texts (Finlay, 2002: 222). The fifth form of reflexive practice identified by Finlay is that of 'discursive deconstruction,' which examines the 'ambiguity of meanings in language and how this impacts on modes of presentation' (2002: 222). Most commonly, this form of reflexivity is demonstrated in experimental texts, however, it may also result in nihilistic representations and language games (2002: 222–4). Despite the critiques of various forms of reflexivity that she reviews, Finlay asserts that reflexive practices are useful for researchers, and provide a way for researchers and readers to evaluate the research process (2002: 225).

Wanda Pillow (2003), writing from a feminist poststructural position, is critical of some of the forms of reflexivity that have been popularized and are now accepted practice for qualitative researchers. Pillow asserts that in situating the 'self' as 'close to the subject,' confessional tales may result in the researcher seeking commonalities with participants (2003: 182). A problem with such disclosures is that they are 'dependent on a knowable subject' and have 'equated the knowing researcher as somehow having 'better' and more 'valid' data' (2003: 184). Pillow argues that research that focuses on giving 'voice' to the other may actually perpetuate the unequal power relationships between privileged researchers and participants, while obscuring the 'colonial' relationship of the researcher–researched (2003: 185). Pillow's response to forms of reflexivity that seek knowable truths about selves and others is to propose the use of 'reflexivities of discomfort,' which acknowledges the tenuous nature of the search for knowledge. This perspective positions reflexive practices 'not as clarity, honesty, or humility, but as practices of confounding disruptions – at times even a failure of our language and practices' (Pillow, 2003: 192).

As Lynch has commented, 'concepts of reflexivity are diverse, and the implications of reflexive inquiry remain unspecified until we learn more about the relevant theoretical investments and contextual applications' (2000: 47). The contradictory and overlapping versions of reflexivity extant in the social sciences have been formulated by researchers with diverse disciplinary interests in anthropology, education, health sciences, psychology, science, and sociology. Researchers who have written about reflexivity situate their work in a variety of epistemological and theoretical traditions, including ethnomethodology, feminism, phenomenology, poststructuralism, and postmodernism. It is safe to say that there are numerous meanings of 'reflexivity,' and one's definition of reflexivity will be informed by both the discipline one comes from, and one's theoretical framing for research. While these multiple forms of reflexivity have proven to be ways that researchers have responded to particular problems in research – including claims for the neutrality and objectivism of scientific knowledge, Western science as a colonizing project, and representation of the Other – demonstrating reflexivity can also be problematic. Criticisms of the outcomes of reflexive practices have been that they have resulted in narcissistic confessions, nihilist textual experimentations, masking of inherent power relationships in research, and claims for more valid and truthful representations of data even while simultaneously critiquing approaches to research that seek objectivity and Truth.

Given that experienced researchers cannot agree on the nature and practices of reflexivity, it is tempting for novice researchers to abandon the concept altogether! Yet, rather than being absolved from responsibility for reflexivity, I hope that readers will be better able to understand the importance of situating oneself within the broad spectrum of social theory, and outlining how one's research design, methods, and researcher stance on reflexivity are informed by particular theoretical positions. One place to begin a reflexive journey is by examining one's 'subjectivity.'

Subjectivity and Qualitative Research

Gary Shank (2006) points out in his historical review of the term that subjectivity has often been viewed in opposition to objectivity, and as such, something to be avoided in scientific research. Nevertheless, there are multiple ways of viewing both 'subjectivity' and 'objectivity.' 'Subjectivity' viewed as a problem means that the private domain of the individual researcher, including thoughts, preconceptions, attitudes, preferences, personal history, and so forth (Shank, 2006: 82) are distorting influences on the researcher's data gathering and analyses that will lead to biased reporting, and therefore must be expunged from both the research process (for example, through controlled forms of information gathering) and representations of findings (for example, through use of third person accounts).

In contrast to a view of subjectivity as a problem to be eradicated, Alan Peshkin (1988) has forwarded the idea that the researcher's subjectivities – or 'subjective-Is' – can be systematically sought out throughout the duration of a project, and openly acknowledged (see Peshkin, 1986, for an example). Thus, in contemporary qualitative research practice, investigation and acknowledgement of one's subjective positions in relation to one's research topic and research participants is routinely seen to be an important aspect of one's apprenticeship as a reflexive researcher, and the absence of subjectivity statements in research reports can be a cause for suspicion on the part of readers (Preissle, 2008).

Bruno Latour espouses the view that objectivity and subjectivity need not be seen as opposites, arguing that '[o]bjectivity does not refer to a special quality of the mind, and inner state of justice and fairness, but to the presence of objects which have been rendered "able" ... to *object* to what is told about them.' (2000: 115, original emphasis). Latour argues that researchers in the social sciences, in order to strive for the kind of objectivity found in the best of the natural sciences, need to allow the:

> subject of study as much as possible able to object to what is said about them, to be as disobedient as possible to the protocol, and to be as capable to raise their own questions in their own terms and not in those of the scientists whose interests they do not have to share! (2000: 116)

Given that objectivity and subjectivity need not be viewed as opposites with objectivity occupying a privileged position, and that subjectivity is something that may be acknowledged rather than treated as a problem, what might be gained from reflexive practices?

For Peshkin, the process of examining one's subjectivities is important because researchers can 'learn about the particular subset of personal qualities that contact with their research phenomenon has released' (1988: 17). Peshkin (1988) suggests that each new project provides an environment in which different sets of subjective-Is may be invoked. While this exploration of subjectivities entails continuous and repeated examination of one's personal experiences and biography as a researcher within the context of each new project, it is not simply an autobiography since it focuses on the relationships and interactions between the researcher and participants (Preissle, 2008).

There are a number of common approaches to examinations of subjectivity, all of which may be used to inform each other. These strategies are frequently used by qualitative inquirers as demonstrations of 'reflexive' practice. These include: (1) subjectivity statements; (2) researcher journals; (3) interviews of the researcher; and (4) analysis of the interviewer's work. Below, I discuss each of these strategies in turn.

Subjectivity Statements

Researchers can critically examine their perspectives and assumptions about key elements of the research project – including theoretical perspectives, personal hypotheses concerning the research findings, and positions in relation to the research participants – through writing subjectivity statements. Writing a subjectivity statement can be a helpful step when one is learning how to design and conduct a research project because it forces a researcher to consider key questions about the impetus for the study and decisions made concerning theories and methods. Thus, even while designing a study, researchers might write a subjectivity statement in order to examine their interests and background with respect to a particular topic.

For example, Ardra Cole and Gary Knowles show how writing a personal history is one way of examining researcher subjectivities (2001: 48–56). They note that this biographical life history of the researcher might focus on prior experiences with the research topic as well as any research on the topic of interest. Time invested in writing this account, they argue, will not only help researchers to understand themselves, but contribute to becoming more comfortable with the writing processes involved in doing research (2001: 49).

Another example of a researcher's investigation of researcher subjectivities is provided by Sofia Villenas (1996), who draws on field notes from her research study as well as reflective narratives of her experiences in graduate school. In her examination of her identities as a Chicana ethnographer, Villenas demonstrates how she was at the same time marginalized and complicit in 'othering' herself and the Latino community that she studied in North Carolina. Villenas describes some of the complexities and messiness inherent in doing qualitative research, and demonstrates that consideration of one's researcher subjectivities is both ongoing and changeable work that may be revisited throughout a research project and career. In the case described by Villenas, the anger and guilt that she experienced from her complicity in being co-opted into 'othering' the community that she studied resulted in her use of a number of subversive and resistance strategies as she attempted to develop transformative research practices.

Another analytic method used to examine the topic of self and subjectivity in relation to a research project is described by a sociologist, Susan Krieger (1985). What is unusual about this account is that the investigation of subjectivity was conducted *after* the data collection phase had concluded and Krieger had left the research setting. Krieger found that she was unable to analyze and write up the data collected in her study of a lesbian social group. Thus, she began a three-step structured process of re-engaging with the data through, first, writing sets of notes that reflected her pre-interview self-assessment, and, second, interview self-assessment with each of the 78 interviewees in her study. A third step included revisiting and analyzing the content of her interview notes, since the interviews for this study, conducted in 1977/8, were not recorded. Through this frank analytic assessment of the part that her 'self' had played in the research process, Krieger was able to complete and publish the study.

As may be seen from this section, subjectivity statements may be developed in the very beginning stages of a study, and then re-visited and developed throughout the research process. In publications it is now common to see subjectivity statements included as part of the research design and methods section of an article, chapter, or book. Yet, feminist philosopher Sandra Harding cautions that simply writing a list of one's social locations is unlikely to meet the requirements of reflexive methods: 'I, the author, am a woman of European descent, a middle-class academic, trained as a philosopher, who has lived all her life in the U.S.' (2007: 54). Harding continues: 'for the researcher to stop her analysis of her social location here, with just the confession, is to leave all the work up to the reader' (2007: 54). Subjectivity statements, then, may be seen as flexible and reflective documents that are subject to change and revision. Depending on the theoretical perspective that researchers take to research, statements may also allow for contradictory, complex, and multi-faceted accounts, as exemplified in the 'messy texts' that have emerged in response to the calls for reflexivity in qualitative research.

Researcher Journals

The researcher journal is usually composed of a series of written entries that record the researcher's reflections, ideas, commentaries, and memos throughout the research process. Anthropologists have long used notebooks in which they have recorded entries by hand, however, with the advent of new technologies, researchers frequently make use of laptop computers and handheld devices such as personal digital assistants, as well as digital audio-recording devices to record and store these kinds of 'jottings.' For researchers undertaking ethnographic fieldwork, researcher journals may be kept separately as an adjunct to field notes, or researchers' responses and personal thoughts about the research process may be threaded throughout field notes (see for example, Emerson et al., 1995; Goodall, 2000: 137–9). Peshkin made use of index cards to jot down his thoughts while in field settings, and, in search of subjectivity, looked for the 'warm and the cool spots, the emergence of positive and negative feelings, the experiences I wanted to avoid, and when I felt moved to act in roles beyond those necessary to fulfill my research needs' (1988: 18).

The researcher journal offers a highly personal respite for contemplation, and researchers may make use of poetry (Cahnmann, 2003), and other idiosyncratic forms of writing which may ultimately be used in a published report from the study. While the reflexive researcher journal has long been an integral part of doing ethnographic fieldwork, it is also used by researchers undertaking interview studies. For example, Cole and Knowles describe the reflexivity journal as essential to doing life history research:

> As soon as possible after a conversation, site visit, or meeting with a research participant, it is important to somehow record impressions, thoughts, ideas, questions, and puzzles arising from those sessions. Whether by talking into a handheld audio-tape recorder, writing in a logbook, or using a word processor, the idea is to review as much of the research encounter as possible. Through the process of reviewing there will likely emerge elements of subjective presence to be noted or monitored. (2001: 90)

Caroline Bradbury-Jones (2007) describes her use of a reflexive journal in her study of the meaning of empowerment for nursing students. In her application of this technique, she used the journal to record her personal thoughts throughout the project, which she later analyzed through applying Peshkin's (1988) notion of 'subjective-Is.'

Similar to subjectivity statements, reflexive journals are a tool that researchers can use to consider their identities as researchers in relation to the various research contexts that they find themselves in. However, the researcher journal is also a place that researchers can use to jot down comments about what occurs during interactions with participants, as well as thoughts, ideas, hunches, and questions that arise during the research process.

Interviewing the Researcher

There are a number of ways that researchers can use interviews strategically to learn more about their subjectivities. In this section I discuss the 'why-interview' and the 'bracketing interview' – both of which interrogate a researcher's assumptions, beliefs and hypotheses about a particular topic.

The Why-interview

Ilja Maso (2003) describes the 'why-interview' as a method that beginning researchers can use to interrogate their initial research interests and questions. According to Maso, 'every researcher has to know what motivated the research question, which beliefs are behind it and of which conceptual framework it is an expression' (2003: 42). There are two key questions in the why-interview. The first concerns the concepts embedded in the question formulation ('what do you mean by each of the concepts embedded in the question?'); and the second focuses on why researchers want to ask the question ('why is this question so important to you?') (Maso, 2003: 42–3). As Maso describes the process, the interviewer probes the interviewee's responses (in this case, the researcher) in order to reveal the:

> concepts the researchers are using, why the earlier formulated question is so important to them and whether the formulated question is a proper 'translation' of what is important to the researchers. (2003: 42)

Corinne Glesne has outlined a similar approach, noting that she asks of her students: 'Why are your research questions, of all the research questions you could ask, of interest to you?' (2006: 120). Asking these kinds of questions is a useful strategy for novice researchers as they begin to formulate research questions, since interrogation of the concepts underlying the formulation of research questions, and why these questions are important will assist in decisions concerning how to focus the topic of investigation and pose significant questions.

The Bracketing Interview

The 'bracketing interview' is a strategy discussed by phenomenological researchers Howard Pollio, Tracy Henley and Craig Thompson (1997: 47–9) in which researchers investigate their presuppositions concerning their research projects by being interviewed themselves by another researcher about their proposed topics of study. The term 'bracketing' is commonly associated with phenomenological research and Max van Manen defines it as 'the act of suspending one's various beliefs in the reality of the natural world in order to study the essential structures of the world' (1990: 175). Although phenomenologists working from different philosophical traditions espouse a range of views on what might be accomplished through bracketing, Pollio et al. (1997: 47–9) assert that it is impossible for researchers to fully 'bracket' or 'suspend' their knowledge of the world. They describe the bracketing interview as follows:

> … the investigator becomes the first person interviewed about the topic of his or her investigation. This is done to provide the researcher with some feel for what it is like to be interviewed on the present topic and to provide a thematic description of his or her present understanding of the phenomenon … the intention is not to have the interviewers become objective – only to have them become more attuned to their presuppositions about the nature and meaning of the present phenomenon and thereby sensitize them to any potential demands they may impose on their co-participants either during the interview or in its subsequent interpretation. (1997: 48)

Although the technique of bracketing interviews is drawn from phenomenological research, this strategy is useful for researchers using other theoretical approaches for a number of reasons. First, it helps researchers reflect on the kinds of information they seek to elicit. Second, researchers also gain a better understanding of what they are asking participants to do in interview settings. Third, this kind of interview can be used by a novice interviewer to practice interviewing skills with a colleague. Bracketing interviewers who are fellow-researchers are able to offer collegial, and perhaps, alternative perspectives to the interviewee concerning his or her topic.

In Activity 6.1 at the end of this chapter, I describe one approach to using the bracketing interview as both a site for practice of interview skills, as well as a source of information from another researcher concerning the interviewee's subjectivities.[1] The activity is described from the interviewer's perspective – in this case the 'researcher' becomes the interviewee – participating in a bracketing interview conducted by another researcher. This approach provides researchers with insights about their proposed research from another perspective, which can assist self-reflection. This exercise can be accomplished while researchers are beginning to develop their research questions, as well as further along in the process when preliminary research questions about prospective topics have been developed.

Liz Rolls and Marilyn Relf (2006) have extended the use of the bracketing interview as a reflexive strategy throughout the life of a project, using it as a means of support for a researcher, in this case, in a study of childhood bereavement services in the UK. In the research described by Rolls and Relf, they recommend bracketing interviews as a means for qualitative researchers to 'process fieldwork events in such a way that *it increases understanding of the phenomena they are studying*' (2006: 302, original emphasis). They claim that bracketing interviews do this by:

> Enabling the researcher to hold the tension of the dialectic process, of investigating and testing the nature of the participant's experience, at the same time as holding and recognizing their own experience, in a way that always relates these to the research data, without entering the researcher's material therapeutically, or allowing the researcher to superimpose their meaning on participants. (2006: 302)

In their development of the bracketing interview drawn from phenomenological work, these researchers have been informed by the model of clinical supervision routinely used in the health sciences. This link to clinical supervision is made explicit in their comment that 'like clinical supervisors, bracketers need to be skilled in understanding such mechanisms as transference and counter transference, projection and parallel process' (Rolls and Relf, 2006: 303), and the authors point out that the person conducting bracketing interviews must be aware of the differences between a supervisory relationship that is academic or personal, and one that involves research. This use of the bracketing interview has considerable potential for researchers dealing with the challenges of studying sensitive topics (see for example, Dickson-Swift et al., 2007). Yet if used in studies of sensitive topics, it seems that the bracketing interviewer must have substantial knowledge and expertise in dealing with both clinical supervision and social science research in order to avoid the pitfall of the interview lapsing into a therapy session for the researcher. In addition, in research on sensitive topics, it is advisable that the bracketing interviewer have sufficient expertise to refer the researcher to sources of assistance should they be necessary.

Another application of the researcher being interviewed is exemplified in work conducted by Juanita Johnson-Bailey (2001). In her research examining narratives of African-American women who had re-entered higher education, she herself was interviewed for the study, and in doing so, became a participant of her own study.

---

[1] I am indebted to Kathleen deMarrais for sharing this pedagogical strategy with me.

In speaking some years after the event, Johnson-Bailey commented that she initially did not want to do this:

> I actually didn't want to do that. That was my professor's idea ... I think it was one of the best things that I've ever done ... I actually thought that since I came up with the questions on the interview guide, I knew the answers. But the interviewing process is such a dynamic one that when we got in the room – I closed doors, and she's asking these questions that I actually wrote – I didn't have prepared answers .... Often the process of telling is a process of coming to understand. And so in answering some of those questions, for the first time I was hearing and knowing things about myself, discovering things about myself, which was really interesting ... If I was going to ask my participants to share their stories and ... not [to] edit out the difficult parts, of course I couldn't do that either. And so I think that in a way it prepared me and sensitized me as to what I was asking of these women. But it also help[ed] me to analyze and to look critically at my own journey, and to make some changes. (Interview conducted 10 May 2007 by author)

In this excerpt, we see how Johnson-Bailey enhanced her understanding of what she was expecting of her participants through participating in a research interview conducted by another researcher using the interview questions that she had developed. Participating in the interview process informed her about not only the interview method, but the kinds of data that she wanted to generate for the study.

One can see from examples provided in this section that there are a number of ways in which researchers can use interviews to investigate their subjectivities. These include being interviewed by another researcher about the background to the topic of interest; being interviewed throughout a project as a means of support, particularly when dealing with sensitive topics; and finally, being interviewed about one's topic with the interview guide that one intends to use with others. Participation in these kinds of interviews can inform researchers about their involvement and personal stake in a project, their subjective-Is, and may also inform the design and methods of the study as it progresses.

Analyzing the Interviewer's Work

Another strategy that researchers can use to consider self and subjectivity in a research project is to critically reflect on their interaction with others within a research interview. By examining the interviewer's interactions in research interviews, researchers have the opportunity to learn more about themselves as co-constructors of data. This in turn may inform the development and design of further research, and the conduct of further interviews.

Once interview questions have been developed, researchers can try these out with a potential participant. After transcribing the interviews, researchers can ask questions of their practice by closely inspecting the interview transcript. In addition to learning about their assumptions as researchers by considering what topics are pursued, and which are overlooked, interviewers can consider design issues. For example, did the interview questions generate the kind of data anticipated? Do questions need to be re-worded? What stands out about the organization of the questions asked within the interview as a whole?

One approach to the work of examining interview transcriptions to inform practice is illustrated by Karen Nairn, Jenny Munro and Anne Smith (2005), who employ Pillow's notion of 'uncomfortable reflexivities.' These researchers examine how close analysis of an apparently 'failed' interview of a group interview of high school students conducted by one of the researchers provided ways to re-consider the research methods used, the data collected, and the 'social relations of the research' (2005: 236). In response to this interview – in which very little usable data content-wise was generated – the researchers went about changing their research design and methods by: (1) involving young people in the construction of interview questions; (2) recruiting students face-to-face, rather than relying on teachers; (3) planning for multiple interviews over time; (4) including youths as interviewers and researchers; (5) conducting interviews outside school environments; and (6) inviting other kinds of data from youths in the form of portfolios including videos, writing, photos, music, and images (2005: 238). In this example, we see how close analysis of and reflection on interview interaction that has gone awry in some way can yield multiple insights that can inform further research on the topic.

Christina Sinding and Jane Aronson (2003) provide another demonstration of how researchers might go about a reflexive examination of interview practice. In their article, they explore entries from their researcher journals as well as interview interactions with caregivers of people dying with cancer and elderly women needing care. These authors highlight the vulnerability of participants and ethical complexities that were made visible in their interview research, and urge researchers to carefully consider the following questions in relation to the use of research interviews:

In this context, what are the norms or standards of conduct?

What kinds of experiences are valued?

How might my interviews expose the disparities between an individual's experience and valued or dominant images?

What personal strategies of accommodation might these discourses or these social policies engender?

How might my interviews unsettle the accommodations individuals have made?

What will I do, when accommodations are unsettled and failures exposed? (2003: 114)

These questions are certainly applicable to other studies, and may be particularly relevant in research examining sensitive issues. Reflexive explorations by qualitative researchers in other fields of study will likely yield many more questions.

The two examples outlined above provide models for other researchers willing to closely analyze puzzling, difficult, or ethically challenging interactions that have occurred in research projects using interviews. Other researchers have provided examples of how they have re-investigated data generated in earlier studies, examined how their own contributions to the interaction contributed to the co-construction of interview data, and explored the implications of this for their studies (see for example, Gadd, 2004; Roulston, 2000; Wang and Roulston, 2007). In Chapter 7, I will explore the topic of analyzing interview interaction methodologically in more detail.

Conclusion

Given that in qualitative interviews the researcher is the instrument, there is no escape from the self. Whether acknowledged or not, researcher selves are implicated in every aspect of a research project – from the formulation and design of a study, to the interview interaction, and analysis and representation of interview data. In this chapter I began by reviewing various perspectives on reflexivity from different theoretical viewpoints. I then outlined a number of reflexive practices that might be used by qualitative interviewers to examine their researcher subjectivities. The task of considering the self in qualitative inquiry is a continuously evolving and ongoing task, and will never be completed. Yet as interviewers, qualitative researchers need to be aware of who they are in relation to research projects, and how that might be theorized in ways that are consonant with their epistemological and theoretical assumptions about knowledge production.

A reflexive research practice does not conclude with the design and conduct of interviews – it is also very much part of how we analyze and represent others in reports from our studies. Through combining the various reflexive strategies outlined in this chapter – subjectivity statements, researcher journals, interviews, and analysis of interaction – researchers can explore the particularities of their encounters with others in their examination of research problems, and, in doing so, learn something more about themselves and others. As Robert Emerson, Rachel Fretz and Linda Shaw comment: 'in training the reflexive lens on ourselves, we understand our own enterprise in much the same terms that we understand those we study' (1995: 216).

In Chapter 7 I demonstrate how researchers can investigate their interview practice, the kinds of questions they might ask of interview transcriptions, and discuss how this can inform both the analyses and interpretations of data, as well as research design.

Further Reading

Writing Subjectivity Statements

Cole, A.L. and Knowles, J.G. (eds) (2001) *Lives in Context: The Art of Life History Research*. Walnut Creek, CA: AltaMira Press.
Cole and Knowles provide examples of subjectivity statements that show how their own life histories have informed their current work using life history methods.

Reflexivity and Writing Practices

Denzin, N.K. (1997) *Interpretive Ethnography: Ethnographic Practices for the 21st Century*. Thousand Oaks, CA: Sage.
This text outlines different theoretical positions on reflexivity, and reviews the ways that researchers have used experimental and 'messy' texts to represent research.

Finlay, L. and Gough, B. (eds) (2003) *Reflexivity: A Practical Guide for Researchers in Health and Social Sciences*. Oxford: Blackwell Science.

This edited collection provides examples of how different researchers have addressed the issue of reflexivity in their research.

Goodall, H.L. (2000) *Writing the New Ethnography.* Walnut Creek, CA: Altamira Press. *Goodall provides a series of writing experiments (pp. 42–44, 150) that serve as entrées into creative writing about the self, and considering one's biography and social locations in relation to research interests.*

Goodall, H.L. (2008) *Writing Qualitative Inquiry: Self, Stories, and Academic Life.* Walnut Creek, CA: Left Coast Press.
Here, Goodall provides further practical advice on narrative writing strategies, and how to include the self in writing up qualitative research.

Hertz, R. (ed.) (1997) *Reflexivity and Voice.* Thousand Oaks, CA: Sage.
Hertz's edited collection provides examples of writing that deals with reflexivity and voice from researchers from a range of theoretical perspectives.

Special issues of *Forum: Qualitative Social Research* 3 (3) (2002) and 4 (2) (2003).

Further Examples of Reflexive Accounts and Writing About Self

Behar, R. (1993) *Translated Woman: Crossing the Border with Esperanza's Story.* Boston, MA: Beacon Press.
Chaudhry, L.N. (1997) 'Researching "my people," researching myself: Fragments of a reflexive tale, *International Journal of Qualitative Studies in Education,* 10 (4): 441–53.
Choi, J.-A. (2006) 'Doing poststructural ethnography in the life history of dropouts in South Korea: Methodological ruminations on subjectivity, positionality and reflexivity', *International Journal of Qualitative Studies in Education,* 19 (4), 435–53.
Jordan, A.B. (2006) 'Make yourself at home: The social construction of research roles in family studies', *Qualitative Research,* 6 (2): 169–85.
Mauthner, N.S. and Doucet, A. (2003) 'Reflexive accounts and accounts of reflexivity in qualitative data analysis', *Sociology,* 37 (3): 413–31.
Palmer, J.D. (2006) 'Negotiating the indistinct: Reflections of a Korean adopted American working with Korean born, Korean Americans', *Qualitative Research,* 6 (4): 473–95.

Activity 6.1   Why-interview

Participate in a 'why-interview' (Maso, 2003) with another researcher. In this interview, you will discuss the concepts used in your research questions, and what it is that you want to know by examining each research question.

Interview questions:

- What are your research questions for your study?

For each of the research questions:

- What are the key concepts relevant to this research question?
- What do you mean by this concept?
- Why is this question so important to you?

Activity 6.2   Bracketing interview

Participate in a bracketing interview with another researcher. In this interview, you will discuss your research interests, and what you expect to find in your study.

Interview Questions

1. Tell me about your research topic.
2. Tell me about some of your experiences [concerning the research topic].
3. What have you learned about the topic from your reading in the literature?
4. What do you expect to find from your study?
5. Why to do you think this topic is important?
6. What audiences do you hope to inform with your research?

Instructions to the Interviewer

In this interview, your purpose is to gain as much information as possible from the participant. Therefore, practice using the following kinds of questions with your interviewee:

- Open questions (e.g. tell me about ....)
- Follow-up questions or 'probes' to gain more information

   o You mentioned ... tell me more about that.
   o You mentioned ... can you give me a specific example of that?
   o You mentioned ... what was that like for you?

Try to practice more 'formal' interviewing skills, including listening without interrupting. Demonstrate that you are listening by:

- Eye contact
- Body posture
- Nodding

   Before asking the next question in the list above, consider whether you have 'followed up' or probed the participant's accounts.

   Try to refrain from contributing your own views, opinions, or experiences about the topic to the conversation.

   Work at providing sufficient 'wait-time' with your participant (e.g. count to five before you ask another question).

SEVEN

Examining Interview Talk Methodologically

This chapter introduces:

- An approach to examine *how* interview data are co-constructed by speakers and provides actual examples of interview interaction that demonstrate interviewers *asking multiple questions*; *including possible responses* in questions; *providing insufficient guidance* for interviewees to answer questions; *following up on unanticipated answers*; *clarifying participants' statements*; and *asking questions that include assumptions* concerning participants' life worlds.

Questions asked by interviewers seen in documentaries, satires and news programs are frequently posed for purposes other than gaining information. For example, questions may be asked of interviewees in ways that mock, challenge, provoke, and even ensnare them to respond in certain sorts of ways. Surrounded daily by models of interview practice that may not serve social scientists well in their work as qualitative researchers, how might novice researchers develop their practice and skills as interviewers?

In this chapter, I show how close analysis of interview transcripts is one possible tool for researchers to reflect on and to develop their interview practice. Researchers can develop further sensitivity concerning what they do and say in interaction through inspecting transcriptions via methods drawn from conversation analysis (CA). This method of investigating talk-in-interaction was developed by Harvey Sacks and his colleagues (Sacks, 1992; Schegloff, 2007; Silverman, 1998). CA focuses on examining the conversational resources used by members in everyday interaction (Psathas, 1995; Have, 2007), and was originally used to analyze mundane talk rather than research interviews. More recently, as outlined in Chapter 3 in the section on the constructionist conception of the interview, scholars have used methods drawn from CA and ethnomethodology (EM) (Garfinkel, 1967; Have, 2004) to investigate the generation and analysis of interview data (Baker, 1983, 2002, 2004; Mazeland and Have, 1998; Rapley, 2001, 2004; Roulston, 2006a). In this chapter, I show how this approach might be used by qualitative interviewers to investigate their interview practice.

Asking Questions of Transcriptions

In the following sections, I demonstrate how researchers might begin to ask questions of their own interaction by using the following questions:

- How are questions formulated by the interviewer?
- How do interviewees orient to the interviewer's questions?
- What actions are accomplished in the talk?
- What happens next?

While there are many more questions that interviewers might ask of their transcripts (see, for example, Activity 7.1 at the end of this chapter), the questions listed above provide a useful starting point to examine and understand how interaction is accomplished in interviews. The findings from this kind of methodological analysis can inform the interviewer about him/herself as interviewer and researcher; and his or her contribution to the generation of data. This kind of analysis is a powerful tool that researchers can use to think about their interview practice; and moderate practice in future research interviews; or to think about questions of research design more broadly. Let us look at some examples.

Novice interviewers sometimes find the formulation of clear, open-ended questions and effective follow-up of respondents' accounts with follow-up questions or probes more challenging than anticipated. In the examples that follow, using the tools of CA I examine a variety of interactional phenomena that occurred in qualitative interviews. In discussing these excerpts, I demonstrate how close analysis of transcripts from interviews may be used as a methodological tool to examine one's interview practice. These examples might prompt others to look at their own interview transcripts more closely, for just this kind of detail. In some instances, close analysis reveals that practices deemed to be problematic actually elicit the kind of rich description that is sought from qualitative interviews. The excerpts that follow illustrate the following kinds of interactions:

- asking multiple questions: the 'think-aloud' question;
- including possible responses in questions;
- providing insufficient guidance for interviewees to answer questions;
- following up on unanticipated answers;
- clarifying participants' statements; and
- asking questions that include assumptions concerning participants' life worlds.

Asking Multiple Questions: The 'Think-aloud' Question

I use the term 'think aloud' question to indicate extended question sequences that include repeated and/or reformulated questions posed by the interviewer. These multiple questions often include possible responses, and are frequently replete with repairs, pauses, and restarts. If the interviewer fails to pause to allow the interviewee time to respond, he or she may re-state the question, emphasizing a different or new issue. In response to a think aloud question, the interviewee is called upon to consider multiple questions. In the excerpt below, we see an example of this in which an interviewee skillfully responds to all of the interviewer's questions. The complexity of her responses is highlighted through close line-by-line analysis.

Excerpt 7.1 (see Appendix 3 for full excerpt) is drawn from an interview conducted by a novice interviewer for a phenomenological study of teachers' anger (Liljestrom et al., 2007). The initial guiding question was, 'Think of a specific time when you've experienced anger in a school or classroom setting, and tell me about it.' The interviewee described a lengthy and complex incident in which two sixth grade students were involved. One of the students had thrown the other's book bag away, and after repeatedly asking the perpetrator to pick it up, the teacher confronted the offending student, who justified his position by blaming the other student. In this narrative, the teacher described grabbing the student by the arm. When he pulled away from her, the teacher's long fingernail scratched his arm, and subsequently the student pushed the teacher. The incident escalated to involve the principal, a police investigation, and the students' parents. Excerpt 7.1 occurs after the interviewee's lengthy elaboration of the incident.

At line 1 in Excerpt 7.1.1, the interviewer signals the 'final question' in relation to this narrative, beginning his question with 'do you think?' (line 2). (See Appendix 1 for transcription conventions.)

Excerpt 7.1.1 (2002[1])

1. IR OK (.) and so I guess the last question about this one would be (.) um (.)
2.   do you think (.) I mean 'cos it sounds like a lot of (.) because it could
3.   have been a lot worse=

Rather than complete the question, the interviewer restarts his utterance (lines 2–3), finally formulating an assessment of the prior narrative: 'because it could have been a lot worse.' This utterance, in fact, tends to downgrade the seriousness of the preceding narrative. At line 5, the interviewer finally presents a probing question, which also functions as a formulation of prior talk. With the inclusion of 'but was it?' at the end of this utterance, a closed question is posed (line 6).

Excerpt 7.1.2

5. IR =[from what you're saying (.) and so it sounds like a lot of (.) the anger
6.   you felt was:: maybe not (.) ↑totally apparent to other people but was it↑

At this point, however, the interviewer does not allow time for the interviewee to respond, but immediately poses a reformulated question (lines 7–10) that expands on the intent of the question posed at line 6.

---

[1]The interviewer provided consent for the researchers to use the data to examine how novice researchers develop interview skills.

Excerpt 7.1.3

```
 7. IR  I mean did other people who maybe the other students who saw the
 8.      incident or (.) other (.) the principal or whatever who heard the story
 9.      do you think that they knew like the extent or the ↑level of anger
10.      you were ↑at at that point? or was it something that you felt inside
11.      that maybe (.) didn't really show itself
```

Following this sequence, the interviewer again does not allow time for the interviewee to respond, and follows with a third question at lines 10–11. With no immediate response from the interviewee, the interviewer poses a fourth question.

Excerpt 7.1.4

```
12. IR  I mean do you think it'd be apparent to everyone that you were
13.      really angry at that moment
```

In this sequence, the interviewer has posed multiple questions that emphasize different topics. In summary, four interrelated questions have been asked:

- Q1 concerns whether the teacher's *anger* was *apparent* to others;
- Q2 seeks to find out how aware others were of the *extent* or *level* of the interviewee's anger;
- Q3 concerns whether the interviewee *experienced the anger inside* or whether her *anger was expressed outwardly*;
- Q4 combines the ideas presented in Q1 and Q2 – was it *apparent* to others at the time that the interviewee was *very angry*?

At line 15, the interviewee begins her response with the interviewer's final words 'at that moment.' These words fix the subsequent description within the classroom setting at the time of the initial incident (rather than in other settings described in which the event was recounted to teachers or the principal).

Excerpt 7.1.5

```
15. IE  at ↑that moment I think (.) my students probably knew (.) you know (.)
16.      "O::::h shit" [you know it hit the FA::::N [you know what I'm ↑saying=
17. IR            [mm hm                  [HEH HEH HEH HEY
18. IE  =HEH HEH HEH HEH it's ↑really ↓bad=
```

In this response, the interviewee agrees that her students would have recognized her anger – emphasizing the words, 'O::::h shit' you know it hit the FA::::N.' In effect, this utterance responds to both Q1 and Q4 – yes, her anger was apparent to her students, and with the addition of 'it's really bad' at line 18, Q2 concerning the extent of her anger is answered. The interviewee initially understates the visibility of her anger to her students by describing it as: 'I think (.) my students probably knew' (line 15), but her laughter, with the addition of 'it's really bad,' demonstrates the irony of the description.

Excerpt 7.1.6

20.   IE =but no::: I don't (.) ((clears throat)) I think the teachers knew (.) how-
21.   they knew I was <u>mad</u> (.) but <u>not</u> from that situation because by the
22.   time I went to the principal=

In the next line, the interviewee's 'but no I don't' appears at first ambiguous. Which of the interviewer's questions is the interviewee responding to? Could the utterance at lines 20–22 mean, 'Yes, other teachers knew she was angry after the fact' but 'No, her anger was not visible to other teachers'? This interpretation seems to be supported by lines 25–34, in which the interviewee claims to have gone back to her classroom and 'Gained her professionalism back' – the anger she had experienced did not become known to other teachers until she had told them about the event later.

The sequence of responses to the interviewer's questions may be summarized as follows: the interviewee's students were aware she was angry (Q1), that she was *very* angry (Q2), since her anger was expressed outwardly (Q3) in the classroom. Other teachers were not aware of the interviewee's anger since she did not express it outside the classroom (Q3), but became aware of it when she chose to tell them about the incident later (Q1 and Q4). This participant's responses provided a portrayal indicating that she was 'in control' of expressing her anger, and could and did behave professionally. The interviewee emphasized her professional abilities as a teacher, describing in detail how she was fully responsible for the incident, and that she had learned from it and would never repeat this error.

What might be learned about the interviewee's experiences from this interviewer's 'think aloud question'? With closer inspection, the talk generated from the interviewer's probes provided considerable detail concerning the interviewee's account. The inclusion of multiple questions and possible responses by the interviewer has implications for data analysis, however. For example, the interviewee's responses need to be considered carefully to show how she responded to each one of the interviewer's questions, and how there are both 'yes' and 'no' responses to the multiple questions. Since there is some ambiguity in responses, without close analysis, it is difficult to discern which question the interviewee was responding to. This analysis shows how the parties to this interaction artfully arranged their talk on a turn-by-turn basis, with the interviewee deftly responding to each of the interviewer's questions, providing a complex, yet precise account of her experiences. Without viewing this interview data as a sequence of talk involving both interviewer and interviewee, it is difficult, however, to discern a precise understanding of the responses to the interviewer's questions.

If interviewers examine the questions they pose in detail as considered here, they might also consider other possible ways of following up on participants' accounts. Useful starters for follow-up questions include:

- Earlier you talked about _____, tell me more about _____.
- In your description, you used the word _____, what do you mean by that?
- You mentioned _____, describe an example of that.

These are just a few of the possible ways that follow up questions can be asked. The common element to these questions is that they (1) use the participant's terms, and (2) are posed as open questions.

Including Possible Responses in the Questions

Even short questions may include possible responses in their formulation, as in Excerpt 7.2 below. These kinds of questions are explicit in offering possible ways for interviewees to take up the topic.

Excerpt 7.2 (May 2004)[2]

1. IR so the people that you've uh that you interface with that you talk wi::th
2.   what kind of feedback do you get from the::m let's say some good
3.   feedback you get and maybe even some bad feedback that you get
4. IE we get very little bad feedback=
5. IR =OK=
6. IE =so far um or I personally have gotten very little bad um people always
7.   enjoy (.) the hospitality of the [Conference] Center=
8. IR =OK=
9. IE =all I get that comment quite often

Excerpt 7.2 is taken from an interview by a student from a qualitative study undertaken for a local conference center to gain feedback on services offered. Students conducted individual interviews with unknown people using a semi-structured interview guide (Roulston et al., 2008).

In the excerpt above, the question posed at lines 1–3 by the interviewer was not on the interview guide. Initially begun as 'What kind of feedback do you get from them?' the interviewer extended the question by suggesting possible ways for the interviewee to respond ('good' and 'bad' feedback.) At line 4, the interviewee first orients to the second part of the question as posed – that is the negative response, 'I personally have gotten very little bad.' She then orients to the 'good' – affirming that 'people always enjoy the hospitality' of the conference center. This is a precise response to the interviewer's question: 'What kind of feedback do you get', in that the interviewee indicates that this is the kind of comment that she receives 'quite often.'

What kind of reply was generated by this interviewer's question? In this particular interview, the interviewee provided a minimal response, with little specific detail about what was 'good' or 'bad.' In her response, however, the interviewee concisely responds to each element of the interviewer's question. The question posed by the interviewer was not drawn from either the interviewee's prior

---

[2]Excerpts 7.2 and 7.3 are drawn from interviews conducted as part of an authentic class project. The interviewer provided consent to use these as illustrations in this text.

talk – as frequently recommended in methods texts – or the interview guide. Further talk could have been possibly generated at this point in the interview by formulating a question using words from the interviewee's prior talk ('You mentioned _____, could you give me a specific example of that?'). This, of course, assumes that further description is 'better.' If the object of qualitative interviews is to generate 'rich descriptions,' then it is useful for interviewers to learn skills that generate these kinds of responses. If the object is to gain 'answers' to 'questions,' then perhaps a more economical means might be used to gain data (e.g. a written or spoken survey).

Alternatively, the interviewer could have returned to the interview guide for assistance. For interviewers who find it difficult to generate extended descriptive accounts in qualitative interviews – studying the ways questions are formulated, and how interviewees respond to different kinds of questions posed may provide insight into how the interviewer's questions generated particular types of interaction.

Yet, even though much of the literature on qualitative interviews suggests that interviewers should refrain from providing possible responses in the questions, and proposes that researchers ask one question at a time, Excerpt 7.3 below shows an intriguing example. Here, the interviewer poses a series of questions concerning room arrangement, asking the interviewee to compare the room in which they are sitting to those of the conference rooms.

Excerpt 7.3 (May 2004)

```
 1. IR  what about the setup of the of the rooms what type of a setup do do you
 2.         generally use or you do you have different types of formats that they run
 3.         say like a conference style we're sitting at in this room or is it classroom
 4.         seats or=
 5. IE  =no actually kind of like theater-style=
 6. IR  =OK=
 7. IE  =that's the way that [the conference] hall is set up permanently=
 8. IR  =OK=
 9. IE  =is theatre style and then um there is a stage at at the front and (.) um our
10.        symposia is really composed ↑mostly of roundtable discussions
11.        and so there is a group of people seated on stage (.) and a moderator
12.        behind a podium there's usually I think six (.) five or six people seated on
13.        stage and the [conference] center setup for that which is the one
14.        we've always used is very very elegant the chairs are not like this
15.        and they're not straight chairs they're they're very nicely appointed
16.        furniture=
17. IR  =mm hm=
18. IE  =and there are tables in between the chairs with flowers um (.) uh
19.        water pitchers (.) and the um (.) the participants in the roundtable are
20.        always miked (.) and the audiovisual people at the [conference] center
21.        are ↑excellent when it comes to that um (.) I don't be- we hardly ever
22.        have any communications type electronic type glitches when it comes to
23.        the sound's always really good and they make people very comfortable
24.        when they have to be clipping on a little microphone (.) so that always
25.        goes off without a hitch
```

In Excerpt 7.3, the interviewer poses two different questions:

- Q1 What type of a setup do you generally use?
- Q2 Do you have different types of formats that they run say like a conference style we're sitting at in this room or is it classroom seats or

In response to the interviewer's questions, the interviewee rejects the options offered in the second question, and responds to the first question, elaborating in great detail on every aspect of the arrangement of the conference setting described. The interviewee's response involves both a description of what 'theater style' entails; and also the conference center staff's work in arranging that, including set-up of the stage; comfort of furniture; decorations; provision of water for tables; audio-visual arrangements and sound requirements; as well as the conference center staff's ease of working with VIPs involved in the event. In effect, this participant provides a strong endorsement for the quality of the services and facilities offered by the conference center even though the interviewer had not sought an evaluative response at this point in the interview.

In Excerpt 7.3, the interviewer's questions have generated a detailed and spontaneous description from the interviewee that responds to the questions concerning room arrangement, as well as what 'always' happens in interviewee's conference planning. This excerpt is particularly useful in showing how talk routinely follows unanticipated paths. While I – along with other writers on interviewing – have proposed to students that 'multiple questions' and questions configured with possible responses in them may be in some ways 'problematic' and are to be avoided, an investigation of Excerpt 7.3 shows otherwise. Puchta and Potter (2004) in their analysis of the work of focus group moderators have shown that the use of a similar device, what they term 'elaborate questions,' may be used as a way to secure participation of group members as new topics are introduced.

From a neo-positivist conception of interviewing, questions that include possible responses are thought to 'lead' the interviewee towards possible responses, thus 'biasing' the data. From a romantic conception of interviewing, again, these kinds of questions provide possible paths for participants to follow in responding to interviewers, and are therefore seen to prevent participants from formulating narrative responses in their own terms. In Excerpt 7.3, a close examination of the participant's response shows that the participant selects the terms with which to formulate her answer, and rejects the options offered by the interviewer. Again, what occurs in this excerpt cannot be extrapolated to make claims about the routine ways in which qualitative interviews are accomplished. Yet this instance shows a possible way in which interview talk might unfold in a way that does not quite align with the prescriptions offered by methodological literature. This excerpt, then, offers a cautionary tale about following prescriptions – guidelines should be taken as just that, guides to practice that must be applied in nuanced ways in specific research contexts given that each and every interview may unfold in unique ways.

Providing Insufficient Guidance for Interviewees to Answer Questions

In Excerpt 7.4, taken from an in-class practice interview of a class mate by a graduate student (Roulston et al., 2003), an interviewee's attempts to clarify the purpose of an interview question are seen to generate difficulties for the interviewer. Below, a non-specific question from the interviewer generated multiple attempts from the interviewee to find an appropriate topic to talk about.

Excerpt 7.4: (May 2001)[3]

```
 1.  IR   so um yeah tell me more about your teaching experiences just within
 2.       the classroom like instruction in the classroom
 3.  IE   OK um (.) do you are you looking at do you want me to talk about
 4.       what I ↑did in the classroom or my experiences of ↑kids in the
 5.       ↑classroom or what would you like me to
 6.  IR   yeah um (.) uh OK
 7.       (4.0)
 8.  IR   uh tell me what you believe about learning
 9.  IE   mmm
10.       (4.0)
11.  IE   in terms of (2.0) the nature of learning? or [in terms of what I want
12.  IR                                               [yes in terms of nature of
13.       learning and how you (.) use this um (.) your belief or employ your
14.       belief into classroom instruction
15.  IE   °OK°
16.       (2.0)
17.  IE   um (3.0) in terms of (4.0) learning theory although I must admit
18.       I desperately need a refresher course on learning theory
19.  IR   mm hm
20.       (4.0)
21.  IE   I (2.0) I see (2.0) um (2.0) I think that the human brain (.) is capable of
22.       different levels of thought and that those structures develop over time
23.       as kids age (.) and that they go from a sensory motor stage through
24.       a concrete operation to a formal operations stage now (.) how did I get
25.       here
26.  IR   how do yourself learn? how do you yourself learn?
```

It is not until lines 12–14 that a topic of talk is clarified. After several questions from the interviewee, the interviewer's initial topic ('teaching experiences') has transformed into a quite different one: 'beliefs about the nature of learning and how it was used in classroom instruction.' After an aborted attempt to respond to this question (lines 17–25), the interviewee comes to a halt, with 'how did I get here.' At this point, the interviewer offers a new topic for discussion: the interviewee's own learning style.

---

[3]Excerpt 7.4 is drawn from an interview in which the students involved provided informed consent to participate in a study examining how novice interviewers develop interview skills.

Excerpt 7.4 shows how an interviewee's responses to this interviewer's question resulted in multiple re-castings of the original question by the interviewer. Following a search for a topic that this interviewee would be willing to talk about, the interviewer eventually suggested a new topic – given that the interviewee in this case had not addressed the interviewer's prior questions in any detail. This sequence of interview interaction shows that simply asking questions of interviewees may not necessarily generate meaningful answers. The problem posed for interviewers, then, is to formulate questions that interviewees are willing and able to respond to in terms that are mutually understood. It is undoubtedly the case that had the interviewer in this instance asked the question posed at lines 1–2 to another person, the interaction would have unfolded differently, and may not have proven to have been problematic as on this occasion. Examining interactions such as this, however, will help interviewers consider the kinds of questions they pose, how participants orient to them, and will provide information about the kinds of questions that participants routinely have problems with, and which may need to be reformulated in future interviews.

Following Up on Unanticipated Responses

As carefully as researchers might formulate their questions prior to conducting open-ended interviews, participants often take them up in ways that the interviewer does not anticipate. Interviewers are then faced with the problem of what to say next. For inexperienced Interviewers, this can be a daunting task – however, by listening carefully, taking up what participants have said already to formulate follow-up questions, and considering whether they have sufficient information to make sense of what participants have said before beginning new topics, they will be able to develop the skills to deal with interviews that do not unfold in routine or expected ways. For example, in the first round of interviews for a qualitative evaluation study, I began each of the semi-structured interviews with an open-ended invitation to interviewees to talk about key concepts involved in the training program, which was the topic of study. For the study I interviewed physicians in a family medicine residency. The first question on the interview guide was aimed to elicit these physicians' understandings of mind body interventions – a central topic of the training program on mind body interventions and spirituality (MB/S) in patient care in which they were involved as part of their residency program. I had posed the question on the interview guide as follows:

What do you think of when you hear the term 'mind-body' interventions?

I had thought very carefully about both how to introduce the interviews to participants I was meeting for the first time, as well as the wording of each question. My purpose in beginning with this question was to provide wide latitude for how the physicians might respond in their own terms to the central concept encompassed by the training program – that of MB interventions. In response to this question, residents provided a range of descriptions that focused on different aspects of MB medicine. For example, some of those interviewed began their responses by naming specific types of interventions, while others focused on particular illnesses and conditions that might be treated with MB interventions. Irrespective of whether residents were in their first, second, or third year, or whether they expressed positive or negative views of the training program, residents interviewed routinely described an understanding of MB interventions that focused on at least one of the following topics: types of MB interventions; illnesses and conditions that might be treated by MB interventions; the connections between patients' thoughts and beliefs (mind) and physical symptoms (body) in healing; holistic treatment of patients in which physicians take into account both the mind and the body; and the role of spirituality in healing.

Excerpt 7.5.1 below shows how one interviewee oriented to this question in a way that was unique among the 24 participants who participated in interviews during the first round of data generation for this study. Rather than begin his response with an understanding of MB interventions that included an orientation to any of the topics listed above, this interviewee began by providing a negative evaluation of mind body medicine (MBM), together with a rationale for why he saw it as an ineffective approach to patient care. In effect, this interviewee oriented to my opening statement introducing the interview at lines 1–3, in which I say that I am 'really interested to learn about your perceptions and opinions about this new training grant that they have here.'

Excerpt 7.5.1 (October 2007)

```
 1.  IR   u::::m so thank- thank you for ↑coming and uh I'm just really interested
 2.        to learn about your perceptions and opinions about this new training
 3.        grant that they have here and what's plan- what they're planning
 4.        to do here at the residency program .hhh um there's quite a bit of
 5.        uh specific terms um mentioned in the grant and I'm just gonna start
 6.        by asking you uh what you think of when you hear these various
 7.        terms and the first one is what do you think of when you hear the
 8.        term mind body interventions
 9.  IE   we:ll (.) I really (.) just doing that because I had to I I I really don't like
10.        this=
11.  IR   =uh huh=
12.  IE   =this part of the medicine I think there is no way we can apply that
13.        when we just have fifteen minutes to see a patient=
14.  IR   =uh huh=
15.  IE   =with hypertension it's like OK I have the patient with five different
16.        problems ↑and he has some (.) other (.) issues so how can I use that
17.        knowledge to:: (.) to help the patient I can't I can't see a way to do
18.        that=
19.  IR   =uh huh=
20.  IE   =and so far I don't think the classes we have the conferences will
21.        help us with that uh=
22.  IR   =uh huh=
23.  IE   =yeah=
```

In this sequence of talk, my utterances as an interviewer demonstrate close, yet non-committal monitoring of talk through use of the continuer 'uh huh.' In lines 20–21, the interviewee concludes his response with a summation of his opinion of the training program, effectively concluding his response to both my first question, and the purpose of the interview as a whole. In this sequence of interaction, the interviewee may be seen to have responded to my opening statements and the initial question in a way that did not elicit descriptions demonstrating how and what he understood MB interventions to be – as occurred in each of the other interviews. In having evaluated both the value of MB medicine and the merit of the training program in his opening utterances, and signaling his resistance to a program that he saw as mandatory, this interviewee had already answered or invalidated many of the questions included on the interview guide before I had asked them.

As an interviewer, at this early point in the interview I was faced with a problem – how could I elicit further descriptions from this participant given that he had responded to the overall purpose of the interview so concisely in several utterances? Given that he had begun by providing an opinion of the training program without specific prompting, how could I reorient the interview to a discussion of the basic terms and concepts as I had hoped for in posing the opening question?

In lines 24–27, I formulated prior talk ('given your assessment that you don't see it as being useful') and asked him to specify his reasoning further. Both my formulation and the way in which the follow-up question is posed may be seen to invite the interviewee to expand on what he has said without siding with his view. While in some senses, this may be taken as being 'impartial' as an interviewer, in fact, by reframing his complaints about the training program ('I really (.) just doing that because I had to'; 'I really don't like this'; 'there is no way we can apply that') as 'you don't see it as being useful'; I have avoided taking up the issues he has raised at this point concerning 'required participation'; and 'learning something that is not practical or useful' – postponing discussion of these complaints to a later point in the interview.

Excerpt 7.5.2 (October 2007)

```
24.  IR   =yeah and so u::m given your assessment that you don't see it as
25.        being useful do you um is this (.) only to do with the the like
26.        the structure of your work in terms of the ti::me you see pat-? or
27.        [<are there other things involved?>
28.  IE   [OK in a different reality          where I would have uh two hours
29.        to see a patient I:: I still don't think I would be interested=
30.  IR   =uh huh=
31.  IE   =in (.) I don't know if it's because I'm not a religious person and
32.        not very spiritual so (.) u::h I really (.) it doesn't (.) I I don't like this=
33.  IR   =uh huh=
34.  IE   =it just just it might be just me but=
35.  IR   =uh huh=
36.  IE   =yeah
```

In this follow up sequence, the interviewee responds to my question concerning 'time spent with patients,' by rejecting this as a reason for the opinion he had provided earlier, taking up the other option I had suggested – 'other things involved' – by wondering aloud if it was because he was not 'a religious person and not very spiritual.' At line 37, I return to the first question, although, in restating it and stressing the word 'mean,' I emphasize that this time I am seeking a definition.

Excerpt 7.5.3 (October 2007)

```
37.  IR   yeah and um what does that mean to you mind-body interventions
38.       (2.0)
39.  IE   mmm:: well I think it it has to be to try and understand the patient
40.       a little bit more? because the patient is (.) it might be someone who
41.       has a spiritual side a::nd how that affects his body like his health
42.       u::h I ↑think it it might work (.) but (.) it's (.) that's not the part of
43.       medicine that I ↓like=
44.  IR   =uh huh=
45.  IE   =so I'm I really (.) I think I can help the ↑patient by using ↑that if I
46.       have the ↑time (.) but I'd rather use other tools and other things to do
47.       what I really (.) like to do
```

In this sequence, the interviewee provides the kind of description I had been hoping to elicit using the first question. Yet the interaction elicited in this sequence as a whole provided useful data for me as interviewer by presenting possible topics to discuss within the interview, as well as giving some insight into the interviewee's reasoning concerning his evaluative statements. 'How' the interviewee has responded to the initial question – by providing his evaluation of the program without prompting from the interviewer – is also analyzable, in that here the interviewee has used the interview context to immediately alert the interviewer to his concerns, and signal the topics that he would like to discuss further in the interview.

Clarifying Participants' Statements

Closed questions are frequently conceptualized as a problem for qualitative interviewers – given that open-ended questions are deemed to elicit the kind of descriptive data that qualitative researchers seek to generate, and closed questions encourage yes/no responses and short answers. Yet, follow-up questions posed in a closed format may be used by interviewers to check their understanding of prior talk. Take, for example, closed questions shown below that I asked of participants in the evaluation study of a training program in MB/S for physicians in a family medicine residency. As mentioned earlier, the purpose of the study was to elicit physicians' perspectives and opinions about a training program in MB/S in which they were involved. The interviews were tightly scheduled, and due to the physicians' schedules, there was little likelihood for the researchers to check their interpretations with interviewees after the interview. In Excerpt 7.6, at lines 1–2, I asked a closed question, which summed up – or 'formulated' – my understanding of talk. Closed questions can lead to yes/no responses, which is how this interviewee began his answer.

Excerpt 7.6 (October 2007)

```
 1.   IR   yeah so u:m (.) am I right in in hearing you that you equate spirituality
 2.         with religious practice?
 3.   IE   (.) yes yes I I I think it's it's y- y- it's it's hard to separate both
 4.         because every time you hear about spirituality it's in the religious
 5.         context↑ like I know that the human being u:::h (.) it it is- it although
 6.         they have like different religions they they it's not (.) really a spiritual
 7.         -tual species (.) I don't know how to say that because it doesn't matter
 8.         where you come from you have it something that you (.) yeah I can't
 9.         differentiate both=
10.   IR   =OK so you don't so you don't differentiate spirituality and religion or
11.         religious practice?=
12.   IE   =no I can't=
13.   IR   =OK=
14.   IE   =I can't understand someone to be spiritual without um believing in a
15.         religion or something=
16.   IR   =uh huh
```

In this sequence, we see the interviewee providing an account for his agreement with the interviewer's formulation of his talk at lines 1–2. Although he agrees with the researcher's formulation that he equates religion with spirituality, the interviewee provides an account for his reasoning for this view (lines 3–9). At lines 10–11, I take up the terms offered by the interviewee to re-state another closed question about the topic being discussed. Here, I use the interviewee's term, 'differentiate,' rather than the term 'equate' used in the opening follow-up question (lines 1–2) – thus a slightly different meaning is conveyed. Again, the interviewee agrees with the formulation that I provide; demonstrating that in this sequence, the interviewer and interviewee have accomplished some degree of intersubjective understanding.

In Excerpt 7.7, I provide a second example of closed questions, which sum up prior talk and call upon the interviewee to assess the accuracy of the interviewer's understanding of what has been discussed. Again, this excerpt is drawn from the evaluation study of a training program in mind body medicine for residents.

Excerpt 7.7: (October 2007)

```
 1.   IR     OK so would I be correct in um (.) paraphrasing what you said
 2.          is=
 3.   IE     =mm hm=
 4.   IR→   =you haven't seen the concrete pieces?=
 5.   IE     =right like=
 6.   IR→   =the specific how to go about doing this?=
 7.   IE     =yes that would be fair=
```

Here again, I formulated talk via two closed questions (lines 4 and 6) to which the participant is asked to respond. In both of the preceding excerpts, the closed questions are specifically marked as formulations of prior talk, and I have sought an assessment from participants as to the accuracy of these formulations. In Excerpt 7.7, rather then provide an account that explicates the participant's understanding of the topic further (as seen in Excerpt 7.6), the interviewee confirms my understanding of his talk.

Although the use of closed questions in open-ended interviews is unlikely to generate the detailed descriptions sought by many qualitative researchers, these excerpts show that they may be valuable resources in instances in which researchers want to accomplish on-site member checking of their understanding of topics discussed. Kvale (1996: 145) suggests that one criteria for 'quality' of interviews is that interviewers check their understandings of talk throughout the interview, and goes so far as to suggest that leading questions are well-suited to 'check repeatedly the reliability of interviewees' answers, as well as to verify the interviewers' interpretations.' In these examples, closed questions were posed purposefully as formulations of prior talk in order to assess the interviewer's understanding of prior interaction in a similar way to that suggested by Kvale. Rather than suggest that these kinds of questions be used in any kind of qualitative interview, researchers might evaluate their use of such a resource in order to use it in a context-sensitive way that will align with their theoretical assumptions about interviewing, and the research purpose of interviews conducted.

Questions that Include Assumptions about Participants' Life Worlds

Excerpt 7.8 below shows an example of how interviewees can take up interviewers' invitations for particular kinds of responses in a way that disagrees with the premise of the question. In that interviewees may demonstrate their disagreement with the premise of interviewers' questions, this sequence of talk unfolds in a way that resembles Excerpt 7.3 shown earlier. In essence, focus group participants in Excerpt 7.8 refuse to answer the question posed. In this focus group that I moderated, I formulated prior talk to segue to a question on the focus group guide – that of a discussion of 'drawbacks' of the training program in which participants were involved (see arrowed utterances). Given that this was an evaluation project in which participants of the study were invited to discuss both positive and negative aspects of a program ('benefits' and 'drawbacks'), this kind of question is commonly used by qualitative researchers, and assumes that participants are able to provide descriptions and opinions about both 'positive' and 'negative' features of a particular experience. Of course, such opinion questions might also be posed without assuming a dimension of experience (see Patton, 2002).

Excerpt 7.8 (October 2007)

1. M→   IE 8's mentioned one of the drawbacks- well actually this is a drawback
2.   →   of maybe ↑implementing it is that of clear guidelines that there's a lack
3.   →   of clear guidelines for practice? is that accurate?=
4. IE8   =mm hm=
5. M   =u:m do you see any drawbacks for u:m this kind of intervention program
6.   being in a residential um residence family residence program (.) training
7.   program?
8. IE8   well I think if we don't try that in a residency then who else is going to

```
9.          try=
10.  M      =uh huh uh huh=
11.  IE8    =so (      ) people are still open for learning=
12.  M      =uh huh=
13.  IE8    =and the patient maybe (helped) come to the expectancy of trying
14.          something new so I think both the investigator and the patient would
15.          be more open to give it a try=
16.  M      =uh huh (.) so any other perspectives on that one? so drawbacks for
17.          actually learning about it?
18.          (2.0)
19.  IE?    mm hm I think it's excellent=
20.  IE?    =yeah I think it's a great opportunity=
21.  M      =uh huh
```

At line 4, interviewee 8 provides assent to the moderator's restatement of his prior talk as 'lack of clear guidelines' for practice. However interviewee 8's response to the next question, in addition to two other group members' responses (lines 8–15, 19–20), indicates that these participants' responses do not align with the basic premise of the question – that participants might have something to say about *both* 'positive' and 'negative' features of the program. Interviewee 8, in lines 8–15, sets the record straight in a way that diverges with my formulation of prior talk as aligning with 'drawbacks.' In lines 19–20, two other participants of the group provide strong endorsement for the view expressed in lines 8–15 by interviewee 8, that there are no drawbacks to the inclusion of the training program in the residency.

This raises the question of whether interviewers should ask questions with prior assumptions embedded in them. In the example provided in Excerpt 7.8, three participants of this group provided positive evaluations in response to a question seeking any negative views (or 'drawbacks'). The data generated are valuable in that it indicates that by disagreeing with the very premise of the question, their positive evaluations may be seen to be even more strongly articulated, than if they had simply responded to the question concerning 'benefits' of the program. Rather than discard such questions from interview protocols altogether, when participants refuse to answer questions (as in Excerpt 7.8), it is useful for researchers to consider what the question was to which they responded. In this case, the question they appear to have responded to is not 'what are the drawbacks of the program?'; but 'what is your opinion of the MB/S training program at the family residency?' Responses such as these, then, might be used to inform the construction of questions for future interviews. That is, for this particular study, in succeeding rounds of data generation, I might purposefully elicit descriptions of the positive facets of the program that are referred to in this sequence by this group of participants.

From a neo-positivist perspective of interviewing, asking questions that include assumptions about participants' life worlds is problematic, because it fails to situate the interviewer as neutral and objective. From a romantic perspective of interviewing, asking these kinds of questions might also be seen as problematic, albeit for different reasons. In providing a priori assumptions to which participants respond, rather than providing interviewees opportunities to set the agenda for talk within the interview, interviewers fail to build rapport with participants through sharing their own experience, and may subsequently instigate disagreement with participants. If the interview is seen from a constructionist perspective, though, these kinds of disagreements are also data to be analyzed. Kvale's advice (2006: 158) that these kinds of leading questions might be used to check the interviewer's understandings of prior talk might well apply. The usefulness of data generated by these kinds of questions, however, is heavily dependent on the researcher's recognition of the ways in which participants disagree with interviewers in both subtle and overt ways.

Other Issues that Might Be Examined

In this chapter I have provided some demonstrations of how one might analyze excerpts from transcripts using methods drawn from conversation analysis. These methodological analyses demonstrate that problematic question formulations as outlined in methodological literature may not actually emerge as problematic under close inspection. The excerpts provided in this chapter represent a minute fragment of the possible interactions that can occur in qualitative interviews, however. By examining closely the conversational resources used by speakers in the generation of research data, individual researchers can account for their part in the construction of research data, and also show how participants of research interviews artfully construct their accounts in response to interviewers' questions.

Such analyses can prompt a number of methodological questions concerning interview research, including:

- What kinds of *actions* are accomplished by speakers? For example, did the interview questions generate particular kinds of conversational sequences (e.g. justifications; excuses, accusations, complaints, praise and so forth)? What might be made of that?
- What kinds of interactional problems were evident in the interview, and how were these produced and managed by speakers?
- Are research interviews the best possible means of generating data to inform one's research questions? Should other methods of data generation be considered (e.g. field notes of observations, naturally occurring data, survey data, documentary data and so forth)?
- What kinds of interactions are facilitated in group talk? Do these serve the purposes of generating talk relevant to the research topic?

Conclusion

Researchers are usually in the business of studying others' talk. Study of one's own interview talk, however, can lead to a mindful consideration of one's role in the generation of data for the study of research questions in the social sciences; in short, a reflective interview practice. Harvey Sacks' (1992, Vol. 2, p. 5) observation that conversational sequences cannot be predicted very far is insightful. While the advice literature in qualitative interviewing advocates certain kinds of 'best' practices that interviewers should follow, there is no way of knowing what will happen in any given interview. 'Good' questioning practices at times do not generate rich, descriptive data. Yet, some participants respond to 'poor' questioning practices in perceptive ways. The aim of analyzing transcripts for reflective purposes is not to illuminate a set of prescriptive rules for others to follow, but for each one of us to mindfully consider our actions and interactions with others.

In Chapter 8, I review a range of possible approaches that might be used to analyze and represent findings from qualitative interviews.

Further Reading

Roulston, K. (2000) 'The management of "safe" and "unsafe" complaint sequences in research interviews', *Text,* 20 (3): 1–39.

Roulston, K., Baker, C. and Liljestrom, A. (2001) 'Analyzing the interviewer's work in the generation of research data: The case of complaints', *Qualitative Inquiry,* 7 (6): 745–72.

Activity 7.1   An exercise in analyzing interview interaction

Transcribe 3–5 minutes of talk from an interview that you have conducted using Jeffersonian transcription conventions (see Appendix 1). Select a segment of interview interaction in which you are talking. For example, you may be summing up what your participant has said, or asking questions. Use the questions below as a guide to thinking further about interview interaction. Appendix 2 provides a glossary of terms used in conversation analysis that will assist in examinations of transcriptions.

Question–answer sequences

- Did the interviewer pose a single question? If not, what other questions did the interviewer ask? Which question did the interviewee respond to? In what order? What might be made of that?
- Did the question posed by the interviewer function as another type of conversational resource? For example, was it also an assessment, or a formulation? If a question also functioned as formulation of prior talk, what ideas were retained? What was deleted? What was transformed?
- Did the interviewer include possible responses in the question? If so, did the interviewee take these up in their response? If not, what happened next?

Answering Questions

- Did the interviewee answer the question at the first possible opportunity?
- Did the interviewee answer this question, or use their turn to initiate a different topic?
- Did the interviewee answer the question with another question?
- Was that question aimed at clarifying the meaning of the previous question?
- If not, how did it relate to the prior utterance?

(Continued)

(Continued)

- What happened next?
- Did the interviewee pause prior to responding? What did the interviewer do next?

Repair

- Were there stumbles, slips, or repairs in the interviewee's response? What might be made of that?
- What about the interviewer's talk – were there stumbles, slips, or repairs? What might be made of that?
- If repair is evident in the transcription, did the interviewer and interviewee successfully demonstrate an understanding of one another's utterances? How was this achieved? If not, what happened next?

Assessments

- Did the interviewer provide assessments of the interviewee's responses? What happened next?

Turn-taking

- How is turn-taking accomplished?
- Does the interviewer always allocate the next turn, or does the interviewee self-nominate?
- How does the interviewer generate the next interview question?
- Was this an interruption; or a transition-relevant place? What happened next?
- Were there any interruptions or overlaps in the Q-A sequence?

Actions in Interviews

- Did the interviewee use extreme case formulations (ECFs) in his or her answers?
- What conversational work did these ECFs accomplish (e.g. complaining, praising, making a case)?
- What are other actions observable in interaction (e.g. excuses, justifications)?

Activity 7.2   Reflecting on interview interaction

Write a reflective statement that focuses on the following issues:

- What does this kind of transcription reveal that is not apparent in your earlier transcription of this interview talk?
- What do you notice about your contribution to the interview interaction?
- Describe the features of the question–answer sequences that you have transcribed.
- How did the participant respond to your utterances and/or silences?
- What have you learned from this exercise about your interaction in the research interview?
- How does this analysis of your interview practice inform you methodologically?

EIGHT

Analyzing and Representing Interview Data

This chapter introduces:

- *Inductive, deductive* and *abductive* reasoning in data analysis.
- Multiple approaches to data analysis and representation, including: *grounded theory, ethnographic* analysis, *narrative* analysis, *phenomenological* analysis, *ethnomethodological* analysis and *conversation* analysis.
- Resources for *deconstructive* approaches to analysis and arts-based approaches to representation.

In this chapter I provide an overview of different approaches to the analysis of interview data. There are many approaches to the analysis of qualitative interview data, and this is reflected in a variety of texts that provide overviews of differing approaches to qualitative data analysis, as well as guidelines for specific approaches to the analysis of qualitative data. Among others, these include grounded theory, ethnographic analysis, narrative analysis, phenomenological analysis, ethnomethodological analysis and conversation analysis, application of Foucauldian theory and poststructural approaches to analysis; as well as alternative approaches to representation of data, including arts-based research and performative inquiry.

It is beyond the scope of the present chapter to provide in-depth reviews of how to analyze qualitative interview data using all of these approaches. Rather, I introduce readers to various families of approaches, including thematic analysis, grounded theory analysis, ethnographic analysis, phenomenological analysis, narrative analysis, and ethnomethodological analysis. I conclude the chapter with brief introductions to further resources for applying poststructural and postmodern lenses to the analysis of data, and the use of creative analytic practices and arts-based approaches to representation.

Qualitative Data Analysis and Reasoning

One way of thinking about qualitative data analysis involves considering the kind of reasoning practice involved: that is, 'inductive,' 'deductive,' and 'abductive' reasoning.

Researchers may analyze interview data using any of these approaches. Inductive analysis is based on the assumption that inferences can be developed by examining empirical data for patterns. Thus, by closely examining qualitative data in the form of documents, field notes, or interview transcripts, the researcher locates patterns and commonalities that contribute to the generation of theory. Inductive reasoning can take into account topics that have been initiated by participants, rather than being driven solely by testing the researcher's questions and hypotheses.

Deductive reasoning involves confirming or falsifying predictive statements about the relationships between variables. When applied to interview data, one approach would be for researchers to use pre-conceptualized codes to reduce the data, and then test whether proposed hypotheses are supported or disconfirmed by the findings from analysis. Thomas Schwandt (2001: 125) points out that qualitative analysis typically involves both inductive and deductive reasoning, given that researchers generate findings through close examinations of data in combination with applications of substantive theories from prior research to inform and develop their analyses.

Whereas inductive reasoning is usually associated with qualitative research, and deductive reasoning with quantitative methods, abductive reasoning is one approach that has been discussed by grounded theorists. Kathy Charmaz (2006: 104) explains that abductive inference involves the researcher considering multiple theoretical explanations for a phenomenon that occurs in the data. The researcher then formulates hypotheses for each possible explanation, and then systematically checks each of these by examining the data, in order to locate the 'most plausible explanation.' Charmaz claims that abductive reasoning may be used by grounded theorists to 'account for surprises, anomalies, or puzzles in the collected data,' and 'invokes imaginative interpretations' through the researcher's formulation of possible accounts (2008: 157).

In this chapter I will focus on inductive or 'bottom-up' approaches to data analysis, given that qualitative researchers seek to generate interpretations from close examinations of data, rather than through analysis of data that has been reduced to numerical form in order to test prior hypotheses about relationships among variables. Readers wanting to learn more about abductive reasoning will find explanations in Charmaz (2006, 2008), and Amanda Coffey and Paul Atkinson (1996).

Thematic Analysis

Of all approaches to the analysis of qualitative data, perhaps one of the most commonly used is that of thematic analysis, given that 'themes' can be generated in a variety of ways. This approach generally entails some form of *data reduction*, through applying codes to the data (for example, as described in grounded theory analysis) or elimination of repetitive or irrelevant data (for example, as described in phenomenological reduction) in order to define conceptual categories; *categorization of data*, through sorting and classification of the codes or data into thematic groupings or clusters, and then finally, *reorganization of the data into thematic representations* of findings through a series of assertions and interpretations. These themes are supported by evidence from the data set in the form of excerpts from interviews that link the researcher's assertions to what was said by speakers in interview contexts. Given that thematic findings may be generated from any number of analytic approaches, I first discuss 'coding' as one method to reduce data.

Coding

'Codes' are labels that researchers apply to sections of data – whether interview transcripts, documents, or field notes – that represent some aspect of the data. Applied to interview data, codes might refer to the topics of talk developed by interviewer and interviewee, as well as how the talk has been produced (for example, stories, complaints, and so forth). Excerpt 8.1 shows some preliminary codes applied to a transcript of an interview with a parent in a study of young children's music preferences (Roulston, 2006b). This excerpt shows a mixture of codes derived directly from words and phrases uttered by the participant (known as 'in-vivo' codes), as well as codes relating to the research questions posed.

Excerpt 8.1 (26 September 2002)

IR: Interviewer

IE: Interviewee (parent, talking about three-year old daughter Angela's music preferences)

IR:	Yeah, I just thought maybe we'll start with, if you can tell me a bit about the kinds of music that she listens to?	Types of music that child listens to
IE:	OK, she's kind of funny. She is a real rock and roll kid I guess. Ever since she was a baby, well when she was a baby the first thing that she really showed an interest in was *Raffi*. We had this one tape I remember. We were driving to Florida for Thanksgiving, so I guess she was eight, ten months old, nine months old. She would be crying and crying, crying, and the only thing that would make her stop crying would be to put in this tape. So we had to listen to *Raffi* over and over and over for the whole eight-hour trip.	Rock and roll Response to music as baby Raffi Car as a place to listen to music Types of music that child listens to
IR:	Wow!	
IE:	So that was kind of her first real putting her foot down about music. Now she is really, she loves *The Beatles*. *The Beatles* have always been a standard and she will find other favorites every one in a while. So right now one of her other favorites are the *B-52s*. And she likes, what gets her interested in is if they sing silly songs and so she'll listen to the silly ones and then listen to the music.	Types of music that child listens to Preference for Beatles Preference for B-52s Silly songs

Analytic codes may also be derived from the researcher's review of literature on the topic, or use schema developed by other researchers. For example, Robert Bogdan and Sari Biklen (2003: 162–8) propose a schema for coding qualitative data that includes paying attention to the following phenomena: setting/context; definition of the situation; perspectives held by the subjects; participants' ways of thinking about people and objects; processes; activities; events; strategies; relationships and social structure; narrative (that is, the structure of the talk); and methods (that is, research procedures). Lofland et al. (2006: chs 6–7) describe another approach that might be used by researchers to focus their analytic questions that combines 'units of social organization' (practices, episodes, encounters, roles, and social types, relationships, groups, organizations, settlements and habitats, and subcultures and lifestyles) with 'substantive aspects' (cognitive, emotional, and hierarchical). According to these authors, there are eight basic questions that might be asked of any combination of units and aspects: these concern frequencies, magnitudes, structures, processes, causes, consequences, and agency. This approach to coding and analysis had been developed from the authors' work as ethnographers, and is one approach to the development of sociological theories.

In selecting codes to label data, analysts are frequently advised to stay close to the data. Indeed, anthropologist Clifford Geertz noted that 'it is not only interpretation that goes all the way down to the most immediate observational level: the theory upon which such interpretation conceptually depends does so also' (1973/2003: 167). Thus, there are various warnings extant to researchers to not force data into pre-formulated coding schemes – in fact, the issue of forcing data to fit codes was central to a dispute between the developers of grounded theory, Anselm Strauss and Barney Glaser (see Kelle, 2005). It is a useful step when beginning coding to write a 'code definition' for the labels applied – this might include the kinds of ideas that are encompassed by the code (that is, inclusion criteria), the exclusion criteria if necessary, and an example of coded text. In this way, the analyst can apply codes in a systematic way while building a 'code dictionary' or 'codebook' that can be used to analyze further transcriptions in a study (Ryan and Bernard, 2000: 781). For example, here are several of the code definitions I used in preliminary analysis of interview data from a study of music teachers' perspectives of gender.

- *Male voice* – includes references to working with the male voice, descriptions of techniques to work with boys' voices, or not knowing how to work with male voice.
- *Mothers and women in children's musical lives* – includes narratives and descriptions of what the teacher has observed in relation to the participation of women in children's musical experience. May include specific narratives about mothers/women with whom the teacher has worked, or the teacher's personal experience.
- *Music education as a gendered profession* – includes descriptions of 'routine' activities involved in music education (e.g. rehearsals, choral festivals, conferences) in which the participant describes the 'gendered' nature of the profession. Data may include descriptions of male teachers, female teachers, and the kinds of activities associated with being male or female in music education.

Although researchers develop different methods of coding data, one strategy is to begin by reading the interview transcriptions and formulate codes by adding notes and labels in the margin of each transcription; meanwhile listing each of the codes applied and definitions in a separate file. There are many computer assisted qualitative data analysis software (CAQDAS) packages that assist this process (see Lewins and Silver, 2007); however, I have found it a useful strategy to begin coding on hard copies of transcriptions before applying codes using electronic means of assistance. After preliminary coding of one transcription, the analyst can move to another transcription using the code dictionary as a starting point, and continuing to add new codes. As codes are developed, earlier transcriptions are checked to see if the emerging concepts are present. Through this iterative and recursive process, the analyst can assemble a list of preliminary codes which will be adjusted, collapsed, and revised as necessary throughout the analytic process. Through methodical, thorough and exhaustive coding, researchers reduce a data set to conceptual elements that may then be sorted into 'categories.'

Data Categorization

A 'category' is an abstract concept that analysts use to organize the codes that have been generated through examination of a data set. The process of coding and re-organizing codes into categories is a creative one in which the analyst plays with the data, and tries out different ways of thinking about how the data might be understood. By reading and re-examining the interview data, codes, and categories, researchers can develop their ideas about the data into assertions that are supported by data excerpts. As an example, here is one of the broader categories that I developed from the data from the study on music teachers' perspectives of gender:

Perspectives of 'gender'

Self as gendered professional
Music education as gendered profession
Perspectives of gender
Elementary teaching as gendered
Fathers and men in children's musical lives
Mothers and women in children's musical lives
Classroom practice:

o Girls
o Boys
o Male voice
o School chorus
o Ethnic and cultural differences
o Children's listening practices

In this list, I have grouped the preliminary codes around a single larger issue, in this case 'perspectives of gender', which provided a starting point for writing about the data. I have found it useful to work with other researchers while coding and categorizing data – this stimulates discussion over decisions concerning coding and categorization, and calls on researchers to justify their decisions, and provide evidence to warrant claims made. Although here I have explained 'coding' and 'categorization' as separate steps, they are more likely to be undertaken concurrently, as these processes inform each other.

Thematic Representation

In published research, thematic approaches to data analysis vary in the level of sophistication demonstrated, and range from description to various levels of theory generation. If researchers code to the interview and/or research questions, then themes generated will orient to these questions, and themes are likely to attend to description. For example, findings that would fit this model might include 'participants' perspectives' concerning the 'benefits' or 'limitations' of some program or phenomenon of study. In this case, researchers might take care to account for data that does not fit the researcher's questions by attending to negative or discrepant data. In this way, researchers can ensure that they report on issues initiated by participants that do not necessarily relate to the researcher's agenda, but are nevertheless important in terms of emergent topics.

Educational anthropologist and ethnographer, Harry Wolcott (1994), in his explanation of qualitative data analysis, describes three dimensions that may all be evident in a report to various degrees: description, analysis, and interpretation. Thematic analysis may draw on each of these ways of presenting qualitative data. In description, the analyst's principal aim is to answer the question: 'What is going on here?' by presenting data from the researcher's observations in fieldwork, or information derived from interviews (Wolcott, 1994: 12). Analysis, in Wolcott's view, focuses on identifying the 'essential features and the systematic description of interrelationships among them' (1994: 12) – how things work. Wolcott argues that analysis may by used to inform evaluative questions – such as 'why a system or program is not working, or how it might be made to work "better"' (1994: 12). For Wolcott, interpretation addresses questions of meanings and contexts: 'How does it all mean? What is to be made of it all?' (1994: 12). Wolcott makes a distinction between analysis and interpretation, arguing that in the latter, 'the researcher transcends factual data and cautious analyses and begins to probe into what is to be made of them' (1994: 36). Wolcott's advice for transforming data via description, analysis, and interpretation is useful for those who want to do thematic analyses, and he provides concrete suggestions for approaches that might be used by researchers to represent their descriptions, analyses, and interpretations of data in reports. His extensive publications also provide examples of how the findings of qualitative studies might be represented thematically.

Grounded Theory Approaches to Analysis

Grounded theory as an approach to the design and conduct of research, and analysis of data has been enormously influential within the field of qualitative inquiry, and the analytic processes described by grounded theorists have also been taken up by qualitative researchers who may not situate their studies as contributions to grounded theory work. For example, many of the coding practices common to thematic analysis have stemmed from the methods first described by Barney Glaser and Anselm Strauss (1967) in their book *The Discovery of Grounded Theory*. Numerous descriptions of analytic processes used in generating grounded theory as well as innovations in the development of this approach have been published since.

In keeping with roots in symbolic interactionism, grounded theorists have examined social processes with a view to developing theories. These types of analyses are examples of 'syntagmatic' searches or contiguity-based relationships, which involve a focus on the 'juxtaposition in time and space, the influence of one thing on another, or relations among parts of a text' in order to see 'actual *connections* between things' (Maxwell and Miller, 2008: 462). How might one start to do this? Again, the answer to this question will depend on the version of grounded theory with which one aligns, given that the developers of grounded theory, Glaser and Strauss, have expounded different visions of grounded theory over time (Glaser, 1978; Glaser and Strauss, 1967; Strauss and Corbin, 1998) and their students have innovated on these approaches in diverse ways (for example, Charmaz, 2000, 2006; Clarke, 2005; Corbin and Strauss, 2008).

Initial and Focused Coding

A proponent of 'constructivist grounded theory,' Charmaz (2000, 2006, 2008) outlines a process of initial or open coding in which the analyst begins to work through the data set adding codes in a line-by-line fashion. Rather than code for themes or topics, as I have described earlier, Charmaz suggests that researchers use gerunds – noun forms of verbs – in order to make 'processes' explicit, 'make connections between codes,' and 'keep analyses active and emergent' (2008: 164). Focused or selective coding is a process whereby analysts examine and refine the codes through a process of locating those that are most significant, or appear more prominently in the data. Tentative explanations concerning the codes are then developed (Charmaz, 2008: 164).

Memo Writing

Memo writing is used widely by qualitative researchers, and is a crucial step in the generation of grounded theory. It involves researchers writing and reflecting on the research process and analytic decision-making, and documenting the development of interpretations throughout a study (see Charmaz, 2006, 2008; Corbin and Strauss, 2008; Glaser, 1978; Strauss and Corbin, 1998, for examples). Researchers usually begin by jotting down ideas and questions, and making connections between data excerpts and interpretations. Systematic record-keeping is advised so that the ideas included in memos may later be developed into manuscripts.

The Constant Comparative Method

The constant comparative method of analysis was first explained by Barney Glaser in an article published in the journal *Social Problems* in 1965, which was subsequently re-printed as a chapter in *The Discovery of Grounded Theory* (1967). The basic strategy used by the researcher is to 'constantly compare' data with data. In Glaser and Strauss's version of the constant comparative method, four steps are outlined:

(1) Comparing incidents applicable to each category;
(2) Integrating categories and their properties;
(3) Delimiting the theory; and
(4) Writing the theory. (Glaser and Strauss, 1967: 105)

The analyst begins by applying codes or categories to the data, each time comparing the data with previous incidents coded in the same way. Charmaz (2000) goes beyond Glaser's description of comparing 'incidents' to expound on further aspects of the data that might be compared:

> (a) comparing different people (such as their views, situations, actions, accounts, and experiences); (b) comparing data from the same individuals with themselves at different points in time; (c) comparing incident with incident; (d) comparing data with category, and (e) comparing a category with other categories. (2000: 515)

By constantly comparing data, the analyst begins to 'generate theoretical properties of the category' (Glaser and Strauss, 1967: 106), and the analyst can begin to expound on the:

> full range of types or continua of the category, its dimensions, the conditions under which it is pronounced or minimized, its major consequences, its relation to other categories, and its other properties. (1967: 106)

Throughout the comparative process, the analyst is advised to write memos explaining his or her developing ideas about the data. In order to 'integrate' categories and their properties, the analyst begins to compare incidents with the properties of the categories that have been developed throughout the coding process (Glaser and Strauss, 1967: 108), and in this way, develops theoretical propositions about the data. Glaser and Strauss (1967: 110) describe this as an 'emergent' process, with the theory beginning to 'solidify,' with fewer and fewer modifications as details of the theoretical propositions are clarified further. In their initial explanation of this analytic approach, they advise that the two requirements for theory are:

> (1) *parsimony* of variables and formulation, and (2) *scope* in the applicability of the theory to a wide range of situations while keeping a close correspondence of theory and data. (1967: 111)

Finally, when theoretical saturation has been achieved – that is new incidents located in the data no longer add aspects to the emergent theory – the analyst can begin to write up the theory using coded data and memos (Glaser and Stauss, 1967: 113).

Axial Coding

One area of possible confusion in grounded theory analysis is that of 'axial coding,' a process described by Strauss and Corbin (1998) that has occasionally been critiqued as overly prescriptive. Although axial coding has sometimes been taken to be a separate method of analysis, Strauss and Corbin seem to have been expounding on the process of coding outlined in the constant comparative method. Strauss and Corbin (1998: 123) explain that they used the term 'axial' because 'coding occurs around the axis of a category, linking categories at the level of properties and dimensions.' In this process, the analyst examines each category in detail in order to ascertain and describe both 'properties' and 'dimensions.' Dey (1999: 52) defines a property as a 'quality common to a whole class but not necessary to distinguish it from others,' and a dimension as some measurable aspect of a category (1999: 52). These concepts are perhaps best explained by using a concrete example provided by Dey:

(1) Something (for example, water) has properties or dimensions but not categories. Analysts assign something to a category depending on the comparisons that might be made with other categories (that is, water could be categorized as a 'beverage' when compared to soda, or alcohol; or a 'fluid' when compared to a gas or solid [1999: 53–4]).
(2) We 'discover' properties and dimensions by observing 'the way something interacts with the environment.' Properties and dimensions may be used as a 'basis for classification' [1999: 43].
(3) When we categorize, 'we make a distinction based on comparison' (1999: 54). Properties and dimensions may be identified without comparing. For example, a *property* of water is its ability to dissolve substances; a *dimension* of water is its depth (1999: 54–5).

The purpose of axial coding, as described by Strauss and Corbin, is to examine and answer questions concerning conditions and consequences – that is 'why or how come, where, when, how, and with what results' in order to 'relate structure to process' (1998: 127), and this process aids in the development of conditional and consequential matrixes (see Strauss and Corbin, 1998: ch. 12). Charmaz (2008: 160–1) cautions that both Glaser's version of theoretical coding (in which he elaborates on 18 different coding families), and Strauss and Corbin's axial coding move towards 'application' rather than 'emergence' of theoretical constructs. Juliet Corbin, in the most recent edition of the text in which she and Strauss explained axial coding, de-emphasizes this form of coding, commenting that any distinction between open coding and axial coding that may have been assumed from earlier writing is 'artificial' (Corbin and Strauss, 2008: 198).

Although various explanations for defining 'properties' and 'dimensions' in relation to coding and categorization appear to be contradictory as described by different authors, the process of thinking about these aspects of data can be helpful in the analytic process. These kinds of questions ask analysts to consider under what conditions particular phenomena arise and to what extent, and help analysts make connections between data that go beyond description.

Ethnographic Analysis

The object of ethnographic analysis is to make sense of particular cultures, including the language or 'folk terms' that members of the culture routinely use, and to generate findings that will provide descriptions, analyses, and interpretations of how members experience and understand their world. Anthropologist James Spradley (1979, 1980) defines ethnographic analysis as '*a search for the parts of a culture, the relationships among the parts, and their relationships to the whole*' (1979: 142, emphasis in original). A number of different strategies informed by cognitive anthropology are used by Spradley to do ethnographic analysis, including domain, taxonomic, and componential analyses. The 'developmental research sequence' outlined by Spradley describes analytic processes *within* the context of data generation, rather than as steps taken *after* data have been generated and collected. Thus, ethnographic interviews are informed by observations in the field, and vice versa. Ethnographic interviews are carried out at multiple points throughout a research project in order to generate specific kinds of descriptions from participants. Thus, descriptive questions generate data that may be subject to 'domain' analysis, structural questions generate data that may be subject to 'taxonomic' analysis, and contrast questions generate data that can be analyzed for components to generate a 'componential analysis.' Each of these three forms of analyses is used by the analyst to 'discover cultural themes,' which are represented in an ethnography. Premised on symbolic interactionist theory, Spradley's approach to analysis aims to explain a culture's language and symbol system in order to unpack the 'cultural meanings' of a particular group or society (1979: 99).

Spradley first advises the beginning ethnographer to locate the 'domains' in a particular culture. A domain is any symbolic category in a culture that includes other categories, and for Spradley, the domain is the first unit of analysis in doing ethnography (1979: 100). Rather then use established lists of categories such as the schema discussed earlier in the section on thematic coding, Spradley suggests that analysts need to derive the domains from the language or 'folk terms' used by the participants in interviews (1979: 103–5). Through a process of looking for 'names for things,' the analyst can identify possible 'cover terms' and include terms used by participants in interviews, before searching for further terms in other interviews (1979: 105). In this way, the analyst can construct a domain analysis, which may be analyzed for semantic relationships. Spradley outlines nine universal relationships (see Table 8.1) that may be used for domain analysis, and for construction of 'structural' questions to be posed in later ethnographic interviews.

Spradley defines a taxonomy as a 'set of categories organized on the basis of a single semantic relationship' (1979: 137). Once again, Spradley outlines a specific

Table 8.1   Types of semantic relationships

Type	Relationship
Strict inclusion	*X* is a kind of *Y*
Spatial	*X* is a place in *Y*, *X* is a part of *Y*
Cause–effect	*X* is a result of *Y*, *X* is a cause of *Y*
Rationale	*X* is a reason for doing *Y*
Location for action	*X* is a place for doing *Y*
Function	*X* is used for *Y*
Means-end	*X* is a way to do *Y*
Sequence	*X* is a step (stage) in *Y*
Attribution	*X* is an attribute (characteristic) of *Y*

Source: From Spradley, *The Ethnographic Interview*, IE. © 1979 Wadsworth, a part of Cengage Learning, Inc. Reproduced by permission. www.cengage.com/permissions

sequence of steps for taxonomic analysis, with the goal of locating the relationships between elements of a particular domain. This systematic search for relationships is followed in Spradley's research sequence by componential analysis, which he defines as a 'systematic search for the attributes (components of meaning) associated with cultural symbols' (1979: 174).

Table 8.2 shows how the semantic relationships outlined by Spradley might be used as a preliminary way to organize topics related in interview data. Here, the 'x is a kind of y' relationship is explored in relation to data from a study of young children's music preferences (Roulston, 2006b).

Table 8.2   Strict inclusion (*X* is a kind of *Y*)

Included terms	Semantic relationship	Cover term
Adult popular music performed by:		
• Janet Jackson		
• Paulena		
• The B-52s		
○ Rock Lobster	is a kind of	preferred music
• The Beatles		
• The Rolling Stones		
• Jimmy Hendrix		
○ 'Purple Haze'		
○ 'Star Spangled Banner'		
○ 'All Along the Watchtower'		
Traditional children's songs		
• 'Twinkle Twinkle Little Star'		
• 'I'm a Little Teapot'		
• 'How Much Is that Doggie in the Window'		
• 'Grandfather's Clock'		
• 'Cowboy Songs'		
Music for children performed by:		
• Raffi		
• Kids Bop		
• The Wiggles		

(Continued)

Table 8.2 *(Continued)*

Included terms	Semantic relationship	Cover term
Adolescent/young adult music performed by:	is a kind of	preferred music
• Britney Spears		
• Backstreet Boys		
• 'NSync		
Movie soundtracks		
• *Shrek*		
• *The Little Mermaid*		
Classical music		
• Tapes for Suzuki violin lessons		
• Beethoven's 5th Symphony		
• Tchaikovsky's Sleeping Beauty		
• Mozart		
Christian music		
• The Fish (radio)		
Children's chorus		

By analyzing data while it is being collected, these analytic strategies can provide the basis for questions that might be asked in succeeding interviews, and inform further data analysis (see Figure 8.1).

An adequate ethnography, according to Spradley, attends to the details of a particular culture and provides an overview of the whole by locating cultural themes. Spradley defines a cultural theme as '*any cognitive principle, tacit or explicit, recurrent in a number of domains and serving as a relationship among subsystems of cultural meaning*' (1979: 186, emphasis in original); and provides nine strategies that might be used by ethnographers to undertake a theme analysis.

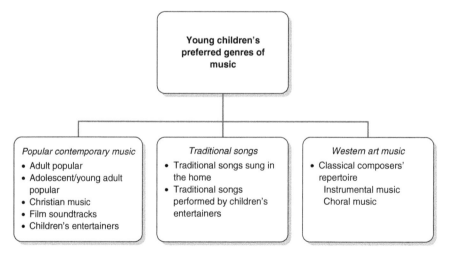

Figure 8.1   Organizing ideas

Spradley's approach to the analysis of ethnographic data – including interviews and field notes of observation – is comprehensive and highly structured. In practice, analysis of ethnographic data is likely to be more flexible then is suggested by the steps of his developmental research sequence (Spradley, 1979, 1980). For example, ethnographers and sociologists Lofland et al. (2006), in their explanation of data analysis, draw on writings from a variety of grounded theorists, in addition to the work of Spradley, and Miles and Huberman (1994) to outline strategies that might be used to do ethnographic analysis, and suggest that analysts ought to 'play with the data' (Lofland et al., 2006: 218) rather than stick too closely to particular forms of theoretical development.

Phenomenological Approaches to Analysis

Like other families of qualitative data analysis, there are multiple ways to conducting phenomenological analysis, informed by different philosophical viewpoints. Clark Moustakas (1994), a transcendental phenomenologist, begins the process of phenomenological reduction – that is, reducing the data to its essential meaning elements – by identifying 'meaning statements' relevant to the object of analysis. Thus, the interview data are reduced by eliminating repetitive statements and data that are irrelevant to the study of a particular lived experience, and focusing and reflecting on statements that reflect the 'horizons' of meaning relevant to the phenomenon. Meaning statements are then clustered into themes, and used to develop textural and structural descriptions of the experience (Moustakas, 1994: ch. 7). Constructing a textural description of an experience involves the researcher deeply reflecting on the phenomenon:

> Such a description, beginning with the Epoche[1] and going through a process of returning to the thing itself, in a state of openness and freedom, facilitates clear seeing, makes possible identity, and encourages the looking again and again that leads to deeper layers of meaning. Throughout, there is an interweaving of person, conscious experience, and phenomenon. In the process of explicating the phenomenon, qualities are recognized and described; every perception is granted equal value, nonrepetitive constituents of experience are linked thematically, and a full description is derived. (Moustakas, 1994: 96)

The next step of the process is to construct a structural description of an experience. Whereas textural descriptions focus on the 'what' of an experience, structural

---

[1]Moustakas (1994) uses the term 'Epoche' to refer to the process in which researchers purposefully refrain from bringing preconceptions to bear on the object of analysis. He writes: '*Epoche* is a Greek word meaning to refrain from judgment, to abstain from or stay away from the everyday, ordinary way of perceiving things. In the natural attitude we hold knowledge judgmentally; we presuppose that what we perceive in nature is actually there and remains there as we perceive it. In contrast Epoche requires a new way of looking at things, a way that requires that we learn *to see* what stands before our eyes, what we can distinguish and describe ... In the Epoche, the everyday understandings, judgments, and knowings are set aside, and phenomena are revisited, freshly, naively, in a wide open sense, from the vantage point of a pure or transcendental ego' (1994: 33, original emphasis).

descriptions focus on the 'underlying and precipitating factors that account for what is being experienced; in other words the 'how' that speaks to conditions that illuminate the 'what' of experience' (Moustakas, 1994: 98). This task is assisted by 'imaginative variation,' in which the researcher seeks 'possible meaning through the utilization of imagination, varying the frames of reference, employing polarities and reversals, and approaching the phenomenon from divergent perspectives, different positions, roles, or functions' (Moustakas, 1994: 98). The final step in the analytic process is to combine the structural and textural descriptions in a creative way that conveys a 'unified statement of the essences of the experience of the phenomenon as whole' (Moustakas, 1994: 100). Moustakas draws on Edmund Husserl to define the meaning of 'essence' as 'that which is common or universal, the condition or quality without which a thing would not be what it is' (1994: 100); although he modifies this definition by noting that essences are never exhausted, and the syntheses constructed by analysts represent 'essences at a particular time and place from the vantage point of an individual researcher' (Moustakas, 1994: 100).

Max van Manen, a hermeneutic phenomenologist, outlines three possible approaches to the 'uncovering' or 'isolation' of thematic aspects of a phenomenon: (1) the wholistic or sententious approach; (2) the selective or highlighting approach; and (3) the detailed or line-by-line approach (1990: 92–3). In the first approach, the analyst reads the whole text, asks: *'What sententious phrase may capture the fundamental meaning or main significance of the text as a whole?'* (van Manen, 1990: 93, emphasis in original); and then writes a phrase to express this meaning. In the selective approach, the analyst asks: *'What statement(s) or phrase(s) seem particularly essential or revealing about the phenomenon or experience being described?'* (van Manen, 1990: 93, emphasis in original). The third approach, similar to the approach described by Moustakas, involves the analyst in a line-by-line reading of the data, asking: *'What does this sentence or sentence cluster reveal about the phenomenon or experience being described?'* (van Manen, 1990: 93, emphasis in original). As the analyst works through the data set, he or she begins writing 'linguistic transformations' to capture the themes (van Manen, 1990: 94). Van Manen describes this as a creative process, in which the author attempts to 'grasp the essence of some experience in a phenomenological description' (1990: 96–7). This process may be assisted by further conversations with participants and collaborative discussions in a research group (van Manen, 1990: 99–100). In this section I have highlighted two approaches to phenomenological analysis as entry points, although other researchers have provided accounts of the steps they have used in accomplishing phenomenological analysis.

Approaches to the Analysis of Narrative

What is narrative? A narrow definition of narrative is that it is a 'story' with a plot – that is 'topically centered and temporally organized' (Riessman, 2008: 5). Defined in this way, a 'narrative' or 'story' can be subjected to various models of structural analysis drawn from sociolinguistics. A broader view of narrative includes life stories involving documents, interviews and observations, or sequences of interviews and conversations (Riessman, 2008: 5–6). From this perspective, different forms of data can be woven into a 'narrative' that represents a 'life' or 'biography.' Narrative researcher Catherine Kohler Riessman underscores that there is no single meaning for what 'narrative' might encompass, and includes 'stories told by research participants,' 'interpretive accounts developed by an investigator,' and 'even the narrative a reader constructs after engaging with the participant's and investigator's narratives' as different layers of what has come to constitute 'narrative' inquiry in the human sciences (2008: 6).

Given this broad spectrum of what is encompassed by 'narrative' work, a useful starting point to consider narrative inquiry as a body of work is provided by Donald Polkinghorne (1995). Polkinghorne proposes two categories of narrative research that he labels as 'analysis of narratives' and 'narrative analysis' that respond, respectively, to two types of cognition identified by psychologist, Jerome Bruner. These are: paradigmatic cognition, and narrative cognition.

Paradigmatic Cognition

Work that employs paradigmatic cognition, in Polkinghorne's view, results in the analysis of participants' narratives or 'stories' for common themes or ideas – a move from 'stories to common elements,' with findings including taxonomies of 'types of stories, characters, or settings' (Polkinghorne, 1995: 12). This form of narrative inquiry can result in representations of thematic findings generated via coding and categorization of data (for example, such as grounded theory). Paradigmatic searches can also involve structural approaches to the analysis of narratives for oral versions of personal experience such as that formulated by William Labov and Joshua Waletzky (1967/1997) (see Table 8.3).

The structural approach to analyzing stories provided by sociolinguists such as Labov and Waletzky reveals how the narrator frames the experience described, the meanings that they make of the event, as well as how they want to convey the

Table 8.3   Elements of narrative structure

Element	Description
Abstract	Summary of the story
Orientation	These clauses orient listeners to person, place, time, and behavioral situation
Complicating action	Information concerning a series of events that comprise a 'complicating action' or 'complication'
Evaluation	The narrator's comment and attitude toward the event; the 'part of the narrative that reveals the attitude of the narrator toward the narrative by emphasizing the relative importance of some narrative units as compared to others' (Labov and Waletzky, 1967/1997: 32).
Resolution	What happened next; outcome of the event
Coda	Closure to story, and return to the present moment

Source: Labov, W. and Waletzky, J. (1967/1997). 'Narrative analysis: Oral versions of personal experience', *Journal of Narrative and Life History, 7* (1–4): 3–38. Reprinted by permission of Taylor & Francis Informa UK Ltd.

events to particular audiences. In Labov and Waletzky's model, the 'evaluation' section of the narrative – which may be infused throughout the narration – is particularly helpful in examining these aspects of story-telling. For example, Table 8.4 includes a narrative told by a music teacher in response to an initial question asking him how he had become a music teacher.

Labov and Waletzky's model is helpful to locate the core elements of the story which the interviewee narrates to describe his inauspicious entrée into the music education profession beginning at the point when as a teenager he had 'no musical aspirations at all.' As a high school student he broke his leg at the end of his junior year, and was recruited to sing in the high school chorus by the choral director simply because he was using the handicap ramp to pass by the music room. In spite of not singing well at multiple auditions, the choral director assigned him to the top singing group the following year – not because of his singing ability, but because of his persistence, in that he had returned every day for a week at the director's request. In this narrative, the interviewee describes a rapid and successful rise in the choir – as a fast learner, he both caught up to the rest of the singers, and became leader of the tenor section, eventually earning a scholarship to attend a music school. The complicating event in this narrative – having a broken leg and failing to shine in multiple auditions, has an unexpected outcome, in that he is chosen for the top group by the choral director. This is a narrative of 'success,' in which the story-teller is discovered by a choral director who provides guidance, and he himself discovers that his initial assessment of his musical ability is inaccurate. Not only does he have 'natural ability,' but he is a 'quick learner,' and with persistence and hard work he succeeds in unanticipated ways.

The structure of a narrative might also be examined using the model proposed by Elinor Ochs and Lisa Capps (2001). Ochs and Capps argue that social science research has focused attention on a 'default' form of narrative with the characteristics that cluster to one end of possibilities: 'one active teller, highly tellable account, relatively detached from surrounding talk and activity, linear temporal and causal organization, and certain, constant moral stance' (2001: 20). These authors chart an approach to the analysis of everyday narratives with characteristics that fall at the other end of the spectrum illustrated by the narrative included in Table 8.4: 'multiple, active co-tellers, moderately tellable account, relatively embedded in surrounding discourse and activity, nonlinear temporal and causal organization, and uncertain fluid moral stance' (Ochs and Capps, 2001: 23).

These kinds of approaches to the analysis of narratives provide information concerning how interviewees position themselves within their stories, as well as how they wish to be heard by their audiences. Riessman (2008) also combines elements of structural analysis and thematic analysis in what she calls a 'dialogic/performance' approach to the analysis of narratives. In this perspective, the focus of analysis is the performative elements of the narrative – here the analyst considers the context of the production of the narrative, the audiences, in addition to both the content of the narrative, and the linguistic resources used by speakers to formulate the story (Riessman, 2008: ch. 5).

Table 8.4 Examining the structure of a narrative

Interviewer's talk is **bolded**

Labov and Waletzky's model	Narrative
Abstract: What was this about?	**The first question is just tell me how you came to be teaching music in a school.**
Abstract/ orientation: When Who Where What	I have always had a love for music, as far as I wanted to be a singer. When I was in middle school, I got involved in the choral program of my church. That was about it. The extent of my musical experience. As a high school student I played soccer. And so I was going to go to college on a soccer scholarship, and get a degree in criminal justice. I had no musical aspirations at all.
Complication Then what happened?	My junior year, I broke my leg, and was not able to play soccer in my senior year. The handicap ramp of my school led you past the chorus room, and one day I was going past the chorus room, the choral director was out in the hallway and I must have been humming or doing something of that nature, and the choral director said, 'Hey boy, you like to sing?' And I said, 'Well I sing at church, but never have I took a class.' And he said, 'Well we're having auditions for the choral program at the college, for the high school next year.' This was the end of my junior year. And he said, 'Won't you come by and audition?' And I said, 'Well OK, that's fine.' Because I had broken my leg, I had nothing to do after school, so it was fine. I went by and auditioned for him, and did pretty horrendous audition, at least according to him it was pretty bad. This was on a Monday, and so at the end of it, I could pretty much tell, he actually even confirmed my suspicions that I was not very good. So I said, 'Well thanks for letting me try.' And he said, 'Well no it's OK. I want you to come back again tomorrow.' And I thought this was strange, because the auditions were on Monday, why would he want me to come back on Tuesday? I returned on Tuesday, and we did it again, the exact same audition, and there was some improvement there, I could tell. But nothing major. At the end of the audition, he asked me to come back on Wednesday. And the same thing on Thursday, and then finally on Friday, he asked me to come back one last time. On Friday, I got a little frustrated with him, and I said, 'Why do you keep asking me to come back?' I'm not a musician, I like to sing. But that's not my forte.' And he said,
Resolution/ result What finally happened?	'I want to see how persistent you'd be at trying something. Because you came back every day, I'm going to put you in my top group for next year.' Which I thought was very strange. But he did, he put me in the top group. I spent the whole summer taking private lessons, because I wanted to get good, since I was going to be in this top group, I thought, well I don't want to embarrass myself. When school started back in my senior year, I was in his top chorus class. And
Evaluation	began to improve, and eventually became section leader of the tenor section of the high school there. By the middle of the year, I had realized that I really did like music, and that I had a natural ability to catch on quick, for someone who
Result	was – most of the kids who were in there had been in at least four years. Some had been in chorus all their, at least since middle school, and here I'd come in my senior year, and was able to catch up to the whole group. So I decided I wanted to do something with music, but I wasn't really sure what, so he recommended that I go to a college to study music. And he recommended _____ College. What I didn't know is that _____ College was considered one of the best music schools in the state of _____ at that time. Um, so I got the application packet, I applied, and went and auditioned. He helped me with my audition, and I received a music scholarship to study at _____ College in _____.

Narrative Cognition

Rather than generating findings and commonalities across cases, a focus on narrative cognition produces 'individual cases' and 'emplotted stories' – a move from 'elements to stories' (Polkinghorne, 1995: 11–12). Polkinghorne has recently clarified the terms used in his 1995 article, commenting that he believes 'analysis of narratives' to be 'what qualitative research is doing'; whereas narrative analysis:

> was looking at an individual life or portion of the life and the final result was a story ... It came from a lot of different sources, but what you tried to end up with was a description of the life movement of a particular person. (Don Polkinghorne, interviewed by Jean Clandinin, in Clandinin and Murphy, 2007: 636)

Clandinin and Murphy explain that narrative analysis 'understands lives as unfolding temporally, as particular events within a particular individual's life' (2007: 636). Whereas in the kinds of coding procedures described in thematic analysis and grounded theory approaches, the analyst focuses on searching each new episode 'as an instance of a general type,' the analyst working from a narrative cognition frame is 'open to the specific and unique elements that make the new episode different from all that have gone before,' and will synthesize data 'by means of a plot into a story or stories ... a history, case study, or biographic episode' (Polkinghorne, 1995: 11–12). Rather than coding data, the research synthesizes elements drawn from different data sources (for example, memoirs, photos, diaries, interviews, archival records) into a narrative with a plot, by asking questions such as, 'How did this happen?' or 'Why did this come about?' (Polkinghorne, 1995: 15). Juanita Johnson-Bailey's book *Sistahs in College: Making a Way Out of No Way* (2001) exemplifies Polkinghorne's 'narrative analysis' approach, with each of the eight chapters presenting a first-person narrative of an African-American woman's re-entry into higher education.

Researchers have continued to innovate and develop ways to do narrative inquiry, and have begun to make use of visual data such as photographs (Bach, 2007) and collage (Luttrell, 2003) among other methods. Riessman points out that narrative inquirers use visual data to both tell stories *with* images, and tell a story *about* images (2008: 141). The deployment of visual data for the purposes of narrative inquiry draws on visual methods in the fields of sociology and anthropology, and there is a wealth of writing on analytic methods that might be used.

Ethnomethodological Analysis and Conversation Analysis

Applications of an ethnomethodological (EM) approach to the analysis of interview data are less common than the analytic approaches described earlier in this chapter, given that the original intent of ethnomethodology was to examine the methods used by members in mundane settings to accomplish ordinary and everyday activities. For this kind of work, video- and audio-recordings of naturally occurring events and everyday activities have been the preferred method of data generation, rather than research interviews. Nevertheless, a growing number of researchers have employed EM analysis to examine how interview talk is accomplished and how research topics are talked into being. Carolyn Baker argues that EM analyses of research interviews attends:

> to *how* participants do the work of conversational interaction, including how they make sense of each other, how they build a 'corpus of interview knowledge,' how they negotiate identities, and how they characterize and connect the worlds they talk about. (2002: 777)

In a related enterprise, sociologist Harvey Sacks (1992) studied conversation, which led to two branches of work: conversation analysis (CA), and membership categorization analysis (MCA) – both of which have been associated to varying degrees with ethnomethodology. Conversation analysis examines sequences of talk-in-interaction in order to look at the conversational resources people use in order to make sense of one another's utterances. Much of the work in CA has focused on developing understanding of the features of multi-party talk, including turn-taking, gaps and overlap, adjacency pairs and preference organization, sequential structure, and repair (see Appendix 2).

As demonstrated in Chapter 7, in order to analyze interview data using conversation analysis, a first step is to transcribe a sequence of interaction in further detail, including gaps, pauses, overlaps, as well as the kinds of slips and repairs of speech that are routinely edited out during transcription of interviews (see Have, 2007; Pomerantz and Fehr, 1997 for further guidance in beginning analysis of this sort). Once a more detailed transcription has been accomplished, the analyst attends to the details of the particular interaction on a turn-by-turn basis. Depending on the features of talk, the analyst can examine any number of phenomena, including turn-taking, sequence organization, repair, pauses, preference organization, topic change, and so forth.

Analysis of interview data might also draw on membership categorization analysis, a method used by EM to examine peoples' reasoning as demonstrated in descriptive practices. With respect to interview talk, researchers can identify the membership categorization devices (MCDs) used by speakers to describe versions of 'social reality built around categories and activities' (Baker, 1997: 131). In seminal papers on the topic, Sacks (1972a, 1972b) described in detail the apparatus by which people 'do descriptions' in ways that are recognizable to others via the use of 'membership categorization devices,' which are collections of 'membership categories' plus 'rules of application.' Sacks' most well-cited example was drawn from a child's story: 'The baby cried. The mommy picked it up.' Sacks explains how in this fragment of talk, the categories of 'baby' and 'mommy' belong to the MCD 'family.' Certain activities are heard as 'category-bound,' for example, babies 'cry,' and mommies 'pick babies up.' As Sacks shows, much more can be made of this short fragment of talk using membership categorization analysis. What is relevant here is that through the use of both CA and MCA, researchers can identify the conversational resources used by speakers to formulate descriptions, the kinds of actions that speakers accomplish through talk, and the moral portrayals and cultural particulars of participants' worlds as portrayed in research interviews.

'Post-'approaches to Analysis

The diverse multiplicity of approaches encompassed by the term 'postmodern theory' (Best and Kellner, 1991, 1997, 2001) represents a 'multi-voiced, multi-hued, clamorous circus' that challenges conventional research methods and its underlying modernist assumptions about what counts as knowledge (Scheurich, 1997: 175), as well as how findings are represented (Denzin, 1997). Researchers working from 'post-' perspectives, including poststructural, postmodern, and deconstructive approaches, are unlikely to outline instructions for how to go about applying these theoretical perspectives to the analysis of data. The epistemological assumptions underlying many of the approaches to analysis that I have reviewed above that seek to help researchers 'produce better accounts, clearer formulations of problems and more efficient solutions' (Stronach and MacLure, 1997: 4) are anathema to researchers with assumptions drawn from poststructural and postmodern discourses. Indeed, Ian Stronach and Maggie MacLure propose that researchers working from poststructural, postmodern, and deconstructive approaches encounter 'disappointment – of certainty, illumination, generality' as both 'choice' and 'inevitability' (1997: 4–5). Thus, there are few explicit guidelines for how to go about doing poststructural, postmodern, or deconstructive analyses. What researchers *do* have to guide their work, however, are many theorists, and a growing number of examples of research that troubles traditional notions of what research is, how it should be conducted, and what it might look like when represented to others.

For example, Stronach and MacLure (1997: ch. 2) provide a postmodern reading of two narrative portraits of a participant in a study in which they were involved. This reading interrogates the texts they produced from their analyses of interview data, and investigates the analytic decisions and writing practices involved in the representation of the interviewee. A number of authors, including Donna Alvermann (2000), Jodi Kaufmann (2007), and Eileen Honan (2007) have experimented with Gilles Deleuze and Félix Guattari's (1987) notion of rhizomes from their book *A Thousand Plateaus: Capitalism and Schizophrenia* to conduct and represent research that employs interview data. In a methodological chapter, James Scheurich and Kathryn McKenzie (2005) examine Michel Foucault's methods in his archaeological and genealogical works, recommending that readers draw on the original sources as a way to begin this kind of work, and providing an extensive list of studies that apply Foucauldian theory. Maggie MacLure (2003: ch. 7) interrogates the 'fabrication' involved in life-history interviewing, as well as providing questions that might be used to 'open up' a text for a deconstructive reading (2003: 82) – these are provided as examples that have guided her own inquiries in a 'loose and dimly felt way' (2003: 82).

These approaches to the analysis and representation of interview data upset the notion of the unitary subject, challenge conventional assumptions and accepted practices of social research, and question the very possibility of arriving at 'results.' Readers are more likely to find 'openings' (Stronach and MacLure, 1997), 'ruins' (St Pierre and Pillow, 2000), partial small-'t' truths, and possibilities for ways of working that refuse prescription and definitive conclusions. Some researchers who draw on postmodern and poststructural theories have also turned to alternative approaches to the representation of data, a topic that I now discuss.

The Arts, Performance, and Qualitative Inquiry

Research known as 'arts-based inquiry' draws on artistic forms from literature and the visual and performing arts to inform the practices involved in conducting qualitative research, as well as to provide alternative modes of representation to traditional scientific papers that open up spaces for communicating with audiences beyond the academy. Thus, scholars have used poetry, visual imagery, and performative inquiry in work variously labeled as 'arts-based inquiry,' 'Scholar-ARTistry,' and 'a/r/tography' (Cahnmann-Taylor, 2008: 6); while others employ performance-based methods such as performance autoethnography, ethnodrama, ethnotheater, readers' theater, dance, and movement for both critical and pedagogical purposes (Leavy, 2008: 344).

What is immediately apparent when reviewing literature on arts- and performance-based methods used by qualitative inquirers is that there is a proliferation of approaches used by researchers in multiple disciplines for a wide variety of purposes. With multiple labels for such work, and diversity in how researchers have taken up and used the arts and performance in their work, like the postmodern approaches to data analysis outlined earlier, while there are as yet few standardized practices, there are a multitude of exemplars to which researchers might refer.

Poetry

Poetry has been used in both sociology and anthropology as a way to represent research findings, and there has been an upsurge in interest from other fields such as health and education (see Prendergast, 2006). Melisa Cahnmann (2003) discusses three ways in which poetry can be used by qualitative researchers to inform their work. First, she reviews poetic devices used by poets in the craft of writing poetry; second, she outlines practices that poets use to develop their ideas (for example, keeping a poetry journal, reading, taking inspirational notes from others' work); and finally, she proposes that poetry provides alternative means for researchers to inform multiple audiences.

Drama

There are a number of scholars who have used dramatic formats for the presentation of research, and this work encompasses a variety of approaches. 'Readers' theater' is a format in which participants participate in readings from scripts to enact some aspect of a research project for pedagogical purposes, or as a way to present the findings from a research project to an audience. Theatre professor, Johnny Saldaña, has drawn on ethnographic data to write scripts for what he variously calls 'ethnotheatre,' 'ethnodrama,' and 'ethnographic performance,' and has provided guidelines for playwriting, dramatization, and performance (Saldaña, 2003). One of Saldaña's plays, *Finding My Place: The Brad Trilogy*, is based on ethnographic data provided by ethnographer, Harry Wolcott (2002).

Closely related to these genres are performance ethnographies, in which scholars combine ethnographic data in the form of interviews and field notes with documentary and visual sources; and autoethnographic performances in which researchers perform work that focuses on personal experience. Denzin (2003a, 2005) has drawn on critical and emancipatory perspectives to argue for performative inquiry as an approach that may be used for decolonizing and emancipatory agendas, and asserts that various forms of political and subversive theater, including 'historical restagings, masquerade, ventriloquism, and double inverted performances' can disrupt colonialist discourses, and contribute to social justice aims (Denzin, 2005: 934).

Fiction

As Susan Krieger (1983) points out in the methodological essay on 'Fiction and social science' that appends her book, *The Mirror Dance: Identity in a Women's Community*, fictionalization has long been used as a narrative strategy by social scientists in the representation of their work. Numerous scholars in multiple disciplines have used fiction as a way of representing their research to others, and it is standard practice in writing up qualitative research to fictionalize names and settings in order to maintain confidentiality for participants. Scholars in the social sciences have used fiction as a way to present their research in alternative ways (see Hecht [1998, 2006] for an example of traditional and fictional representations of findings from a study of street children in Brazil).

For social scientists who seek to represent realist accounts, unitary truths, and facts concerning reality, performance inquiry, research poetry, and fictional representations of social science research are to be resisted. David Silverman, for example, has written extensively about qualitative research methods, yet goes so far as to state that 'the experimental writing, sometimes including poetry, that increasingly populates some academic journals is, strictly speaking, bullshit' (2007: 139), and proposes an 'anti-bullshit' agenda for qualitative research, calling for research that exemplifies the qualities of clarity, reason, beauty and truth (2007: 139–42). Many proponents of arts-based inquiry and creative analytic practices would argue with the use of these criteria to judge the quality of their work. The viewpoint expressed by Silverman and others is situated in direct opposition to that taken by many researchers working from postmodern perspectives; and it seems unlikely that social scientists from either position will convince one another of the merit of their arguments any time soon. As I have argued throughout this text, social researchers must make informed decisions about the purpose of their research, the audiences to whom they wish to speak, how they want to go about designing, conducting and representing their work to others, and justify those to others.

Conclusion

Novices to qualitative data analysis are sometimes surprised to find that making sense of qualitative data is a very time-consuming process requiring considerable thought and reflection. At such times, it is helpful to remember that few complex endeavors are easy the first time through. With practice, beginning researchers will find that they will become more adept at applying these processes – whatever method is selected. With persistent effort, along with reference to relevant literature and exemplars related to the approach selected, the painstaking work involved in qualitative data analysis will be rewarded.

In the final chapter, I conclude with accounts from experienced researchers about their interview practices. As will be quickly apparent, these researchers do not follow prescriptions or rules, but might be thought of as having 'evolved their perspective on the basis of prior actions and experiences' as in the case of the 'proficient performers' or 'experts' who simply 'do what works' as described in the Dreyfus model of human learning (Flyvbjerg, 2001: 16–17). By designing and conducting an interview study using guiding questions that have been suggested in earlier chapters, novice researchers will advance their skills to develop and accomplish competence as researchers and interviewers.

Further Reading

Overviews of Qualitative Data Analysis

Bauer, M.W. and Gaskell, G. (eds) (2000) *Qualitative Researching with Text, Image and Sound: A Practical Handbook*. London: Sage.

Coffey, A. and Atkinson, P. (1996) *Making Sense of Qualitative Data: Complementary Research Strategies*. Thousand Oaks, CA: Sage.

Ezzy, D. (2002) *Qualitative Analysis: Practice and Innovation*. Crows Nest, NSW: Routledge.

Miles, M.B. and Huberman, A.M. (1994) *Qualitative Data Analysis: An Expanded Sourcebook*, 2nd edn. Thousand Oaks, CA: Sage.

Silverman, D. (2001) *Interpreting Qualitative Data: Methods for Analysing Talk, Text, and Interaction*, 2nd edn. London: Sage.

Grounded Theory Approaches to Data Analysis

Charmaz, K. (2006) *Constructing Grounded Theory: A Practical Guide Through Qualitative Analysis*. London: Sage.

Corbin, J. and Strauss, A. (2008) *Basics of Qualitative Research: Techniques and Procedures for Developing Grounded Theory*, 3rd edn. Los Angeles, CA: Sage.

Dey, I. (1999) *Grounding Grounded Theory: Guidelines for Qualitative Inquiry*. San Diego, CA: Academic Press.

Glaser, B.G. (1978) *Theoretical Sensitivity*. Mill Valley, CA: Sociology Press.

Glaser, B.G. and Strauss, A.L. (1967) *The Discovery of Grounded Theory: Strategies for Qualitative Research*. New York: Aldine de Gruyter.

Strauss, A.L. and Corbin, J. (1998) *Basics of Qualitative Research: Grounded Theory Procedures and Techniques*, 2nd edn. Newbury Park, CA: Sage.

Ethnographic Analysis

Lofland, J., Snow, D., Anderson, L. and Lofland, L.H. (2006) *Analyzing Social Settings: A Guide to Qualitative Observation and Analysis*, 4th edn. Belmont, CA: Wadsworth/Thomson.

Spradley, J. (1979). *The Ethnographic Interview*. Fort Worth, TX: Harcourt Brace Jovanovich College Publishers.

Wolcott, H.F. (1994) *Transforming Qualitative Data: Description, Analysis, and Interpretation*. Thousand Oaks, CA: Sage.

Narrative Analysis

Chase, S.E. (2005) 'Narrative inquiry: Multiple lenses, approaches, voices', in N.K. Denzin and Y.S. Lincoln (eds), *The Sage Handbook of Qualitative Research* 3rd edn. Thousand Oaks, CA: Sage. pp. 651–80.

Clandinin, D.J. (ed.) (2007) *Handbook of Narrative Inquiry: Mapping a Methodology*. Thousand Oaks, CA: Sage.

Clandinin, D.J. and Connelly, F.M. (2000) *Narrative Inquiry: Experience and Story in Qualitative Research*. San Francisco, CA: Jossey-Bass.

Cortazzi, M. (1993) *Narrative Analysis*. London: Falmer.

Riessman, C. (2008) *Narrative Methods for the Human Sciences*. Los Angeles, CA: Sage.

Phenomenological Analysis

Dahlberg, K., Drew, N. and Nystrom, M. (2001) *Reflective Lifeworld Research*. Lund: Studentlitteratur.

Hycner, R.H. (1985) 'Some guidelines for the phenomenological analysis of interview data', *Human Studies*, 8: 279–303.

Moustakas, C. (1994) *Phenomenological Research Methods*. Thousand Oaks, CA: Sage.

van Manen, M. (1990) *Research Lived Experience: Human Science for an Action Sensitive Pedagogy*. London: State University of New York Press.

Ethnomethodology

Francis, D. and Hester, S. (2004) *An Invitation to Ethnomethodology: Language, Society and Interaction*. London: Sage.

Have, P.t. (2004) *Understanding Qualitative Research and Ethnomethodology*. London: Sage.

Conversation Analysis

Have, P.t. (2007) *Doing Conversation Analysis: A Practical Guide*, 2nd edn. Los Angeles, CA: Sage.

Hutchby, I. and Wooffitt, R. (1998) *Conversation Analysis: Principles, Practices and Applications*. Cambridge: Polity Press.

Membership Categorization Analysis

Baker, C.D. (2002) 'Ethnomethodological analyses of interviews', in J.F. Gubrium and J.A. Holstein (eds), *Handbook of Interviewing: Context and Method.* Thousand Oaks: Sage. pp. 777–95.

Baker, C.D. (2004) 'Membership categorization and interview accounts', in D. Silverman (ed.), *Qualitative Research: Theory, Method and Practice,* 2nd edn. London: Sage. pp. 162–76.

Sacks, H. (1972a) 'An initial investigation of the usability of conversation data for doing sociology', in D. Sudnow (ed.), *Studies in Social Interaction.* New York: The Free Press. pp. 31–74.

Sacks, H. (1972b) 'On the analyzability of stories by children', in J.J. Gumperz and D. Hymes (eds), *Directions in Sociolinguistics: The Ethnography of Communication.* Oxford: Blackwell. pp. 325–45.

Postmodern and Poststructural Approaches to Analysis

Scheurich, J.J. (1997) *Research Method in the Postmodern.* London: The Falmer Press.

Scheurich, J.J. and McKenzie, K.B. (2005) 'Foucault's methodologies: Archeaology and genealogy', in N.K. Denzin and Y.S. Lincoln (eds), *The Sage Handbook of Qualitative Research,* 3rd edn. Thousand Oaks, CA: Sage. pp. 841–68.

Stronach, I. and MacLure, M. (1997) *Educational Research Undone: The Postmodern Embrace.* Buckingham: Open University Press.

Arts-based Research

Cahnmann-Taylor, M. and Siegesmund, R. (eds) (2008) *Arts-based Research in Education: Foundations for Practice.* New York: Routledge.

Kouritzin, S.G., Piquemal, N.A.C. and Norman, R. (eds) (2009) *Qualitative Research: Challenging the Orthodoxies in Standard Academic Discourse(s).* New York: Routledge.

Neilsen, L., Cole, A.L. and Knowles, J.G. (eds) (2001) *The Art of Writing Inquiry.* Halifax, Novia Scotia: Backalong Books and Centre for Arts-informed Research.

Poetry

Faulkner, S.L. (2007) 'Concern with craft: Using Ars Poetica as criteria for reading research poetry', *Qualitative Inquiry,* 13 (2): 218–34.

Glesne, C. (1997) 'That rare feeling: Re-presenting research through poetic transcription', *Qualitative Inquiry,* 3 (2): 202–21.

Ohlen, J. (2003) 'Evocation of meaning through poetic condensation of narratives in empirical phenomenological inquiry into human suffering', *Qualitative Health Research,* 13 (4): 557–66.

Prendergast, M. (2006) 'Found poetry as literature review: Research poems on audience and performance', *Qualitative Inquiry,* 12 (2): 369–88.

Richardson, L. (2002) 'Poetic representation of interviews', in J. Gubrium and J.A. Holstein (eds), *Handbook of Interview Research: Context and Method.* Thousand Oaks, CA: Sage. pp. 877–92.

Readers Theater

Donmoyer, R. and Yennie-Donmoyer, J. (1995) 'Data as drama: Reflections on the use of readers theater as a mode of qualitative data display', *Qualitative Inquiry,* 1 (4): 402–28.

Maher, J. (2006) *Most Dangerous Women: Bringing History to Life Through Readers' Theater.* Portsmouth, NH: Heinemann.

Ethnotheatre, Ethnodrama
and Performance Ethnography

Denzin, N. (2003) *Performance Ethnography: Critical Pedagogy and the Politics of Culture*. Thousand Oaks, CA: Sage.

Mienczakowski, J. (2001) 'Ethnodrama. Performed research: Limitations and potential', in P. Atkinson, A. Coffey, S. Delamont, J. Lofland and L. Lofland (eds), *Handbook of Ethnography*. London: Sage. pp. 468–76.

Saldaña, J. (2003) 'Dramatizing data: A primer', *Qualitative Inquiry*, 9 (2): 218–36.

Spry, T. (2001) 'Performing autoethnography: An embodied methodological praxis', *Qualitative Inquiry*, 7 (6): 706–32.

Fiction

Banks, A. and Banks, S.P. (eds) (1998) *Fiction and Social Research*. Walnut Creek, CA: Altamira Press.

Caulley, D.N. (2008) 'Making qualitative research reports less boring', *Qualitative Inquiry*, 14 (3): 424–49.

Clough, P. (2002) *Narratives and Fictions in Educational Research*. Buckingham: Open University Press.

Wolf, M. (1992) *A Thrice Told Tale: Feminism, Postmodernism and Ethnographic Responsibility*. Stanford, CA: Stanford University Press.

Activity 8.1   Reading research: Approaches to analysis

Select a method of data analysis that you are interested in and locate several reports of qualitative studies that have used this approach to data analysis and representation. Read each article, paying particular attention to how the author/s described what they did in order to analyze, interpret, and represent the data.

- What theoretical and conceptual frameworks are described by the author/s?
- What information concerning the analytic process is included?
- How are interview data incorporated into the findings section?
- Is it possible to follow the process described by the author to transform data from transcriptions to a report of findings?
- How convincing did you find the reports? Why?

Activity 8.2   Preliminary coding

Develop preliminary codes using an interview transcript that you have completed. For each code, write a 'code definition' and include a sample of data exemplifying the label. Sort the codes into 'clusters' or 'categories.' Using another transcription from the same study, repeat the process of coding beginning with the codes already generated, and adding new ones. Check the first transcript to see if there are data relevant to the new codes.

- Are there ways in which the codes and categories might be revised?
- What assertions might be made from the data?
- Do you have evidence in the transcripts that contradict the assertions?

Activity 8.3   Examining stories

Locate a 'story' with a beginning, middle, and end in your interview data. Examine the structure of the narrative to locate the key elements (abstract, complication, resolution). How are the people and events characterized by the speaker? Consider the narrator's 'evaluation' of the story – what meanings does the teller ascribe to the narrative?

Activity 8.4   Creative analytic practices

Laurel Richardson (1994, 1999) has written about a variety of 'creative analytic practices' that researchers might use to represent your data. Choose one of these approaches (for example, poetry, fiction, readers' theater, performance ethnography and so forth) to represent interview data. Consider what has been omitted from this telling and what understandings have been added.

NINE

Final Thoughts:
Learning How to Interview

This chapter introduces:

- Qualitative researchers' accounts of their interview practice, including their *research purposes*, their views on *'good' practice*, how they deal with *challenges in interviews*.
- Advice to beginning researchers learning to conduct interviews, including *preparing for the interview*; attending to *research design and question formulation*; *being a good listener*; and *being skeptical*.

Experienced researchers with whom I have talked describe how they have learnt how to interview over time, and how they have experimented with different approaches to the design and conduct of their research. As I have discussed earlier, even while research interviews consist of sequences of questions to be asked of research participants, there are numerous ways to go about designing and conducting interviews, and analyzing, interpreting, and representing interview data. There is no 'correct' way to design and conduct an interview study; although there are more or less effective ways of eliciting data for the purposes of answering specific research questions as judged by particular communities of research practice.

In this chapter I close by reviewing some of the issues highlighted by eight qualitative researchers with whom I have talked about interviewing. By sharing what other qualitative researchers do and say about their work, I hope to demonstrate to readers the variety of practices extant within the field of qualitative inquiry, as well as the kinds of things that novice researchers can do as they experiment with various approaches to interviewing as a method to generate data for research purposes.

Qualitative Researchers' Accounts
of their Interview Practice

The qualitative researchers that I talked to described using interviews for a variety of purposes, including establishing dialogue; constructing historical accounts; and studying questions to do with people's feelings, emotions, perspectives, experiences, and life stories. They talked about using a wide range of interview structures and forms of interviewing including life story, oral history, semi-structured and conversational interviews, phenomenological interviews, photo elicitation, ethnographic interviews, and focus groups. One researcher rejected the use of any of these labels for her work, preferring the term 'interview' to describe her use of this method. All of the researchers that I talked to viewed qualitative interviews as being integral to the development of their research agendas, although several discussed how they made use of data other than interviews.

To provide a glimpse of why these researchers choose to use the interview as a method, I quote three researchers who articulate different research agendas. First, Derrick Alridge situates his work within the disciplinary field of history:

> As a historian, much of my research focuses on the Civil Rights Movement, and the Civil Rights Movement as conceptualized by most historians begins in 1954, and goes up to about 1968 to 1970. So, as you know, many of the people that were involved in the Civil Rights Movement are still living today. So I thought that it would be a very rich source of data for us to talk to people who were actually involved in Civil Rights activities, protests, what have you. So that's how I came into using oral histories as a form of data in my work. (Interview conducted September 4, 2007 by author)

Here, Alridge talks about using the interview method to collect oral histories that he uses to construct historical accounts of events and activities related to the Civil Rights Movement in the US.

Another researcher, Thomas Hébert, who is a qualitative researcher working within the field of gifted and creative education, uses life-story interviews, but rather than constructing historical accounts, he focuses on capturing life stories in order to examine individuals' personal experiences as they relate to research questions pertinent to the field of gifted and creative education. He describes this as a 'natural match' with his personal interests:

> So I think interviewing (laughingly) has just been a natural match for the biography fanatic that I am. So capturing people's life stories is important to me, and I think I enjoyed that early experience [in coursework in graduate school] of interviewing and developing a relationship with these characters and it was a lot of fun, and from there, my dissertation work, depended tremendously on interviews ... (Interview conducted 6 April 2007 by author)

Finally, Sharan Merriam, a researcher in the field of adult education, describes the interview method as the most appropriate means of answering the questions about adult development that she seeks to examine. In her view, interviews are the most powerful and effective means of learning about people's feelings, opinions, perspectives, and personal experiences:

> Typically the questions ... I tend to ask to guide a study can only be answered through interviews ... I do work on learning transformation, [adult] learning and [adult] development, those kind of things ... you can't really observe so I mean ... there

is no other way to get that information other than interviewing. I think it's ... probably the most powerful qualitative research technique, certainly most used in most
studies. So I think it depends on your question. If you are asking about interaction
patterns in a classroom, you can watch those, but if you are asking about someone's
feelings, opinion, perspective, understanding of an experience ... it's hard to observe
that. So, it has to be an interview. (Interview conducted 3 April 2007 by author)

While researchers I talked with discussed the theoretical perspectives that
informed their work, not all made the links between these perspectives and how
they used interviewing explicitly. Whereas some expressed a pragmatic or eclectic
view of their use of interviews – that is, they talked of using interviews of varying
structures for particular kinds of research purposes in diverse projects – two
researchers explicitly linked the theoretical perspectives they employed with their
view of interviewing as a 'dialogue' (in this case, philosophical hermeneutics and
critical theory, and feminist theory). Several researchers talked about the interview
as an encounter in which speakers co-construct data together, and situated their use
of interviews within a 'constructionist' perspective. What may be noted in these
accounts is the differing degrees to which researchers from different disciplinary
backgrounds situate their use of interviews in particular theoretical traditions.

'Good' Practice in Interviewing

Commonalities emerged in these qualitative researchers' accounts of what 'good'
interviewing looked like. Good practice in interviewing was seen to involve appropriate preparation; demonstration of appropriate respect for participants; intensive
listening on the part of the interviewer; development of thoughtful interview guides
that used appropriate question formulation with fewer, rather than more, questions;
posing of short, open-ended questions; flexibility on the part of the interviewer to
deviate from prior plans when necessary; and effective use of follow up questions
within interviews to elicit the participants' understandings of topics.

When asked to describe a 'satisfying' interview, a number of researchers
described having had 'rich' interviews that were 'articulate' and 'complete,' or
expressions of 'authentic experiences' of the interviewees. Participants who provided 'very rich descriptions' and who were able to articulate their views and perspectives concerning the researchers' topics were seen to provide data that could
be used effectively in reporting findings from studies. In some senses, 'good interviews' were sometimes described by researchers as involving participants who had
a wealth of knowledge and who were open to talking about their experiences in
interviews. Researchers categorized many of these satisfying interviews as those in
which they learned much from interviewees, and several researchers described
how their understandings of the topics of study were transformed by their interactions with participants.

While 'good' interviews might involve a combination of 'good practice' and
'articulate' participants, 'rich' data might also be generated from challenging interviews. Researchers commented that interviews did not necessarily always go to

plan, or run smoothly. Yet challenging interviews could also be those in which researchers learned a great deal, and generated much useful data.

Dealing with Challenges in Qualitative Interviewing

Researchers described a variety of challenges that they had encountered in interviews, including procedural and technical challenges, issues related to the topic of research; and interviewer–interviewee relationships. Procedural and technical challenges related to unexpected events and interruptions occurring within interviews, or the impacts of contexts that interfered with establishing rapport with participants. Participants described addressing procedural and technical issues by learning how to be flexible in dealing with unexpected events, and preparing adequately in order to avoid problems.

Challenges relating to the research topic included how researchers dealt with difficult emotional issues that emerged in the interview (such as participants' personal hardships and problems); how researchers work with research topics that had deep personal significance; interviewing participants about abstract topics that they found difficult to talk about; or for which the interviewer found it challenging to find the right questions to elicit relevant data; or interviewing participants who may not accurately remember events, or seem not to be truthful. When dealing with difficult and sensitive topics initiated by participants, researchers discussed two approaches – two talked about maintaining a neutral viewpoint as interviewer, but expressing empathy with participants; while another researcher discussed fully engaging in emotional expressions with a participant. Speaking particularly of novice researchers, one researcher suggested that it might be wise for them to not pursue topics of research in which they have a high emotional investment as beginning projects. Two researchers commented that doubtful information provided by participants could be verified via other sources.

Challenges to do with the relationship between interviewer and interviewee included interviewing people who are different to the researcher (for example, in class, race, ethnicity, cultural background, generation, gender, education, status); lack of shared understanding or shared language between interviewer and interviewee with which to discuss topics; interviewing participants who do not appear to be reflective, or are not able to articulate their experiences to an interviewer; interviewing people who may not want to talk to the interviewer; or interviewing participants who volunteer for a study, but may have not had the experience that is required in order to participate fully in the interview. Several researchers identified children and adolescents as being potentially problematic populations for older researchers to work with, and these problems could be exacerbated if participants were of a different race, ethnicity, or cultural background than the researcher.

Researchers described a range of strategies to deal with the challenges involved in the development of trusting relationships with interviewees. Several researchers talked about recognizing the limitations of who they could and could not effectively interview, and what topics they could and could not elicit adequate data about, and account for that in the design and conduct of a study. This involved a number of options including: not conducting interviews or doing research with those groups with whom they felt they would not be able to develop relationships that would allow for effective interviewing; working to manage personal responses to the differences between self and others; conducting multiple interviews over time; doing more preparation for the interview in order to get to know participants and establish a shared language to talk with them; finding ways to establish commonality with participants in order to enhance rapport (such as introducing personal experiences, as in feminist approaches to interviewing; or immersing oneself in the participants' culture, as in ethnographic work); establishing relationships with gatekeepers to assist in developing relationships with participants; working with an insider to a group as a co-researcher; and modifying the research design in order to generate other kinds of data, or use alternative kinds of interview strategies (for example, involving participants as co-researchers to interview others).

What might be made of qualitative researchers' accounts of their interview practices? First, these researchers provide a wide range of accounts concerning their practice – they speak about using a multiplicity of interview forms and structures, and experimenting with different approaches. Second, although the group collectively represented many decades of research experience, each described challenges that they faced in their own interviewing practices and unanticipated issues that had arisen in their research projects. Third, these researchers described learning how to conduct research interviews more effectively over time – this most frequently included learning how to listen more intently to participants, learning how to formulate questions more effectively, and becoming more flexible in dealing with unexpected occurrences. Finally, there are no short cuts to learning how to interview – these researchers agreed that practice, and reflection on that practice was the most effective way to learn how to interview. I close by reviewing four pieces of advice offered by my colleagues.

Advice from Qualitative Interviewers

In talking with researchers who use qualitative interviews in their work and who teach coursework in qualitative methods, I asked them what advice they give their students. Their replies to this question can be synthesized into four principles:

(1) prepare for the interview;
(2) attend to research design and question formulation;
(3) be a good listener; and
(4) be skeptical.

These final pieces of advice are interrelated, and were frequently discussed in relation to one another. Below I highlight some of what these researchers said about these issues.

Prepare for the Interview

As described in Chapter 5, preparation may include learning about the topic one is studying, doing one's homework concerning the participant in relation to the context of the research, and searching for relevant background information. Another aspect of preparation is that of rehearsing the interview questions through practicing the interview itself. Judith Preissle describes the importance of preparation for interviews as follows:

> Even if you're going to do the most open, phenomenological interview, decide what you're going to ask ahead of time. Rehearse it. Try it out with people you're not really going to use information from. Make your changes accordingly. [11 second pause] Prepare, prepare yourself in a way that will free you to focus on your respondent. (Interview conducted 26 June 2007 by author)

Linda Harklau, a researcher in applied linguistics who was trained in anthropological fieldwork, also discussed practice as an essential part of developing skills as an interviewer:

> In terms of overall interviewing practices I think practice is probably what gets you there. I always have students go out and do interviews, and see how they did, and I don't know if you can learn it except by doing ... I think that some people have an easier time with interviewing as a method than others, because [some people are] natural talkers that really have a hard time not jumping in when people are talking ... Then there's other people that ... start out with this sort of psychologist, psychiatrist, sort of clinician attitude ... [that interviewees] will find really off-putting ... They have to find a way to ... get rid of that. (Interview conducted 4 June 2008 by author)

Although researchers can be prepared, they learn by doing. Similarly to other colleagues who I have talked with, both of these researchers emphasize that the only way to learn how to interview is by practice.

Attend to Research Design and Question Formulation

In Chapters 1 and 2, I outlined a number of different approaches to individual and group interviews. These forms of interviews varied in the kinds of questions asked. Across qualitative interviews, however, there are some commonalities concerning the kinds of questions posed. Qualitative inquirers lean towards the use of fewer, open-ended questions, in contrast to employing lengthy protocols that offer possible response options as used in standardized surveys. Kathleen deMarrais, an educational ethnographer and experienced teacher of qualitative research methods, advises her students to work on the research design to develop effective interview questions:

> One thing would be to really get your design in place. So what is it that you want to know? And you may not know that. You may not even be able to start with the design.

You may want to start with an idea ... you're interested in a topic, and you don't really even know enough about it, so go to that literature and read that literature, but also try an interview out. Try an interview out with someone that you may even know, and see what comes up. And in the questions that you've drafted out, are they really going to get to what you want to know for your study. Are they going to work for you? Will it get you to the focus of the study? (Interview conducted 23 May 2008 by author)

Once again, we see in this advice the need for preparation as integral in designing a study. deMarrais also stressed the need for interviewers to learn how to ask fewer, open questions, advice with which Sharan Merriam concurs:

[Don't] have too many questions ... fewer, broader, open questions. 'Tell me about.' 'Give me an example of.' 'What was your experience doing such and such?' (Interview conducted 3 April 2007 by author)

Asking questions effectively is enormously important as an interviewer – but equally important is to listen carefully to what participants say.

Be a Good Listener

Interviewers must learn how to listen respectfully to others, and value what they say. This involves focusing on the participants' stories, and being flexible with enacting the interview guide so that participants can speak without being interrupted by an interviewee bound up in asking particular questions on the interview protocol. In her work with novice interviewers, Juanita Johnson-Bailey also highlights being prepared, and learning to listen respectfully to participants:

I would say be prepared and value listening, value silence, and be respectful. I think too many people are not respectful of the process, respectful of the people that they are interviewing. Find that place where you connect with them. I think when you find that place of connection you can get so much more. I think there's a flow that's established when there is a connection. (Interview conducted 10 May 2007 by author)

Melissa Freeman, a qualitative methodologist who works from a philosophical hermeneutical perspective, also foregrounds the importance of developing listening skills, adding that researchers must learn how to ask open questions that seek descriptions of the phenomenon under examination.

You as an interviewer have to really learn to listen ... it's not about you. It's about allowing that participant to really share, and it's about you asking them in ways that allow you to understand what they're trying to say .... I think a lot of ... new researchers have this idea that the answers will suddenly be there, and they want to get at those answers. They don't understand that you get at all the experiences, and the answers come through the process of analysis and interpretation. So listening well [and] respecting what your participants can contribute, is to me ... really important ...

Think about your questions through the experience itself .... And if you think about your interview questions as ways into the experience of the phenomenon, topic, or whatever, then your interview questions becomes a much more open, looser way of getting into [the topic]. (Interview conducted 21 March 2007, by author)

Derrick Alridge also stresses the importance of not allowing interview protocols to drive the interview:

... you have to be flexible and let the ... interviewee tell their story, because they're going to answer the question, but it's not number one, or number two on the interview protocol. (Interview conducted 4 September 2007, by author)

Through developing intensive listening skills, and through practice, interviewers can learn how to use interview protocols as guides to conversations, rather than as instruments that dictate the topic of talk in ways that do not fit with how participants want to talk about their experiences.

What is necessary in order to enact the three principles described above in the various forms of interviews described in Chapters 1 and 2 will likely vary among projects and researchers. Therefore, a certain amount of skepticism concerning all advice is warranted.

Be Skeptical

The advice to 'be skeptical' is gleaned from my colleague Judith Preissle, who highlights the fact that all lists of advice work in some cases, but not in others. Preissle explains:

... there's always going to be an exception. When would you not prepare? Well, when you have an opportunity to just get an interview, and you don't have any time to prepare. I mean there are going to be times when you might deliberately choose not to prepare. When don't you listen? Well, when you're interviewing that 85-year-old who goes way off and tells you about ... his argument with his daughter, when you're trying to get him to talk about what he remembers from his schooling. You know, that's probably an appropriate time to ... intervene, OK. There are shy people in the world who just, if you let there be too much silence, they freeze up even more. So it's better to be a little chatty at least until you build a relationship. (Interview conducted 26 June 2007 by author)

A certain amount of skepticism concerning advice is healthy for all researchers reading methods texts, given that what works for one researcher may not necessarily work for another; and what works in one context will be unhelpful elsewhere. Whether researchers choose to use research interviews or not, how they go about doing that work will differ according to individual purposes. What is certain, however, is that opportunities for qualitative interviewing abound.

To conclude, the researchers that I spoke with expressed passion and a continuing curiosity for the topics that they study. Asking questions in interviews is one method to study the research questions that intrigue us. In this book, I have suggested that by asking questions of ourselves, and the interview methods that we seek to use, we as qualitative researchers can collectively advance the practice of qualitative interviewing. Am I advocating that anything goes? Most certainly not. Instead, I recommend that qualitative researchers reflect on their practices as interviewers. This includes considering questions such as:

- Who am I as a researcher?
- What are my assumptions concerning knowledge production?
- What are my subject positions in relation to my research topics and participants?
- How do I ask interview questions?
- What are the implications of my interview practice for the data generated?
- What are the implications of my theoretical assumptions concerning research for how data might be analyzed, interpreted and represented?

By making connections to the theories and disciplinary bodies of knowledge that inform our work, I argue that qualitative researchers and interviewers can contribute research of significance and quality to the world around us.

Further Reading

Walford, G. (2007) 'Classification and framing of interviews in ethnographic interviewing', *Ethnography and Education*, 2 (2), 145–57.
This article provides a glimpse into how seven prominent researchers who have published ethnographies describe their use of the interview method.

APPENDIX ONE

Transcription Conventions

Interviewer:	IR
Interviewee:	IE
(really)	unclear words spoken, best guess
( )	unclear words spoken, inaudible
(( ))	transcriber's description
[	two speakers' talk overlaps at this point
[	
=	no interval between turns ('latching')
?	interrogative intonation
(2.0)	pause timed in seconds
(.)	small untimed pause
we::ll	prolonged syllable or sound
why	emphasis or stressed word or syllable
REALLY	word spoken noticeably louder than surrounding talk
°yes°	words spoken noticeably softer than surrounding talk
<I have to go>	words spoken noticeably faster than surrounding talk
heh heh	laughter syllables
fun(h)ny	words spoken laughingly
.hhh	in-breath
hhh.	out-breath
↑	upward rise in intonation
↓	downward fall in intonation

APPENDIX TWO

Terms Used in
Conversation Analysis

Assessment: An utterance that expresses an opinion or evaluation. The 'preferred' response is that of agreement. Below, an interviewer (IR) provides a positive 'assessment' of an interviewee's selection of the 'event' she will describe in response to the IR's prior question:

1. IE   OK well I guess I'll just do the most recent one I just had one this month
2. IR   Oh OK that's great

Adjacency pair: A 'paired sequence of talk' such as summons and response, greeting–greeting, question and answer, invitation and response, accusation and denial. An adjacency pair includes two turns by different speakers. The 'first pair part' provides a slot for a 'second pair part'; however the utterance of a second pair part may not necessarily follow immediately after a first pair part. An example of an adjacency pair in the form of question–answer sequence:

1. IR   Could he have organized it differently?
2. IE   He could have got somebody else in

Extreme case formulation: a formulation expressed in an 'extreme' case (e.g. 'brand new,' 'never,' 'always,' 'every'). ECFs have been found to be used to legitimize claims, construct complaints, do praise, put forward a case in an argument, defend a position, or blame others (Pomerantz, 1986).

1. IE   =we could rea::d music they could read and they would you know I
2.   could put a brand new (.) uh song a pentatonic song=

Formulations: Formulations are statements that 'sum up' the on-going talk, or 'characterize states of affairs already described or negotiated (in whole or in part) in the preceding talk' (Heritage and Watson, 1979: 126). The properties of formulations are that they preserve information, delete information, and transform what has been said in prior interaction. Below, the interviewer formulates prior talk, and poses this as a question to the interviewee, who agrees, and expands on the formulation.

```
1.  IR   so do you find because of this (.) um (.) I guess compression of more
2.       classes into the same period of time that you're just doing less and less?
3.       (1.0)
4.  IE   oh yes it's it's not half as good it's about a quarter as good you know=
```

Preference: The concept of 'preference' refers to interactional events in which 'alternative, but nonequivalent, courses of action are available to participants' (Sacks, 1973, cited by Atkinson and Heritage 1984: 53). 'The central insight [of preference organization] is that not all the potential second parts to a first part of an adjacency pair are of equal standing: there is a ranking operating over the alternatives such that there is at least one *preferred* and one *dispreferred* category of response ... In essence, preferred seconds are *unmarked* – they occur as structurally simpler turns; in contrast dispreferred seconds are *marked* by various kinds of structural complexity. Thus dispreferred seconds are typically delivered: (1) after some significant delay; (2) with some preface marking their dispreferred status, often the particle *well*; (3) with some account of why the preferred second cannot be performed.' (Levinson, 1983: 307, emphasis in original; see also Atkinson and Heritage, 1984: 53)

Recipient design: People orient to and demonstrate sensitivity to multiple features of talk in designing it for co-present parties. These include word selection, topic selection, ordering of sequences, and opening and closing conversations (Sacks et al., 1974: 727).

Repair: The moves people make to correct what they think are mistakes. Mistakes include ones that the speaker has made, or ones that others have made. Repair organization addresses problems in speaking, hearing, or understanding in conversation. Repair has two broad classes: self-repair and other repair. 'Repair is used to negotiate meaning and allows speakers to resolve trouble in speaking, hearing, or understanding' (Schegloff et al., 1977: 361).

Second story: People routinely tell stories that are interactionally relevant to stories told by others. A story narrated by a speaker that resembles the features of a story told by a prior speaker is a 'second story' (Sacks, 1992).

Turn-taking:
Turn constructional unit: The basic 'building block' of multi-party talk is a TCU, or turn. TCUs may include sentences, clauses, and phrases, and are shaped by intonation. Speakers accomplish actions via TCUs, and a single TCU may involve more than one action (Schegloff, 2007: 3–4).

Transition-relevance place: The point at which a possible completion of a TCU is hearable by parties to the talk. A speaker transition may or may not take place at this point (Schegloff, 2007: 4).

APPENDIX THREE

Excerpt 7.1 (March 2002)

IR: Interviewer
IE: Interviewee

1. IR OK (.) and so I guess the last question about this one would be (.) um (.)
2.   do you think (.) I mean 'cos it sounds like a lot of (.) because it could
3.   have been a lot worse=
4.   =[mm hm mm hm
5.   =[from what you're saying (.) and so it sounds like a lot of (.) the anger
6.   you felt was:: maybe not (.) ↑totally apparent to other people but was it↑
7.   I mean did other people who maybe the other students who saw the
8.   incident or (.) other (.) the principal or whatever who heard the story
9.   do you think that they knew like the ex<u>tent</u> or the ↑level of anger
10.   you were ↑at at that point? or was it something that you felt inside
11.   that maybe (.) didn't really show itself
12.   (2.0)
13. IR I mean do you think it'd be apparent to everyone that you were
14.   <u>really</u> angry at that moment
15. IE at ↑<u>that</u> moment I <u>think</u> (.) my <u>students</u> probably <u>knew</u> (.) you know (.)
16.   "O::::h shit" [you know it hit the FA::::N [you know what I'm ↑saying=
17. IR   [mm hm   [HEH HEH HEH HEY
18.   =HEH HEH HEH HEH it's ↑really ↓bad=
19. IR =uh huh=
20. IE =but ↑no::: I don't (.) ((clears throat)) I think the teachers knew (.) how-
21.   they knew I was ↑<u>mad</u> (.) but <u>not</u> from that situation because by the
22.   time I went to the principal=
23. IR =mm hm=
24. IE =and told the principal what had happened and then he took over
25.   the situation (2.0) and I went back to my cla::ss like I said and tried to
26.   hold that pro↑<u>fess</u>ionalism=
27. IR =mm hm=
28. IE =and try to ↑gain my my professionalism back (.) I don't
29.   think you could <u>tell</u> that I was very angry until I I told you everybody
30.   when I talked to my <u>mentor</u> teachers and the other teachers and
31.   I told them what had happened or a couple of them <u>found</u> <u>out</u>=
32. IR =mm hmm=
33. IE =what had happened because of the students of course the students will
34.   tell you
35. IR heh heh heh heh=
36. IE =HEH HEH HEH

APPENDIX FOUR

Further Resources

Examples of Syllabi for Qualitative Course Work and Interview Courses

http://www.coe.uga.edu/syllabus/qual/index.html
http://www.qualitativeresearch.uga.edu/QualPage/teachingqual.htm
http://www.nova.edu/ssss/QR/syllabi.html

Sample Rubrics for Interview Assignments

Roulston, K., deMarrais, K. and Lewis, J. (2003) 'Learning to interview in the social sciences', *Qualitative Inquiry*, 9 (4): 643–68.

Designing an Authentic Interview Project

Roulston, K., McClendon, V. J., Thomas, A., Tuff, R., Williams, G. and Healy, M. (2008) 'Developing reflective interviewers and reflexive researchers', *Reflective Practice*, 9 (3): 231–43.

References

Abell, J., Locke, A., Condor, S., Gibson, S. and Stevenson, C. (2006) 'Trying similarity, doing difference: The role of interviewer self-disclosure in interview talk with young people', *Qualitative Research,* 6 (2): 221–44.

Adams, C. and van Manen, M. (2008) 'Phenomenology', in L.M. Given (ed) *The Sage Encyclopedia of Qualitative Research Methods.* Vol. 2,. Thousand Oaks, CA: Sage. pp. 614–19.

Agar, M. and McDonald, J. (1995) 'Focus groups and ethnography', *Human Organization,* 54 (1): 78–86.

Alford, R.R. (1998) *The Craft of Inquiry: Theories, Methods, Evidence.* New York: Oxford University Press.

Alridge, D. (2007) Interview by K. Roulston. University of Georgia, Athens, GA.

Alvermann, D.A. (2000) 'Researching libraries, literacies and lives: A rhizoanalysis', in E.A. St Pierre and W.S. Pillow (eds), *Working the Ruins: Feminist Poststructural Theory and Methods in Education.* New York & London: Routledge. pp. 114–29.

Alvesson, M. (2003) 'Beyond neopositivists, romantics, and localists: A reflexive approach to interviews in organizational research', *Academy of Management Review,* 28 (1): 13–33.

Angrosino, M. (1998) *Opportunity House: Ethnographic Stories of Mental Retardation.* Walnut Creek: Altamira Press.

Arendell, T. (1997) 'Reflections on the researcher–researched relationship: A woman interviewing men', *Qualitative Sociology,* 20 (3): 341–68.

Ashmore, M. (1989) *The Reflexive Thesis: Wrighting Sociology of Scientific Knowledge.* Chicago: The University of Chicago Press.

Atkinson, J.M. and Heritage, J. (eds) (1984) *Structures of Social Action: Studies in Conversation Analysis.* Cambridge: Cambridge University Press.

Atkinson, P. and Coffey, A. (2002) 'Revisiting the relationship between participant observation and interviewing', in J.F. Gubrium and J.A. Holstein (eds), *Handbook of Interview Research: Context and Method.* Thousand Oaks, CA: Sage. pp. 801–14.

Atkinson, P. and Silverman, D. (1997) 'Kundera's immortality: The interview society and the invention of the self', *Qualitative Inquiry,* 3 (3): 304–25.

Bach, H. (2007) 'Composing a visual narrative inquiry', in D.J. Clandinin (ed.), *Handbook of Narrative Inquiry: Mapping a Methodology.* Thousand Oaks, CA: Sage. pp. 280–307.

Baker, C.D. (1983) 'A "second look" at interviews with adolescents', *Journal of Youth and Adolescence,* 12 (6): 501–19.

Baker, C.D. (1984) 'The "search for adultness": Membership work in adolescent–adult talk', *Human Studies,* (7): 301–23.

Baker, C.D. (1997) 'Membership categorization and interview accounts', in D. Silverman (ed), *Qualitative Research: Theory, Method and Practice.* London: Sage. pp. 130–43.

Baker, C. D. (2000) 'Locating culture in action: Membership categorisation in texts and talk', in A. Lee and C. Poynton (eds), *Culture and Text: Discourse and Methodology in Social Research and Cultural Studies.* St Leonards: Allen & Unwin. pp. 99–113.

Baker, C.D. (2002) 'Ethnomethodological analyses of interviews', in J.F. Gubrium and J.A. Holstein (eds), *Handbook of Interviewing: Context and Method.* Thousand Oaks, CA: Sage. pp. 777–95.

Baker, C.D. (2004) 'Membership categorization and interview accounts', in D. Silverman (ed.), *Qualitative Research: Theory, Method and Practice*, 2nd edn. London: Sage. pp. 162–76.

Banks, A. and Banks, S.P. (eds) (1998) *Fiction and Social Research*. Walnut Creek, CA: Altamira Press.

Barbour, R. (2007) *Doing Focus Groups*. London: Sage.

Barbour, R. and Kitzinger, J. (eds) (1999) *Developing Focus Group Research: Politics, Theory and Practice*. London: Sage.

Bartlett, J., Iwasaki, Y., Gottlieb, B., Hall, D. and Mannell, R. (2007) 'Framework for Aboriginal-guided decolonizing research involving Métis and First Nations persons with diabetes', *Social Science and Medicine,* (65): 2371–82.

Beck, C.T. (2005) 'Benefits of participating in internet interviews: Women helping women', *Qualitative Health Research,* 15 (3): 411–22.

Behar, R. (1993) *Translated Woman: Crossing the Border with Esperanza's Story*. Boston, MA: Beacon Press.

Bellah, R.N., Madsen, R., Sullivan, W.M., Swidler, A. and Tipton, S.M. (1985) *Habits of the Heart: Individualism and Commitment in American Life*. Berkeley, CA: University of California Press.

Bell-Scott, P. and Johnson-Bailey, J. (1998) *Flat-footed Truths: Telling Black Women's Lives*. New York: Henry Holt.

Best, A.L. (2003) 'Doing race in the context of feminist interviewing: Constructing whiteness through talk', *Qualitative Inquiry,* 9 (6): 895–914.

Best, S. and Kellner, D. (1991) *Postmodern Theory: Critical Interrogations*. London: Macmillan.

Best, S. and Kellner, D. (1997) *The Postmodern Turn*. New York: The Guilford Press.

Best, S. and Kellner, D. (2001) *The Postmodern Adventure: Science, Technology, and Cultural Studies at the Third Millennium*. New York: The Guilford Press.

Bishop, R. (2005) 'Freeing ourselves from neocolonial domination in research: A Kaupapa Maori approach to creating knowledge', in N.K. Denzin and Y.S. Lincoln (eds), *The Sage Handbook of Qualitative Research,* 3rd edn. Thousand Oaks, CA: Sage. pp. 109–38.

Bloor, M., Frankland, J., Thomas, M. and Robson, K. (2001) *Focus Groups in Social Research*. Thousand Oaks, CA: Sage

Bogdan, R.C. and Biklen, S.K. (2003) *Qualitative Research for Education: An Introduction to Theory and Methods*, 4th edn. Boston, MA: Pearson Education Group.

Bourdieu, P., Accardo, A., Balazs, G., Beaud, S., Bonvin, F., Bourdieu, E., et al. (1999) *The Weight of the World: Social Suffering in Contemporary Society* (P.P. Ferguson, S. Emanuel, J. Johnson and S.T. Waryn, Trans.). Stanford, CA: Stanford University Press. (Original work published 1993)

Bradbury-Jones, C. (2007) 'Enhancing rigour in qualitative health research: Exploring subjectivity through Peshkin's I's', *Journal of Advanced Nursing,* 59 (3): 290–98.

Brenner, M. (1985) 'Survey interviewing', in M. Brenner, J. Brown and D. Canter (eds), *The Research Interview: Uses and Approaches*. London: Academic Press. pp. 9–36.

Briggs, C. (1986) *Learning How to Ask: A Sociolinguistic Appraisal of the Role of the Interview in Social Science Research*. Cambridge: Cambridge University Press.

Brinkmann, S. (2007) 'Could interviews be epistemic? An alternative to qualitative opinion polling', *Qualitative Inquiry,* 13 (8): 1116–38.

Brinkmann, S. and Kvale, S. (2005) 'Confronting the ethics of qualitative research', *Journal of Constructivist Psychology,* (18): 157–81.

Brody, G., Ge, X., Kim, S.Y., Murry, V.M., Simons, R.L., Gibbons, F.X., Gerrard, M. and Conger, R.D. (2003) 'Neighborhood disadvantage moderates associations of parenting and older sibling problem attitudes and behavior with conduct disorders in African American children', *Journal of Consulting and Clinical Psychology,* 71 (2): 211–22.

Bucholtz, M. (2000) 'The politics of transcription', *Journal of Pragmatics,* 32 (10): 1439–65.

Bucholtz, M. and Du Bois, J. (n.d.) *Transcription in Action: Resources for Representation of Linguistic Interaction.* Available at: http://www.linguistics.ucsb.edu/projects/transcription/representing (accessed 24 July 2008).

Cahnmann, M. (2003) 'The craft, practice, and possibility of poetry in educational research', *Educational Researcher,* 32 (3): 29–36.

Cahnmann-Taylor, M. (2008) 'Arts-based research: Histories and new directions', in M. Cahnmann-Taylor and R. Siegesmund (eds), *Arts-based Research in Education: Foundations for Practice.* New York: Routledge. pp. 3–15.

Charmaz, K. (1997) 'Identity dilemmas of chronically ill men', in A. Strauss and J. Corbin (eds) *Grounded Theory in Practice.* Thousand Oaks, CA: Sage. pp. 35–62.

Charmaz, K. (2000) 'Grounded theory: Objectivist and constructivist methods', in N. Denzin and Y.S. Lincoln (eds), *Handbook of Qualitative Research,* 2nd edn. Thousand Oaks, CA: Sage. pp. 509–35.

Charmaz, K. (2002) 'Qualitative interviewing and grounded theory analysis', in J. Gubrium and J.A. Holstein (eds), *Handbook of Interview Research.* Thousand Oaks, CA: Sage. pp. 675–94.

Charmaz, K. (2006) *Constructing Grounded Theory: A Practical Guide Through Qualitative Analysis.* London: Sage.

Charmaz, K. (2008) 'Grounded theory as an emergent method', in S.N. Hesse-Biber and P. Leavy (eds), *Handbook of Emergent Methods.* New York: The Guilford Press. pp. 155–70.

Chiseri-Strater, E. (1996) 'Turning in upon ourselves: Positionality, subjectivity, and reflexivity in case study and ethnographic research', in P. Mortensen and G.E. Kirsch (eds), *Ethics and Representation in Qualitative Studies of Literacy.* Urbana, IL: National Council of Teachers of English. pp. 115–33.

Chubbuck, S.M. and Zembylas, M. (2008) 'The emotional ambivalence of socially just teaching: A case study of a novice urban schoolteacher', *American Educational Research Journal,* 45 (2): 274–318.

Clandinin, D.J. and Murphy, M.S. (2007) 'Looking ahead: Conversations with Elliot Mishler, Don Polkinghorne, and Amia Lieblich', in D.J. Clandinin (ed.), *Handbook of Narrative Inquiry: Mapping a Methodology.* Thousand Oaks, CA: Sage. pp. 632–50.

Clarke, A.E. (2005) *Situational Analysis: Grounded Theory after the Postmodern Turn.* Thousand Oaks, CA: Sage.

Clark-Ibáñez, M. (2004) 'Framing the social world with photo-elicitation interviews', *American Behavioral Scientist,* 47 (12): 1507–27.

Clough, P. (2002) *Narratives and Fictions in Educational Research.* Buckingham: Open University Press.

Coffey, A. and Atkinson, P. (1996) *Making Sense of Qualitative Data: Complementary Research Strategies.* Thousand Oaks, CA: Sage.

Cole, A.L. and Knowles, J.G. (eds) (2001) *Lives in Context: The Art of Life History Research.* Walnut Creek, CA: Altamira Press.

Corbin, J. and Strauss, A. (2008) *Basics of Qualitative Research: Techniques and Procedures for Developing Grounded Theory,* 3rd edn. London: Sage.

Corsaro, W.A. and Molinari, L. (1990) 'From seggiolini to discussione: The generation and extension of peer culture among Italian preschool children', *International Journal of Qualitative Studies in Education,* 3 (3): 213–30.

Davidson, C.R. (2009) 'Transcription: Imperatives for qualitative research', *International Journal of Qualitative Methods,* 8 (2): 35–52. Available at: http://ejournals.library.ualberta.ca/index.php/IJQM/article/view/4205/5401 (accessed 27 September 2009).

Davis, L. (2004) 'Risky stories: Speaking and writing in colonial spaces', *Native Studies Review,* 15 (1): 1–31.

Davis, M., Bolding, G., Hart, G., Sherr, L. and Elford, J. (2004) 'Reflecting on the experience of interviewing online: Perspectives from the internet and HIV study in London', *AIDS Care*, 16 (8): 944–52.

Deleuze, G. and Guattari, F. (1987) *A Thousand Plateaus: Capitalism and Schizophrenia* (B. Massumi, Trans.). Minneapolis, MN: University of Minnesota Press. (Original published 1980)

Delgado Bernal, D. (1998) 'Using a Chicana feminist epistemology in educational research', *Harvard Education Review*, 68 (4): 555–79.

deMarrais, K. (2008) Interview by K. Roulston. University of Georgia, Athens.

Denzin, N.K. (1997) *Interpretive Ethnography: Ethnographic Practices for the 21st Century*. Thousand Oaks, CA: Sage.

Denzin, N.K. (2001) 'The reflexive interview and a performative social science', *Qualitative Research*, 1 (1): 23–46.

Denzin, N.K. (2003a) *Performance Ethnography: Critical Pedagogy and the Politics of Culture*. Thousand Oaks, CA: Sage.

Denzin, N.K. (2003b) 'Reading and writing performance', *Qualitative Research*, 3 (2): 243–68.

Denzin, N.K. (2005) 'Emancipatory discourses and the ethics and politics of interpretation', in N.K. Denzin and Y.S. Lincoln (eds), *The Sage Handbook of Qualitative Research*, 3rd edn. Thousand Oaks, CA: Sage. pp. 933–58.

DeVault, M.L. (1990) 'Talking and listening from women's standpoint: Feminist strategies for interviewing and analysis', *Social Problems*, 37 (1): 96–116.

DeVault, M.L. and Gross, G. (2007) 'Feminist interviewing: Experience, talk, and knowledge', in S.N. Hesse-Biber (ed.), *Handbook of Feminist Research: Theory and Praxis*. Thousand Oaks, CA: Sage. pp. 143–54.

DeWalt, K.M. and DeWalt, B.R. (2002) *Participant Observation: A Guide for Fieldworkers*. Walnut Creek, CA: AltaMira Press.

Dexter, L. (1970) *Elite and Specialized Interviewing*. Evanston, IL: Northwestern University Press.

Dey, I. (1999) *Grounding Grounded Theory: Guidelines for Qualitative Inquiry*. San Diego, CA: Academic Press.

Dickson-Swift, V., James, E. L., Kippen, S. and Liamputtong, P. (2007) 'Doing sensitive research: What challenges do qualitative researchers face?', *Qualitative Research*, 7 (3): 327–53.

Dinkins, C.S. (2005) 'Shared inquiry: Socratic-hermeneutic interpre-viewing', in P. M. Ironside (ed.), *Beyond Method: Philosophical Conversations in Healthcare Research and Scholarship*. Madison, WI: University of Wisconsin Press. pp. 111–47.

Donmoyer, R. and Yennie-Donmoyer, J. (1995) 'Data as drama: Reflections on the use of readers theater as a mode of qualitative data display', *Qualitative Inquiry*, 1 (4): 402–28.

Douglas, J.D. (1985) *Creative Interviewing*. Beverly Hills, CA: Sage.

Dunaway, D.K. (1996) 'The interdisciplinarity of oral history', in D.K. Dunaway and W.K. Baum (eds), *Oral History: An Interdisciplinary Anthology*, 2nd edn. Walnut Creek, CA: Altamira Press. pp. 7–22.

Duneier, M. (2000) *Sidewalk*. New York: Farrar, Straus & Giroux.

Duranti, A. (1997) *Linguistic Anthropology*. Cambridge: Cambridge University Press.

Egan, J., Chenoweth, L. and McAuliffe, D. (2006) 'Email-facilitated qualitative interviews with traumatic brain injury survivors: a new and accessible method', *Brain Injuries*, 20 (12): 1283–94.

Eisner, E.W. (1997) 'The promise and perils of alternative forms of data representation', *Educational Researcher*, 26 (6): 4–10.

Emerson, R.M., Fretz, R.I. and Shaw, L.L. (1995) *Writing Ethnographic Fieldnotes*. Chicago, IL: The University of Chicago Press.

Esposito, N. (2001) 'From meaning to meaning: The influence of translation techniques on Non-English focus group research', *Qualitative Health Research,* 11 (4): 568–79.

Farquhar, C. and Das, R. (1999) 'Are focus groups suitable for "sensitive topics"?', in R.S. Barbour and J. Kitzinger (eds), *Developing Focus Group Research: Politics, Theory and Practice.* London: Sage. pp. 47–63.

Faulkner, S.L. (2007) 'Concern with craft: Using Ars Poetica as criteria for reading research poetry', *Qualitative Inquiry,* 13 (2): 218–34.

Faulkner, S.L. (2005) 'Method: Six poems', *Qualitative Inquiry,* 11 (6): 941–49.

Ferguson, A.A. (2001) *Bad boys: Public Schools in the Making of Black Masculinity.* Ann Arbor, MI: The University of Michigan Press.

Finch, J. (1984) 'It's great to have someone to talk to': The ethics and politics of interviewing women, in C. Bell and H. Roberts (eds), *Social Researching: Politics, Problems, Practice.* London: Routledge & Kegan Paul. pp. 70–87.

Finlay, L. (2002) 'Negotiating the swamp: The opportunity and challenge of reflexivity in research practice', *Qualitative Research,* 2 (2): 209–30.

Finlay, L. and Gough, B. (eds) (2003) *Reflexivity: A Practical Guide for Researchers in Health and Social Sciences.* Oxford: Blackwell Science.

Fischer, C.T. and Wertz, F.J. (2002) 'Empirical phenomenological analyses of being criminally victimized', in A.M. Huberman and M.B. Miles (eds), *The Qualitative Researcher's Companion.* Thousand Oaks, CA: Sage. pp. 275–304. (Reprinted from *Duquesne Studies in Phenomenological Psychology,* (3): 135–58, by A. Giorgi, R. Knowles and D.L. Smith (eds), 1980, Duquesne University Press).

Flyvbjerg, B. (2001) *Making Social Science Matter: Why Social Inquiry Fails and How it Can Succeed Again.* Cambridge: Cambridge University Press.

Foddy, W. (1993) *Constructing Questions for Interviews and Questionnaires: Theory and Practice in Social Research.* Cambridge: Cambridge University Press.

Fontana, A. and Prokos, A.H. (2007) *The Interview: From Formal to Postmodern.* Walnut Creek, CA: Left Coast Press.

Fordham, S. (1996) *Blacked Out: Dilemmas of Race, Identity, and Success at Capital High.* Chicago, IL: University of Chicago Press.

Freeman, M. (2000) 'Knocking on doors: On constructing culture', *Qualitative Inquiry,* 6 (3): 359–69.

Freeman, M. (2006) 'Nurturing dialogic hermeneutics and the deliberative capacities of communities in focus groups', *Qualitative Inquiry,* 12(1), 81–95.

Freeman, M. (2007) Interview by K. Roulston. University of Georgia, Athens.

Freeman, M. (2008) 'Hermeneutics', in L.M. Given (ed), *The Sage Encyclopedia of Qualitative Research Methods.* Vol. 1. Thousand Oaks, CA: Sage. pp. 81–95.

Freeman, M., deMarris, K., Preissle, S., Roulston, K. and St Pierre, E. (2007) 'Standards of evidence in qualitative research: an incitement to discourse', *Educational Researcher,* 36(1): 1–8.

Frey, J.H. and Fontana, A. (1993) 'The group interview in social research', in D.L. Morgan (ed.), *Successful Focus Groups: Advancing the State of the Art.* Newbury Park, CA: Sage. pp. 20–34.

Frith, H. and Harcourt, D. (2007) 'Using photographs to capture women's experiences of chemotherapy: Reflecting on the method', *Qualitative Health Research,* 17 (10): 1340–50.

Frohmann, L. (2005) 'The framing safety project: Photographs and narratives by battered women', *Violence Against Women,* 11 (11): 1396–419.

Gadd, D. (2004) 'Making sense of interviewee–interviewer dynamics in narratives about violence in intimate relationships', *International Journal of Social Research Methodology,* 7 (5): 383–401.

Garfinkel, H. (1967) *Studies in Ethnomethodology.* Englewood Cliffs, NJ: Prentice-Hall.

Gee, J.P. (1999) *An Introduction to Discourse Analysis*. London: Routledge.

Geertz, C. (2003) 'Thick description: Toward an interpretive theory of culture', in Y.S. Lincoln and N.K. Denzin (eds), *Turning Points in Qualitative Research: Tying Knots in a Handkerchief*. Walnut Creek, CA: Altamira Press. pp. 143–68.

Genovese, B.J. (2004) 'Thinking inside the box: The art of telephone interviewing', *Field Methods,* 16 (2): 215–26.

Gergen, M.M. and Gergen, K.J. (2000) 'Qualitative inquiry: Tensions and transformations', in N. Denzin and Y. Lincoln (eds), *Handbook of Qualitative Research*, 2nd edn. Thousand Oaks, CA: Sage. pp. 1025–46.

Glaser, B.G. (1978) *Theoretical Sensitivity*. Mill Valley, CA: Sociology Press.

Glaser, B.G. and Strauss, A.L. (1967) *The Discovery of Grounded Theory: Strategies for Qualitative Research*. New York: Aldine de Gruyter.

Glesne, C. (2006) *Becoming Qualitative Researchers: An Introduction*, 3rd edn. Boston, MA: Pearson Education.

Goodall, H.L. (2000) *Writing the New Ethnography*. Walnut Creek, CA: Altamira Press.

Green, J., Franquiz, M. and Dixon, C. (1997) 'The myth of the objective transcript: transcribing as a situated act', *TESOL Quarterly,* 31 (1): 172–76.

Gubrium, J.F. and Holstein, J.A. (2002) 'From the individual interview to the interview society', in J.F. Gubrium and J.A. Holstein (eds), *Handbook of Interview Research: Context and Method*. Thousand Oaks, CA: Sage. pp. 1–32.

Gunsalus, C.K., Bruner, E.M., Burbules, N.C., Dash, L., Finkin, M. and Goldberg, J.P., et al. (2007) 'The Illinois white paper: Improving the system for protecting human subjects: Counteracting IRB "mission creep"', *Qualitative Inquiry,* 13 (5): 617–49.

Guterman, L. (1 September 2006) 'Digging into the roots of research ethics: How a Canadian ethnobotanist became a champion of research that advances the lot of indigenous peoples', *The Chronicle of Higher Education*. Available at: http://www.chronicle.com/weekly/v53/i02/02a02401.htm

Hamilton, R.J. and Bowers, B.J. (2006) 'Internet recruitment and e-mail interviews in qualitative studies', *Qualitative Health Research,* 16 (6): 821–35.).

Hammersley, M. (2003) 'Recent radical criticism of interview studies: Any implications for the sociology of education', *British Journal of Sociology of Education,* 24 (1): 119–26.

Hammersley, M. and Gomm, R. (2008) 'Assessing the radical critique of interviews', in M. Hammersley (ed.), *Questioning Qualitative Inquiry: Critical Essays*. Los Angeles, CA: Sage. pp. 89–100.

Harding, S. (1987) 'Introduction: Is there a feminist method?', in S. Harding (ed.), *Feminism and Methodology: Social Science Issues*. Bloomington, IN: Indiana University Press. pp. 1–14.

Harding, S. (2007) 'Feminist standpoints', in S.N. Hesse-Biber (ed.), *Handbook of Feminist Research: Theory and Praxis*. Thousand Oaks, CA: Sage. pp. 45–70.

Harklau, L. (2008) Interview by K. Roulston. University of Georgia, Athens.

Hasson, F., Keeney, S. and McKenna, H. (2000) 'Research guidelines for the Delphi survey technique', *Journal of Advanced Nursing,* 32 (4): 1008–15.

Have, P.T. (2004) *Understanding Qualitative Research and Ethnomethodology*. London: Sage.

Have, P.T. (2007) *Doing Conversation Analysis: A Practical Guide*, 2nd edn. London: Sage.

Hébert, T. (2007) Interview by K. Roulston. University of Georgia, Athens.

Hecht, T. (1998) *At Home in the Street: Street Children of Northeast Brazil*. Cambridge: Cambridge University Press.

Hecht, T. (2006) *After Life: An Ethnographic Novel*. Durham, NC: Duke University Press.

Heritage, J.C. and Watson, D.R. (1979) 'Formulations as conversational objects', in G. Psathas (ed.), *Everyday Language: Studies in Ethnomethodology*. New York: Irvington. pp. 123–62.

Herman-Kinney, N.J. and Verschaeve, J.M. (2003) 'Methods of symbolic interactionism', in L.T. Reynolds and N.J. Herman-Kinney (eds), *Handbook of Symbolic Interactionism.* Boulder, CO: AltaMira Press. pp. 213–52.

Hermanowicz, J.C. (2002) 'The great interview: 25 strategies for studying people in bed', *Qualitative Sociology,* 25 (4): 479–99.

Hesse-Biber, S.N. and Leavy, P.L. (2007) *Feminist Research Practice: A Primer.* Thousand Oaks, CA: Sage.

Hester, S. and Francis, D. (1994) 'Doing data: The local organization of a sociological interview', *British Journal of Sociology,* 45 (4): 675–95.

Hoffman, E. (2007) 'Open-ended interviews, power, and emotional labor', *Journal of Contemporary Ethnography,* (36): 318–46.

Holstein, J.A. and Gubrium, J.F. (1995) *The Active Interview* (Vol. 37). Thousand Oaks, CA: Sage.

Holstein, J.A. and Gubrium, J.F. (2004) 'The active interview', in D. Silverman (ed.), *Qualitative Research: Theory, Method and Practice,* 2nd edn. London: Sage. pp. 140–61.

Honan, E. (2007) 'Writing a rhizome: An (im)plausible methodology', *International Journal of Qualitative Studies in Education,* 20 (5): 531–46.

Hoppe, M.J. and Wells, E.A. (1995) 'Using focus groups to discuss sensitive topics with children', *Evaluation Review,* 19 (1): 102–14.

Houtkoop-Steenstra, H. (2000) *Interaction and the Standardized Survey Interview: The Living Questions.* Cambridge: Cambridge University Press.

Houtkoop-Steenstra, H. and Antaki, C. (1997) 'Creating happy people by asking yes–no questions', *Research on Language and Social Interaction,* 30 (4): 285–313.

Howell, J.T. (1973) *Hard living on Clay Street: Portraits of Blue Collar Families.* Prospect Heights, IL: Waveland Press.

Humphreys, L. (1970) *Tearoom Trade: Impersonal Sex in Public Places.* Chicago, IL: Aldine.

Iseke-Barnes, J. (2003) 'Living and writing indigenous spiritual resistance', *Journal of Intercultural Studies,* 24 (3): 211–38.

Iwasaki, Y., Bartlett, J. G., Gottlieb, B. and Hall, D. (2009) 'Leisure-like pursuits as an expression of Aboriginal cultural strengths and living actions', *Leisure Sciences,* 31: 158–73.

James, N. (2007) 'The use of email interviewing as a qualitative method of inquiry in educational research', *British Educational Research Journal,* 33 (6): 963–76.

James, N. and Busher, H. (2006) 'Credibility, authenticity and voice: Dilemmas in online interviewing', *Qualitative Research,* 6 (3): 403–20.

Johnson, T.S. (2008) 'Qualitative research in question: A narrative of disciplinary power with/in the IRB', *Qualitative Inquiry,* 14 (2): 212–32.

Johnson-Bailey, J. (1999) 'The ties that bind and the shackles that separate: Race, gender, class and color in a research process', *International Journal of Qualitative Studies in Education,* 12 (6): 659–70.

Johnson-Bailey, J. (2001) *Sistahs in College: Making a Way out of No Way.* Malabar, FL: Krieger Press.

Johnson-Bailey, J. (2007) Interview by K. Roulston. University of Georgia, Athens.

Kamberelis, G. and Dimitriadis, G. (2005) 'Focus groups: Strategic articulations of pedagogy, politics, and inquiry', in N. Denzin and Y.S. Lincoln (eds), *The Sage Handbook of Qualitative Research,* 3rd edn. Thousand Oaks, CA: Sage. pp. 887–907.

Kaufmann, J. (2007) 'Transfiguration: A narrative analysis of male-to-female transsexual', *International Journal of Qualitative Studies in Education,* 20 (1): 1–13.

Keats, D.M. (2000) *Interviewing: A Practical Guide for Students and Professionals.* Buckingham: Open University Press.

Kelle, U. (2005) '"Emergence" vs. "forcing" of empirical data: A crucial problem of "grounded theory" reconsidered', *Forum: Qualitative Social Research,* 6 (2): Available at: http://www.qualitative-reseafch.net/fqs.texte/2-05/05-2-27-e.htm

Kezar, A. (2003) 'Transformational elite interviews: Principles and problems', *Qualitative Inquiry,* 9 (3): 395–415.

Kirby, P. (2004) *A Guide to Actively Involving Young People in Research: For Researchers, Research Commissioners, and Managers.* Available at: http://www.invo.org.uk/pdfs/Involving_Young_People_in_Research_151104_FINAL.pdf (accessed 6 August 2008).

Kitzinger, J. and Barbour, R.S. (1999) 'Introduction: The challenge and promise of focus groups', in R.S. Barbour and J. Kitzinger (eds), *Developing Focus Group Research: Politics, Theory and Practice.* London: Sage. pp. 1–20.

Koosimile, A.T. (2002) 'Access negotiation and curriculum change: Lessons from Botswana', *International Journal of Qualitative Studies in Education,* 15 (2): 205–23.

Krieger, S. (1983) *The Mirror Dance: Identity in a Women's Community.* Philadelphia, PA: Temple University Press.

Krieger, S. (1985) 'Beyond "subjectivity": The use of the self in social science', *Qualitative Sociology,* 8 (4): 309–24.

Krueger, R.A. (1998) *Developing Questions for Focus Groups.* (Focus Group Kit 3). Thousand Oaks, CA: Sage.

Krueger, R.A. and Casey, M.A. (2000) *Focus Groups: A Practical Guide for Applied Research.* Thousand Oaks, CA: Sage.

Kvale, S. (1996) *InterViews: An Introduction to Qualitative Research Interviewing.* Thousand Oaks, CA: Sage.

Kvale, S. (1999) 'The psychoanalytic interview as qualitative research', *Qualitative Inquiry,* 5 (1): 87–113.

Kvale, S. (2006) 'Dominance through interviews and dialogues', *Qualitative Inquiry,* 12 (3): 480–500.

Kvale, S. and Brinkmann, S. (2009) *InterViews: Learning the Craft of Qualitative Research Interviewing,* 2nd edn. London: Sage.

Labov, W. and Waletzky, J. (1997) 'Narrative analysis: Oral versions of personal experience', *Journal of Narrative and Life History,* 7 (1–4): 3–38. (Reprinted from *Essays on the Verbal and Visual Arts,* pp. 12–44, edited by June Helm, 1967, Seattle, WA: University of Washington Press.)

Lather, P. (2004) 'Critical inquiry in qualitative research: Feminist and poststructural perspectives: Science "After Truth"', in K. deMarrais and S.D. Lapan (eds), *Foundations for Research: Methods of Inquiry in Education and the Social Sciences.* Mahwah, NJ: Lawrence Erlbaum Associates. pp. 203–16.

Lather, P. and Smithies, C. (1997) *Troubling the Angels: Women Living with HIV/AIDS.* Boulder, CO: Westview Press.

Latour, B. (2000) 'When things strike back: A possible contribution of "science studies" to the social sciences', *British Journal of Sociology,* 51 (1): 107–23.

Lauer, M. (2006) 'A defiant Britney Spears takes on the tabloids', interview transcript available at: http://www.msnbc.msn.com/id/13347509// (accessed 11 August 2006).

Leavy, P. (2008) 'Performance-based emergent methods', in S.N. Hesse-Biber and P. Leavy (eds), *Handbook of Emergent Methods.* New York: The Guilford Press. pp. 343–57.

LeCompte, M.D. and Preissle, J. (1993) *Ethnography and Qualitative Design in Educational Research,* 2nd edn. San Diego, CA: Academic Press.

Lee, R. (2004) 'Recording technologies and the interview in sociology, 1920–2000', *Sociology,* 38 (5): 869–89.

Levinson, S. (1983) *Pragmatics.* Cambridge: Cambridge University Press.

Lewins, A. and Silver, C. (2007). *Using Software in Qualitative Research.* Los Angeles, CA: Sage.

Liljestrom, A., Roulston, K. and deMarrais, K. (2007) 'There's no place for feeling like this in the workplace: Women teachers' anger in school settings', in P. Schutz and R. Pekrun (eds), *Emotion in Education.* Amsterdam: Academic Press. pp. 267–84.

Lincoln, Y.S. and González y González, E.M. (2008) 'The search for emerging decolonizing methodologies in qualitative research: Further strategies for liberatory and democratic inquiry', *Qualitative Inquiry*, 14 (5): 784–805.

Lincoln, Y.S. and Tierney, W. (2004) 'Qualitative research and institutional review boards', *Qualitative Inquiry*, 10 (2): 219–34.

Litoselliti, L. (2003) *Using Focus Groups in Research*. London: Continuum.

Little, D.E. (2002) 'Women and adventure recreation: Reconstructing leisure constraints and adventure experiences to negotiate continuing participation', *Journal of Leisure Research*, 34 (2): 157–77.

Lofland, J., Snow, D., Anderson, L. and Lofland, L.H. (2006) *Analyzing Social Settings: A Guide to Qualitative Observation and Analysis*, 4th edn. Belmont, CA: Wadsworth/ Thomson.

Luttrell, W. (2003) *Pregnant Bodies, Fertile Minds: Gender, Race, and the Schooling of Pregnant Teens*. New York: Routledge.

Lynch, M. (2000) 'Against reflexivity as an academic virtue and source of privileged knowledge', *Theory, Culture and Society*, 17 (3): 26–54.

Lynn, J. and Jay, A. (eds) (1987) *The Complete Yes Prime Minister: The Diaries of the Right Hon. James Hacker*. London: BBC Books.

Macbeth, D. (2001) 'On "reflexivity" in qualitative research: Two readings: and a third', *Qualitative Inquiry*, 7 (1): 35–68.

MacLure, M. (2003) *Discourse in Educational and Social Research*. Buckingham: Open University Press.

MacPhail, A. (2001) 'Nominal group technique: A useful method for working with young people', *British Educational Research Journal*, 27 (2): 161–70.

Maso, I. (2003) 'Necessary subjectivity: Exploiting researchers' motives, passions and prejudices in pursuit of answering "true" questions', in L. Finlay and B. Gough (eds), *Reflexivity: A Practical Guide for Researchers in Health and Social Sciences*. Oxford: Blackwell Science. pp. 39–51.

Mathison, S. (1988) 'Why triangulate?', *Educational Researcher*, 17 (2): 13–17.

Maxwell, J.A. and Miller, B.A. (2008) 'Categorizing and connecting strategies in qualitative data analysis', in S.N. Hesse-Biber and P. Leavy (eds), *Handbook of Emergent Methods*. New York: Guilford Press. pp. 461–77.

Maynard, D., Houtkoop-Steenstra, H., Schaeffer, N.C. and Zouwen, J.v.d. (eds) (2002) *Standardization and Tacit Knowledge: Interaction and Practice in the Survey Interview*. New York: John Wiley & Sons.

Maynard-Tucker, G. (2000) 'Conducting focus groups in developing countries: Skill training for local bilingual facilitators', *Qualitative Health Research*, 10 (3): 396–410.

Mazeland, H. and Have, P.t. (1998) 'Essential tensions in (semi-)open research interviews', in I. Maso and F. Wester (eds), *The Deliberate Dialogue: Qualitative Perspectives on the Interview*. Brussels: VUB University Press. pp. 87–113.

McCracken, G. (1988) *The Long Interview*. Beverley Hills, CA: Sage.

Merriam, S. (2007) Interview by K. Roulston. University of Georgia, Athens.

Merton, R.K. (1990) 'Introduction to the second edition', in R.K. Merton, M. Fiske and P.L. Kendall (eds), *The Focused Interview: A Manual of Procedures*, 2nd edn. New York: The Free Press. pp. xiii–xxxiii. (Original work published 1956.)

Merton, R.K., Fiske, M. and Kendall, P.L. (1990) *The Focused Interview: A Manual of Problems and Procedures*, 2nd edn. New York: The Free Press. (Original work published 1956.)

Meyer, M.J. (2009) 'Transcendence: The journey from hard data into artistic depiction: Theatre as representation', in S.G. Kouritzin, N.A C. Piquemal and R. Norman (eds), *Qualitative Research: Challenging the Orthodoxies in Standard Academic Discourse(s)*. New York: Routledge. pp. 83–102

Mienczakowski, J. (2001) 'Ethnodrama: performed research: limitations and potential', in P. Atkinson, A. Coffey, S. Delamont, J. Lofland and L. Lofland (eds), *Handbook of Ethnography*. London: Sage. pp. 468–76.

Miles, M.B. and Huberman, A.M. (1994) *Qualitative Data Analysis: An Expanded Sourcebook*, 2nd edn. Thousand Oaks, CA: Sage.

Miller, R.L. (2000) *Researching Life Stories and Family Histories*. London: Sage.

Mishler, E. (1986) *Research Interviewing: Context and Narrative*. Cambridge, MA: Harvard University Press.

Mishler, E. (1999) *Storylines: Craftartists Narratives of Identity*. Cambridge, MA: Harvard University Press.

Morgan, D.L. (ed.) (1993) *Successful Focus Groups: Advancing the State of the Art*. Newbury Park, CA: Sage.

Morgan, D.L. (1997) *Focus Groups as Qualitative Research*, 2nd edn. Newbury Park, CA: Sage.

Morgan, D.L. (2002) 'Focus group interviewing', in J.F. Gubrium and J.A. Holstein (eds), *Handbook of Interview Research: Context and Method*. Thousand Oaks, CA: Sage. pp. 141–60.

Morgan, D.L. and Krueger, R.A. (1998) *The Focus Group Kit*. Thousand Oaks, CA: Sage.

Moss, P. (2007) 'Emergent methods in feminist research', in S.N. Hesse-Biber (ed.), *Handbook of Feminist Research: Theory and Praxis*. Thousand Oaks, CA: Sage. pp. 371–90.

Moss, W. (1996) 'Oral history: An appreciation', in D.K. Dunaway and W.K. Baum (eds), *Oral History: An Interdisciplinary Anthology*, 2nd edn. Walnut Creek, CA: Altamira Press. pp. 107–20. (Reprinted from *American Archivist 40*, October 1977.)

Moustakas, C. (1994) *Phenomenological Research Methods*. Thousand Oaks, CA: Sage.

Nairn, K., Munro, J. and Smith, A.B. (2005) 'A counter-narrative of a "failed" interview', *Qualitative Research*, 5 (2): 221–44.

Naples, N.A. (1996) 'A feminist revisiting of the insider/outsider debate: The "outsider phenomenon" in rural Iowa', *Qualitative Sociology*, 19 (1): 83–106.

National Research Council (2002) *Scientific Research in Education*. R.J. Shavelson and L. Towne (eds). Committee on Scientific Principles for Education Research. Washington, DC: National Academy Press.

Nikander, P. (2008) 'Working with transcripts and translated data', *Qualitative Research in Psychology*, 5: 225–31.

Nyden, P., Figert, A., Shibley, M. and Burrows, D. (eds) (1997) *Building Community: Social Science in Action*. Thousand Oaks, CA: Pine Forge Press.

Oakley, A. (1981) 'Interviewing women: A contradiction in terms', in H. Roberts (ed.), *Doing Feminist Research*. London: Routledge. pp. 30–61.

Oakley, A. (1998) 'Gender, methodology and people's ways of knowing: Some problems with feminism and the paradigm debate in social science', *Sociology*, 32 (4): 707–31.

Oakley, A. (2000) *Experiments in Knowing: Gender and Method in the Social Sciences*. New York: The New Press.

Ochs, E. (1979) 'Transcription as theory', in E. Ochs and B. Shieffelin (eds), *Developmental Pragmatics*. New York: Academic Press. pp. 43–72.

Ochs, E. and Capps, L. (2001) *Living Narrative: Creating Lives in Everyday Storytelling*. Cambridge, MA: Harvard University Press.

Oliver, D.G., Serovich, J.M. and Mason, T.L. (2005) 'Constraints and opportunities with interview transcription: Towards reflection in qualitative research', *Social Forces*, 84 (2): 1273–89.

Paoletti, I. (2001) 'Membership categories and time appraisal in interviews with family caregivers of disabled elderly', *Human Studies*, (24): 293–325.

Patton, M.Q. (2002) *Qualitative Research and Evaluation Methods*, 3rd edn. Thousand Oaks, CA: Sage.

Peshkin, A. (1986) *God's Choice: The Total World of a Fundamentalist Christian School*. Chicago, IL: University of Chicago.

Peshkin, A. (1988) 'In search of subjectivity: One's own', *Educational Researcher*, 17 (7): 17–22.

Pillow, W.S. (2003) 'Confession, catharsis, or cure? Rethinking the uses of reflexivity as methodological power in qualitative research', *International Journal of Qualitative Studies in Education,* 16 (2): 175–96.

Platt, J. (2002) 'The history of the interview', in J.F. Gubrium and J.A. Holstein (eds), *Handbook of Interview Research: Context and Method*. Thousand Oaks, CA: Sage. pp. 33–54.

Poland, B.D. (2002) 'Transcription quality', in N. Denzin and Y.S. Lincoln (eds), *Handbook of Interview Research: Context and Method*. Thousand Oaks, CA: Sage. pp. 629–50.

Polkinghorne, D.E. (1995) 'Narrative configuration in qualitative analysis', *International Journal of Qualitative Studies in Education*, 8 (1): 5–23.

Pollio, H.R., Henley, T.B. and Thompson, C.J. (1997). *The Phenomenology of Everyday Life: Empirical Investigations of Human Experience*. Cambridge: Cambridge University Press.

Pollock, M. (2004) *Colormute: Race Talk Dilemmas in an American School*. Princeton, NJ: Princeton University Press.

Pomerantz, A. (1986) 'Extreme case formulations: A way of legitimizing claims', *Human Studies,* (9): 219–29.

Pomerantz, A. and Fehr, B.J. (1997) 'Conversation analysis: An approach to the study of social action as sense making practices', in T.A. van Dijk (ed.), *Discourse as Social Interaction*. London: Sage. pp. 64–91.

Potter, J. and Hepburn, A. (2005) 'Qualitative interviews in psychology: Problems and possibilities', *Qualitative Research in Psychology*, (2): 281–307.

Powers, W.R. (2005) *Transcription Techniques for the Spoken Word*. Lanham, MD: Altamira Press.

Preissle, J. (2007) Interview by K. Roulston. University of Georgia, Athens.

Preissle, J. (2008) 'Subjectivity statement', in L.M. Given (ed.), *The Sage Encyclopedia of Qualitative Research Methods*, Vol. 2. Thousand Oaks, CA: Sage. pp. 844–45.

Prendergast, M. (2006) 'Found poetry as literature review: Research poems on audience and performance', *Qualitative Inquiry,* 12 (2): 369–88.

Psathas, G. (1995) *Conversation Analysis: The Study of Talk-in-interaction*. Thousand Oaks, CA: Sage.

Psathas, G. and Anderson, T. (1990) 'The "practices" of transcription in conversation analysis', *Semiotica,* (78): 75–99.

Puchta, C. and Potter, J. (2004) *Focus Group Practice*. London: Sage.

Rapley, T. (2001) 'The art(fulness) of open-ended interviewing: Some considerations on analysing interviews', *Qualitative Research,* 1 (3): 303–23.

Rapley, T. (2004) 'Interviews', in C. Seale G. Gobo J. Gubrium and D. Silverman (eds), *Qualitative Research Practice*. London: Sage. pp. 15–33.

Reinharz, S. (1992) *Feminist Methods in Social Research*. New York: Oxford University Press.

Reinharz, S. and Chase, S.E. (2002) ‚Interviewing women', in J. Gubrium and J.A. Holstein (eds), *Handbook of Interviewing: Context and Method*. Thousand Oaks, CA: Sage. pp. 221–38.

Richardson, L. (1994) 'Writing: A method of inquiry', in N.K. Denzin and Y.S. Lincoln (eds), *Handbook of Qualitative Research*. Thousand Oaks, CA: Sage. pp. 516–29.

Richardson, L. (1999) 'Feathers in our CAP',. *Journal of Contemporary Ethnography,* 28 (6): 660–68.

Richardson, L. (2002) 'Poetic representation of interviews', in J. Gubrium and J.A. Holstein (eds), *Handbook of Interview Research: Context and Method.* Thousand Oaks, CA: Sage. pp. 877–92.

Riessman, C.K. (1987) 'When gender is not enough: Women interviewing women', *Gender and Society,* 1 (2): 172–207.

Riessman, C.K. (1990) *Divorce talk.* New Brunswick, NJ: Rutgers University Press.

Riessman, C. (2008) *Narrative Methods for the Human Sciences.* Los Angeles, CA: Sage.

Ritchie, D.A. (2003) *Doing Oral History: A Practical Guide,* 2nd edn. Oxford: Oxford University Press.

Robinson, N. (1999) 'The use of focus group methodology – with selected examples from sexual health research', *Journal of Advanced Nursing,* 29 (4): 905–13.

Rolls, L. and Relf, M. (2006) 'Bracketing interviews: Addressing methodological challenges in qualitative interviewing in bereavement and palliative care', *Mortality,* 11 (3): 286–305.

Roulston, K. (2000) 'The management of 'safe' and 'unsafe' complaint sequences in research interviews', *Text,* 20 (3): 1–39.

Roulston, K. (2001) 'Investigating the cast of characters in a cultural world', in A. McHoul and M. Rapley (eds), *How to Analyse Talk in Institutional Settings: A Casebook of Methods.* London: Continuum. pp. 100–12.

Roulston, K. (2004) 'Ethnomethodological and conversation analytic studies', in K.B. deMarrais and S.D. Lapan (eds), *Foundations for Research: Method of Inquiry in Education and the Social Sciences.* Mahwah, NJ: Lawrence Erlbaum Associates. pp. 139–60.

Roulston, K. (2006a) 'Close encounters of the 'CA' kind: A review of literature analyzing talk in research interviews', *Qualitative Research,* 6 (4): 535–54.

Roulston, K. (2006b) 'Qualitative investigation of young children's music preferences', *International Journal of Education & the Arts,* 7 (9). Available at: http://ijea.asu.edu/v7n9/ (accessed 10 December 2006).

Roulston, K., deMarrais, K. and Lewis, J. (2003) 'Learning to interview in the social sciences', *Qualitative Inquiry,* 9 (4): 643–68.

Roulston, K., McClendon, V.J., Thomas, A., Tuff, R., Williams, G. and Healy, M. (2008) 'Developing reflective interviewers and reflexive researchers', *Reflective Practice,* 9 (3): 231–43.

Rubin, H.J. and Rubin, I.S. (2005) *Qualitative Interviewing: The art of hearing Data,* 2nd edn. Thousand Oaks, CA: Sage.

Ryan, G.W. and Bernard, H.R. (2000) 'Data management and analysis methods', in N.K. Denzin and Y.S. Lincoln (eds), *Handbook of Qualitative Research,* 2nd edn. Thousand Oaks, CA: Sage. pp. 769–802.

Rymes, B. (2001) *Conversational Borderlands: Language and Identity in an Alternative Urban High School.* New York: Teachers College Press.

Sacks, H. (1972a) 'An initial investigation of the usability of conversation data for doing sociology', in D. Sudnow (ed.), *Studies in Social Interaction.* New York: The Free Press. pp. 31–74

Sacks, H. (1972b) 'On the analyzability of stories by children', in J.J. Gumperz and D. Hymes (eds.), *Directions in Sociolinguistics: The Ethnography of Communication.* Oxford: Blackwell. pp. 325–45

Sacks, H. (1992) *Lectures on Conversation.* Oxford: Blackwell.

Sacks, H., Schegloff, E.A. and Jefferson, G. (1974) 'A Simplest systematics for the organization of turn-taken over for conversation', *Language,* 50: 696–735.

Saldaña, J. (2003) 'Dramatizing data: A primer', *Qualitative Inquiry,* 9 (2): 218–36.

Sandstrom, K.L., Martin, D.D. and Fine, G.A. (2003) 'Symbolic interactionism at the end of the century', in G. Ritzer and B. Smart (eds.), *Handbook of Social Theory.* London: Sage. pp. 217–31.

Schaeffer, N.C. and Maynard, D. (2002) 'Standardization and interaction in the survey interview', in J.F. Gubrium and J.A. Holstein (eds), *Handbook of Interview Research: Context and Method*. Thousand Oaks, CA: Sage. pp. 577–602.

Schegloff, E.A. (2007) *Sequence Organization in Interaction: A Primer in Conversation Analysis Volume I*. Cambridge: Cambridge University Press.

Schegloff, E.A., Jefferson, G. and Sacks, H. (1977) 'The preference for self-correction in the organization of repair in conversation', *Language,* 53 (2): 361–82.

Scheurich, J.J. (1995) 'A postmodernist critique of research interviewing', *International Journal of Qualitative Studies in Education,* 8 (3): 239–52.

Scheurich, J.J. (1997) *Research Method in the Postmodern*. London: The Falmer Press.

Scheurich, J.J. and McKenzie, K.B. (2005), Foucault's methodologies: Archeaology and genealogy', in N.K. Denzin and Y.S. Lincoln (eds), *The Sage Handbook of Qualitative Research*, 3rd edn. Thousand Oaks, CA: Sage. pp. 841–68.

Schwandt, T.A. (2001) *Dictionary of Qualitative Inquiry*, 2nd edn. Thousand Oaks, CA: Sage.

Seale, C. (1999) *The Quality of Qualitative Research*. London: Sage.

Seidman, I. (2006) *Interviewing as Qualitative Research: A Guide for Researchers in Education and the Social Sciences*, 3rd edn. New York: Teachers College.

Shank, G. (2006) *Qualitative Research: A Personal Skills Approach,* 2nd edn. Upper Saddle River, NJ: Pearson Education.

Silverman, D. (1998) *Harvey Sacks: Social Science and Conversation Analysis*. Cambridge: Polity Press.

Silverman, D. (2001) *Interpreting Qualitative Data: Methods for Analysing Talk, Text, and Interaction*, 2nd edn. London: Sage.

Silverman, D. (2005) *Doing Qualitative Research: A Practical Handbook*, 2nd edn. London: Sage.

Silverman, D. (2007) *A Very Short, Fairly Interesting and Reasonably Cheap Book about Qualitative Research.* Los Angeles, CA: Sage.

Sinding, C. and Aronson, J. (2003) 'Exposing failures, unsettling accommodations: Tensions in interview practice,' *Qualitative Research,* 3 (1): 95–117.

Smith, D.E. (1987) *The Everyday World as Problematic: A Feminist Sociology*. Boston, MA: Northeastern University Press.

Smith, L.T. (1999) *Decolonizing Methodologies: Research and Indigenous Peoples*. London: Zed Books.

Smith, L.T. (2005) 'On tricky ground: Researching the native in the age of uncertainty', in N.K. Denzin and Y.S. Lincoln (eds), *The Sage Handbook of Qualitative Research*, 3rd edn. Thousand Oaks, CA: Sage. pp. 85–108.

Smithson, J. (2000) 'Using and analysing focus groups: Limitations and possibilities', *International Journal of Social Research Methodology,* 3 (2): 103–19.

Spradley, J. (1970) *You Owe Yourself a Drunk: An Ethnography of Urban Nomads*. Prospect Heights, IL: Waveland.

Spradley, J. (1979) *The Ethnographic Interview*. Fort Worth, TX: Harcourt Brace Jovanovich College Publishers.

Spradley, J. (1980) *Participant Observation*. New York: Holt, Rinehart & Winston.

Spradley, J. and Mann, B.J. (1975) *Cocktail Waitress Woman's Work in a Man's World*. New York: McGraw-Hill.

Stewart, D.W., Shamdasani, P.N. and Rook, D.W. (2007) *Focus Groups: Theory and Practice* (Vol. 20). Thousand Oaks, CA: Sage.

St Pierre, E.A. and Pillow, W.S. (eds) (2000) *Working the Ruins: Feminist Poststructural Theory and Methods in Education*. New York: Routledge.

Strauss, A.L. and Corbin, J. (1998) *Basics of Qualitative Research: Grounded Theory Procedures and Techniques*, 2nd edn. Newbury Park, CA: Sage.

Stronach, I. (2006) 'Enlightenment and the 'heart of darkness': (neo)imperialism in the Congo, and elsewhere', *International Journal of Qualitative Studies in Education,* 19 (6): 757–68.

Stronach, I. and MacLure, M. (1997) *Educational Research Undone: The Postmodern Embrace.* Buckingham: Open University Press.

Suchman, L. and Jordan, B. (1990) 'Interactional troubles in face-to-face survey interviews', *Journal of the American Statistical Association,* (85): 232–41.

Tang, N. (2002) 'Interviewer and interviewee relationships between women', *Sociology,* 36 (3): 703–21.

Tanggaard, L. (2007) 'The research interview as discourses crossing swords: The researcher and apprentice on crossing roads', *Qualitative Inquiry,* 13 (1): 160–76.

Tanggaard, L. (2008) 'Objections in research interviewing', *International Journal of Qualitative Methods,* 7 (3). Available at: http://ejournals.library.ualberta.ca/index.php/IJQM/article/view/1827/3449 (accessed 22 May 2009)

Temple, B. (1997) 'Watch your tongue: Issues in translation and cross-cultural research', *Sociology,* 31 (3): 607–18.

Temple, B. and Edwards, R. (2002) 'Interpreters/translators and cross-language research: Reflexivity and border crossings', *International Journal of Qualitative Methods,* 1 (2): Article 1. Available at: http://www.alberta.ca/~ijqm (accessed 6 June 2006).

Temple, B. and Young, A. (2004) 'Qualitative research and translation dilemmas', *Qualitative Research,* 4 (2): 161–78.

Trinh, T., Minh-ha (1992) 'Surname Viet, given name Nam', in Trinh T. Minh-ha (ed.), *Framer Framed.* New York: Routledge. pp. 49–91.

Trinh, T., Minh-ha (Writer and Director) and Bourdier, J.-P. (Associate Producer) (1989) *Surname Viet, Given Name Nam* [Documentary]. (Available from Women Make Movies, www.wmm.com).

van Manen, M. (1990) *Research Lived Experience: Human Science for an Action Sensitive Pedagogy.* London: State University of New York Press.

Villenas, S. (1996) 'The colonizer/colonized Chicana ethnographer: Identity, marginalization, and co-optation in the field', *Harvard Education Review,* 66 (4): 711–31.

Walzer, S. and Oles, T.P. (2003) 'Accounting for divorce: Gender and uncoupling narratives', *Qualitative Sociology,* 26 (3): 331–49.

Wanat, C.L. (2008) 'Getting past the gatekeepers: Differences between access and cooperation in public school research', *Field Methods,* 20 (2): 191–208.

Wang, J. and Roulston, K. (2007) 'An alternative approach to conceptualizing interviews in HRD research', *Human Resource Development Quarterly,* 18 (2): 179–210.

Waters, A. (ed.) (2000) *On Jordan's Stormy Banks: Personal Accounts of Slavery in Georgia.* Winston-Salem, NC: John F. Blair.

Weiss, R.S. (1994) *Learning from Strangers: The Art and Method of Qualitative Interview Studies.* New York: The Free Press.

Wenger, G.C. (2002) 'Interviewing older people', in J. Gubrium and J.A. Holstein (eds), *Handbook of Interviewing: Context and Method.* Thousand Oaks, CA: Sage. pp. 259–78.

Wengraf, T. (2001) *Qualitative Research Interviewing: Biographic Narrative and Semi-Structured Methods.* London: Sage.

Westheimer, J. and Kahne, J. (2004) 'What kind of citizen? The politics of educating for democracy', *American Educational Research Journal,* 41 (2): 237–70.

Wilkinson, S. (1998) 'Focus group methodology: A review', *International Journal of Social Research Methodology,* 1 (3): 181–203.

Wilkinson, S. (1999) 'How useful are focus groups in feminist research?', in R.S. Barbour and J. Kitzinger (eds), *Developing Focus Group Research: Politics, Theory, and Practice.* Thousand Oaks, CA: Sage. pp. 64–78.

Wilkinson, S. (2004) 'Focus group research', in D. Silverman (ed.), *Qualitative Research: Theory, Method and Practice*, 2nd edn. London: Sage. pp. 177–99.

Wolcott, H.F. (1973) *The Man in the Principal's Office: An Ethnography*. New York: Holt, Rinehart & Winston.

Wolcott, H.F. (1994) *Transforming Qualitative Data: Description, Analysis, and Interpretation*. Thousand Oaks, CA: Sage.

Wolcott, H.F. (1995) *The Art of Fieldwork*. Walnut Creek, CA: Altamira Press.

Wolcott, H.F. (2002) *Sneaky Kid and its Aftermath: Ethics and Intimacy in Fieldwork*. Walnut Creek, CA: Altamira Press.

Wolgemuth, J.R. and Donohue, R. (2006) 'Toward an inquiry of discomfort: Guiding transformation in "emancipatory" narrative research', *Qualitative Inquiry,* 12 (5): 1022–39.

Woolgar, S. (ed.) (1988a) *Knowledge and Reflexivity*. London: Sage.

Woolgar, S. (1988b) 'Reflexivity is the ethnographer of the text', in S. Woolgar (ed.), *Knowledge and Reflexivity*. London: Sage. pp. 14–34.

Yow, V.R. (2005) *Recording Oral History: A Guide for the Humanities and Social Sciences,* 2nd edn. Walnut Creek, CA: Altamira Press.

Zeller, R.A. (1993) 'Focus group research on sensitive topics: Setting the agenda without setting the agenda', in D.L. Morgan (ed.), *Successful Focus Groups: Advancing the State of the Art*. Newbury Park, CA: Sage.

Zhao, Y. and Frank, K.A. (2003) 'Factors affecting technology uses in schools: An ecological perspective', *American Educational Research Journal,* 40 (4): 807–40.

Author Index

Potter, J., 2, 89
Powers, W.R., 109
Preissle, J., 119–20, 181, 183
Prendergast, M., 169
Psathas, G., 8, 109, 130
Puchta, C., 35, 45, 47–8, 137

Rapley, T., 60, 130
Reinharz, S., 21–2
Richardson, L., 63–4, 89, 175
Riessman, C.K., 22, 62, 162–4
Ritchie, D.A., 24–6
Robinson, N., 43
Rolls, L., 124
Roulston, K., 46, 59, 61–2, 126, 130, 135,
    138, 151, 159
Rubin, H.J., 58
Ryan, G.W., 152
Rymes, B., 98

Sacks, H., 10, 42, 60, 130, 146, 167, 187
Saldaña, J., 63, 170
Sandstrom, K.L., 79
Schaeffer, N.C., 10
Schegloff, E.A., 130, 187
Scheurich, J.J., 2, 63, 168
Schwandt, T.A., 150
Seale, C., 83–5, 94
Seidman, I., 6, 17, 68
Shank, G., 119
Silverman, D., 2, 56, 59–60, 62, 89,
    130, 170
Sinding, C., 126
Smith, D.E., 21

Smith, L.T., 68–71
Smithson, J., 35
Spradley, J., 19–20, 158–61
Stewart, D.W., 34–5, 37, 44
St. Pierre, E.A., 169
Strauss, A., 152, 155–7
Stronach, I., 68, 168–9
Suchman, L., 10, 15

Tang., N., 22
Tanggaard, L., 27–8
Temple, B., 108–9
Trinh, T., Minh-ha, 9, 63

van Manen, M., 17, 162
Villenas, S., 120

Walzer, S., 62
Wanat, C.L., 97–8
Wang, J., 126
Waters, A., 25
Weiss, R.S., 6, 54
Wenger, G.C., 100
Wengraf, T., 6
Westheimer, J., 54–5
Wilkinson, S., 22, 35
Wolcott, H.F., 6, 21, 85, 154, 170
Wolgemuth, J.R., 65, 67
Woolgar, S., 116

Yow, V.R., 23

Zeller, R.A., 42
Zhao, Y., 54

Subject Index

feminist interviews, 21–3, 29–30, 32, 37–9
fiction, 63–5, 170–1, 174
focus groups, 35–50
   confidentiality, 40
   designing research using focus
      groups, 37–9
   developing questions and topic
      guides, 42–5
   dialogic interaction, 38–9
   managing interaction, 45–8
   purposes, 36–7
   recruitment and organization, 39–41
   scheduling, 41–2
   sensitive topics, 42
   single source of data, 38
   used in conjunction with other
      methods, 38
follow up questions, 12–14, 134–5, 139–44
formal interviews, 9, 35
formulating research questions, 76–80

gaining consent, 96–8
'good' practice in interviewing, 178–9
grounded theory approaches to analysis, 76,
   79, 155–8, 163, 171–2, *see also* axial
   coding, constant comparative method,
   memo writing
group interviews, *see* brainstorming, Delphi
   groups, focus groups, nominal groups

identifying a topic, 74–6
informal interviews, 9, 19, 35, 86
Institutional Review Board, 97
interviewing the researcher, 122–5, 128–9,
   see also bracketing interviews,
   why-interviews
interviews, *see* conceptions of interviews,
   dialogic interviews, ethnographic
   interviews, feminist interviews, formal
   interviews, group interviews, informal
   interviews, life story interviews, oral
   history interviews, phenomenological
   interviews, practice, semi-structured
   interviews, structured interviews,
   unstructured interviews
   definition, 10
   forms, 9
   online, 10
   questions, *see* question formulation
   structure, 14–16

leading questions, 137, 146
life story interviews, 25–6, 30, 32, 168
listening, 182
longevity in the field, 84, 87
longitudinal studies, 83

membership categorization analysis,
   62, 167, 173
member checking, 85, 87

narrative approaches to analysis, 62,
   162–6, 172
   narrative cognition, 166
   paradigmatic cognition, 163–4
natural interviews, 35, *see* informal interviews
naturally-occurring data, 86, 89
neo-positivist conception of
   interviewing, 52–5
   addressing quality, 86–7
   critiques, 55
   exemplars, 54–5, 72
   posing interview questions, 137, 145
neutrality, *see* researcher neutrality
nominal groups, 34

objectivity, 28, 119
observations, 19, 86
open questions, 12–14
oral history interviews, 23–4, 30, 32

phenomenological analysis, 161–2
phenomenological interviews, 16–19, 29,
   31, 172
photo elicitation, 29–30
plausibility, *see* quality in interview studies
poetry, 63, 169, 173
'post-' approaches to analysis,
   168–70, 173
postmodern conception of interviewing, 63–5
   addressing quality, 89
   critiques, 64
   exemplars, 64–65, 72
practice, *see also* asking questions of
   transcriptions, 'good' practice in
   interviewing, preparing for interviews
   advice on interview practice, 180–4
preparing for interviews, 102–4, 180–1
probes, *see* follow up questions
purposes of research, 76–80

quality in interview studies, 83–94, 144, *see*
   also audit trail, data sessions, 'good'
   practice in interviews, longevity in the
   field, member checking, researcher
   neutrality, subjectivity statements,
   triangulation
question–answer sequences, 10–11
question formulation, 11–14, 181–2, *see also*
   asking questions of transcriptions
questions, *see* closed questions, descriptive
   questions, elaborate questions, leading
   questions, open questions

readers theater, 173
reasoning, 149–50
recording interviews, 103–4
recruitment, 39–41, 98–9
reflexivity, 89, 116–18, 126–8, *see also*
  analyzing the interviewer's work,
  interviewing the researcher, researcher
  journals, subjectivity statements,
reliability, *see* quality in interview studies
replication, 87
research design, Chapter 4, 181–2, *see also*
  identifying a topic, formulating research
  questions, quality in interview studies,
  question formulation
researcher neutrality, 87
researcher journals, 121–2
research questions, *see* formulating
  research questions
romantic conception of interviewing, 55–9
  addressing quality, 88
  critiques, 59
  exemplars, 58–9, 72
  posing interview questions, 137, 145–6

sampling, 81–3
scheduling interviews, 41–2, 99–102
selection, 81–3
  comprehensive selection, 82
  criterion-based selection, 81–2
semi-structured interviews, 14–15
sensitive topics, 42, 124
Socratic-Hermeneutic Inter-view, 18–19
special topics and populations
  children, 110
  elites, 102, 111
  men, 100, 111
  women, 110–11

special topics and populations *cont.*
  older people, 100, 111
  participants who are ill, 111
  race and culture, 100, 112
  sexual orientation, 111
standardized interviews, *see* structured
  interviews
stimulus texts, 29–30
structured interviews, 10, 14–15
subjectivity, 55, 58, 119–20
  subjectivity statements, 84, 88–9,
    120–1, 127

thematic analysis and representation, 150–4
therapeutic interview, 66
transcription, 60–1, 88, 105–7, 109–10
transferability, *see* quality in interview studies
transformative conception of interviewing,
  65–8
  addressing quality, 89
  critiques, 68
  exemplars, 67–8, 73
translated data, 108–9
triangulation, 83–4
  data triangulation, 84, 86–7
  investigator triangulation, 84
  methodological triangulation, 84, 86
  theoretical triangulation, 84
trustworthiness, *see* quality in interview
  studies

unstructured interviews, 14–16

validity, 90, *see also* quality in interview
  studies

why-interviews, 122–3, 128